TIME **LIFE** ®
BOOKS

Other Publications:

THE KODAK LIBRARY OF CREATIVE PHOTOGRAPHY
GREAT MEALS IN MINUTES
THE CIVIL WAR
PLANET EARTH
COLLECTOR'S LIBRARY OF THE CIVIL WAR
LIBRARY OF HEALTH
CLASSICS OF THE OLD WEST
THE EPIC OF FLIGHT
THE SEAFARERS
WORLD WAR II
HOME REPAIR AND IMPROVEMENT
THE OLD WEST
LIFE LIBRARY OF PHOTOGRAPHY (revised)
LIFE SCIENCE LIBRARY (revised)

For information on and a full description of any
of the Time-Life Books series listed above, please write:

Reader Information
Time-Life Books
541 North Fairbanks Court
Chicago, Illinois 60611

*This volume is one of a series that explains and demonstrates
how to prepare various types of food, and that offers in each
book an international anthology of great recipes.*

Breads

BY
THE EDITORS OF TIME-LIFE BOOKS

TIME-LIFE BOOKS/ALEXANDRIA, VIRGINIA

Cover: A cylindrical loaf of yeast-leavened white bread is cut into thick slices, revealing a fine, light texture that results from thorough kneading and two slow risings *(pages 14-17)*. Before baking, the loaf was slashed in a checkerboard pattern to increase the bread's crust, and brushed with beaten egg white to give it a light glaze.

Time-Life Books Inc.
is a wholly owned subsidiary of
TIME INCORPORATED

Founder: Henry R. Luce 1898-1967

Editor-in-Chief: Henry Anatole Grunwald
President: J. Richard Munro
Chairman of the Board: Ralph P. Davidson
Corporate Editor: Jason McManus
Group Vice President, Books: Joan D. Manley

TIME-LIFE BOOKS INC.

Editor: George Constable. *Executive Editor:* George Daniels. *Director of Design:* Louis Klein. *Board of Editors:* Dale M. Brown, Thomas A. Lewis, Robert G. Mason, Peter Pocock, Gerry Schremp, Gerald Simons, Rosalind Stubenberg, Kit van Tulleken, Henry Woodhead. *Director of Administration:* David L. Harrison. *Director of Research:* Carolyn L. Sackett. *Director of Photography:* John Conrad Weiser. *Design:* Anne B. Landry (art coordinator); James J. Cox (quality control). *Research:* Phyllis K. Wise (assistant director), Louise D. Forstall. *Copy Room:* Diane Ullius. *Production:* Celia Beattie, Gordon E. Buck

President: Reginald K. Brack Jr. *Senior Vice President:* William Henry. *Vice Presidents:* George Artandi, Stephen L. Bair, Robert A. Ellis, Juanita T. James, Christopher T. Linen, James L. Mercer, Joanne A. Pello, Paul R. Stewart

THE GOOD COOK

The original version of this book was created in London for Time-Life International (Nederland) B.V.
European Editor: Kit van Tulleken. *Photography Director:* Pamela Marke. *Chief of Research:* Vanessa Kramer. *Special Projects Editor:* Windsor Chorlton. *Chief Sub-Editor:* Ilse Gray. *Production Editor:* Ellen Brush. *Quality Control:* Douglas Whitworth

Staff for *Breads:* *Series Editor:* Alan Lothian. *Series Coordinator:* Liz Timothy. *Head Designer:* Rick Bowring. *Text Editor:* Norman Kolpas. *Anthology Editor:* Josephine Bacon. *Staff Writers:* Alexandra Carlier, Jay Ferguson, Ellen Galford, Thom Henvey. *Designer:* Mary Staples. *Researchers:* Tim Fraser, Deborah Litton. *Sub-Editors:* Katie Lloyd, Sally Rowland. *Design Assistants:* Sally Curnock, Ian Midson. *Editorial Department:* Kate Cann, Debra Dick, Beverly Doe, Philip Garner, Aquila Kegan, Lesley Kinahan, Linda Mallett, Molly Sutherland, Julia West, Helen Whitehorn

U.S. Staff for *Breads:* *Series Editor:* Gerry Schremp. *Assistant Editor:* Ellen Phillips. *Designer:* Ellen Robling. *Chief Researcher:* Barbara Fleming. *Picture Editor:* Adrian Allen. *Text Editor:* Mark Steele. *Staff Writer:* David Schwartz. *Researchers:* Pamela Gould (techniques), Patricia Kim (anthology). *Assistant Designer:* Peg Schreiber. *Copy Coordinators:* Allan Fallow, Tonna Gibert, Nancy Lendved. *Art Assistants:* Robert Herndon, Mary L. Orr. *Picture Coordinator:* Alvin Ferrell. *Editorial Assistants:* Brenda Harwell, Patricia Whiteford. *Special Contributor:* Susan Perry (text)

CHIEF SERIES CONSULTANT

Richard Olney, an American, has lived and worked for some three decades in France, where he is highly regarded as an authority on food and wine. Author of *The French Menu Cookbook* and of the award-winning *Simple French Food*, he has also contributed to numerous gastronomic magazines in France and the United States, including the influential journals *Cuisine et Vins de France* and *La Revue du Vin de France*. He has directed cooking courses in France and the United States and is a member of several distinguished gastronomic and oenological societies, including L'Académie Internationale du Vin, La Confrérie des Chevaliers du Tastevin and La Commanderie du Bontemps de Médoc et des Graves. Working in London with the series editorial staff, he has been basically responsible for the planning of this volume, and has supervised the final selection of recipes submitted by other consultants. The United States edition of The Good Cook has been revised by the Editors of Time-Life Books to bring it into complete accord with American customs and usage.

CHIEF AMERICAN CONSULTANT
Carol Cutler is the author of a number of cookbooks, including the award-winning *The Six-Minute Soufflé and Other Culinary Delights* (republished as *Cuisine Rapide*). During the 12 years she lived in France, she studied at the Cordon Bleu and the École des Trois Gourmandes, and with private chefs. She is a member of the Cercle des Gourmettes, a long-established French food society limited to just 50 members, and a charter member of Les Dames d'Escoffier, Washington Chapter.

SPECIAL CONSULTANT
Judith Olney, author of *Comforting Food*, *Summer Food* and *The Joy of Chocolate*, received her culinary training in England and France. In addition to conducting cooking classes, she regularly contributes articles to gastronomic magazines. She has been responsible for some of the step-by-step photographic sequences in this volume.

PHOTOGRAPHER
Tom Belshaw was born near London and started his working career in films. He now has his own studio in London. He specializes in food and still-life photography, undertaking both editorial and advertising assignments. *Aldo Tutino* has worked in Milan, New York City and Washington, D.C. He has received a number of awards for his photographs from the New York Advertising Club. *Alan Duns* was born in the north of England and studied at the Ealing School of Photography. He has undertaken many advertising assignments, but specializes in food photography. His work has appeared in major British publications.

INTERNATIONAL CONSULTANTS
GREAT BRITAIN: *Jane Grigson* has written a number of books about food and has been a cookery correspondent for the London *Observer* since 1968. *Alan Davidson* is the author of several cookbooks and the founder of Prospect Books, which specializes in scholarly publications about food and cookery. *Pat Alburey* is a Member of the Association of Home Economists of Great Britain. She has been responsible for many of the step-by-step photographic sequences in this volume. *Jean Reynolds*, who prepared many of the breads for the photographs in this volume, is from San Francisco. She trained as cook in the kitchens of several of France's great restaurants. FRANCE: *Michel Lemonnier*, the cofounder and vice president of Les Amitiés Gastronomiques Internationales, is a frequent lecturer on wine and vineyards. GERMANY: *Jochen Kuchenbecker* trained as a chef, but has worked for 10 years as a food photographer in several European countries before opening his own restaurant in Hamburg. *Anne Brakemeier* is the co-author of a number of cookbooks. ITALY: *Massimo Alberini* is a well-known food writer and journalist, with a particular interest in culinary history. His many books include *La Tavola all'Italiana*, *4000 Anni a Tavola* and *100 Ricette Storiche*. THE NETHERLANDS: *Hugh Jans* has published cookbooks and his recipes appear in a number of Dutch magazines. THE UNITED STATES: *Julie Dannenbaum*, the director of a cooking school in Philadelphia, Pennsylvania, also conducts cooking classes at the Gritti Palace in Venice, Italy, and at The Greenbrier in White Sulphur Springs, West Virginia. She is the author of several cookbooks and numerous magazine articles. *Robert Shoffner*, wine and food editor of The Washingtonian magazine since 1975, has written many articles on cuisine.

Correspondents: Elisabeth Kraemer (Bonn); Margot Hapgood, Dorothy Bacon (London); Miriam Hsia, Susan Jonas, Lucy T. Voulgaris (New York); Maria Vincenza Aloisi, Josephine du Brusle (Paris); Ann Natanson (Rome). Valuable assistance was also provided by: Judy Aspinall, Lesley Coleman, Karin B. Pearce (London); Carolyn T. Chubet, Christina Lieberman (New York); Mimi Murphy (Rome).

Library of Congress CIP data, page 176.

CONTENTS

The Symbol of Sustenance

According to Hindu scriptures, "Everything is food, but bread is the great mother." Throughout the ages, its status as the most fundamental of fare has been celebrated by countless worshippers, writers and thinkers. Bread is almost a synonym for civilized sustenance.

Not the least of its virtues is variety. Most people think of bread simply as a dough made of wheat flour and water and baked in an oven. The fact is that bread can be based on any of a multitude of flours other than wheat. It can be spiced or sweetened, enriched, flavored or filled. Loaves and rolls may be unleavened and pancake flat, or lightened by baking soda or baking powder instead of the usual leavening, yeast. Some breads are cooked on a griddle, some are deep fried. Bagels are poached before baking (pages 58-59).

The range of home-baked breads includes cakelike French brioche, chewy Mexican tortillas, dense German pumpernickel, flaky Danish pastries, plump English crumpets and paper-thin Indian chappatis—to mention only a few of the possibilities. There are breads that are made for breakfast—pancakes, waffles and doughnuts—and Parker House or cloverleaf rolls for dinner. Middle Eastern pita breads provide pockets that can be stuffed with fillings; Scotland's black bun is a yeasty fruitcake enclosed in a wrapping of plain bread.

This volume is a guide to the preparation of bread in all of its guises. The book begins with the basics—an explanation of flours (pages 8-9) and yeasts (pages 10-11) and, in Chapter 1, step-by-step demonstrations of how to mix, knead, shape and bake simple, yeast-leavened loaves and rolls. The next two chapters show how to embellish yeast dough with butter and eggs or with flavorings and special handling methods. Finally, Chapter 4 illustrates the wide variety of breads that can be made without yeast. All these lessons will enable you to use any of the 201 recipes in the Anthology starting on page 90—a collection that spans many centuries and lands and draws on the world's most distinguished cookery writers.

The genesis of bread

Laced with mystery and magic, the history of bread is older than the recorded history of mankind. Archeologists trace the origin of bread to a primitive, gluey dough of water and wild cereal grains, beaten between rocks to crack their husks, that was shaped into flat cakes and cooked by wandering hunter-gatherers on stones heated in open fires. In time, the nomadic peoples of the Middle East learned to cultivate local grains—wheat, barley, millet—and became the world's first farmers.

Using crude mortars, they ground grains into coarse flours and sifted, or bolted, them through woven baskets to separate out the bran husks, called chaff (diagram, page 7).

The flours improved, but breads remained unleavened until about 4,000 years ago, when some perceptive baker—probably an Egyptian—observed that if an uncooked dough was left unattended for a few hours, often it would begin to bubble and give off a sour smell. When the dough was cooked, it produced a somewhat raised bread that was lighter in texture and more palatable than one made from a fresh mix. Pursuing this lead, breadmakers soon found that a small piece of soured dough from a previous mixture could raise a fresh dough. These pieces were the first sourdough starters (pages 10-11)—natural leavenings that many modern cooks also nurture from baking to baking.

Although the ancients did not understand it, the bubbling and rising of their doughs was caused by yeasts—living single-celled fungi. These fungi, which float about freely in the air, are microscopic: 3,200 billion yeast cells weigh only a pound [½ kg.]. In the warm, moist atmosphere of a dough, with the carbohydrates—or starches—of the flour to nourish them, the cells flourish. As they grow and reproduce, the yeasts convert the starches into carbon dioxide gas and alcohol. The carbon dioxide inflates the dough, giving it a porous texture. When the dough is baked, the carbon dioxide forms at a faster rate to further lighten the bread; meanwhile, the alcohol escapes through evaporation, sending out a rich, "fresh-baked" aroma.

If the dough is made with wheat flour, kneading it increases the action of the yeast dramatically. Unlike other grains, wheat contains significant amounts of proteins called glutenin and gliadin. When moistened, they combine to form the elastic substance known as gluten. Kneading bonds the gluten chemically with up to twice its weight in water and turns it into a three-dimensional meshwork that traps the gas released by yeast.

The master bakers of the ancient world

The Egyptians were not content with merely leavening their dough. Using techniques that are still employed today, they flavored loaves with sweet or aromatic herbs, enriched them with honey or eggs, and shaped them in diverse ways. Hieroglyphs and loaves found preserved in the tombs of pharaohs show more than 50 different forms, some intricately braided, others sculpted to resemble birds, fish, cows and even miniature pyramids. To give breads the all-around, radiant heat they need to cook evenly, the Egyptians also developed special ovens, shaped like beehives or barrels and divided into two compartments, a lower one for the fire, an upper one for the loaves.

It was the Romans, with their engineering skills, who perfected the first rotary mills, or querns, for turning wheat into bread flour. These mills consisted of two large, circular stones, set one atop the other. The lower stone was solid and stationary. The upper stone had a hollow center into which the miller poured grain. As the upper stone was rotated—by slaves or animals during the early days of the mills' use, later by the flowing water of a stream or river—the grain was crushed. The resulting meal was then bolted through finely woven cloth to produce a relatively pure, yellowish flour.

A similar rotary system for turning wooden paddles inside a large stone bowl to mix and knead dough made it possible for the Romans to produce bread in commercial quantities. By the time of Christ, Rome had more than 250 bakeries and produced more than half a million loaves daily. Two hundred years later, the government nationalized bakeries so that it could issue free loaves. The populace, reported the Roman satirist Juvenal, "longs eagerly for just two things—bread and circuses."

Roman legions introduced wheat and the art of breadmaking throughout the Empire, but wheat did not grow easily where winters were severe or the soil was rocky. After Rome fell and trade within Europe stopped, white loaves became a luxury only the privileged classes could enjoy. For most Europeans, the daily bread was made from rye or millet or—in the northernmost countries such as Scotland and Sweden—from oats or barley.

The settling of the New World changed that. Colonists adopted the native corn as a base for bread, with an enthusiasm not shared by the Old World. At the same time, they cleared farm land and soon were producing wheat crops so bountiful that even the poor of Europe could enjoy part of the largesse. By the time of the Revolutionary War, wheat was America's leading export. In 1776, some 75 tons of wheat were shipped overseas from George Washington's Mount Vernon farm alone.

Improving the product

The 19th Century was a kind of Golden Age for breadmakers: Improved milling processes, new wheat varieties and dependable leavenings enabled commercial and home bakers alike to refine their breads and produce them with ease.

Even when wheat was milled twice and bolted through silk gauze, the result was a yellowish flour of uneven texture, flecked with bran and germ. Millers knew that steel rollers could grind wheat finer than stones would, but it was not until James Watts invented the steam engine in 1769 that adequate power was available to turn such rollers. By 1834 a Swiss, Jacob Sulzburger, had developed a steam-powered roller mill; by 1870 a Minneapolis inventor, Edmund La Croix, had improved the process with a purifier to separate the middlings—bran, germ and coarse particles—from the fine particles that form a smooth-textured white flour. In such a mill, high-speed rollers cracked rather than crushed the wheat; the grain was passed through screens of increasing fineness, then air currents drew off impurities from the middlings. Next, the bran and germ were sifted out, and the coarse particles were rolled, sifted, and perhaps purified again. This process is used today in many mills.

About the same time that milling was improved, a new type of wheat, adapted to cold climates, was brought from Russia's Ukraine and became the major crop of America's vast Midwestern plains. Wheats are divided into two major categories—hard and soft. The soft varieties, like the early wheats used by the Egyptians and Romans, yield a flour relatively low in gluten proteins. Hard varieties—of which the highly successful Russian strain is one—are gluten rich. Although soft-wheat flour produces tender bread, only hard-wheat flour can withstand the manipulation required to develop the strong, gas-trapping meshwork required for a high-rising loaf. Today, the most commonly used flours are so-called bread flour—made with hard wheat only—and all-purpose flour, which combines hard and soft wheats and has a wide range of cooking uses, including breadmaking. Both types allow bakers to readily produce yeast loaves with a fine, uniform and light texture.

Even fine wheat flours vary in color from yellow to cream when freshly milled. At this stage, the flour produces a sticky dough that cannot rise fully. Once, the problem was solved by storing the flour for a minimum of 30 days; as it aged, its color faded to white and its components matured to make handling easier. Storing flour, however, was expensive and often resulted in insect infestation. Toward the close of the 19th Century, millers began to treat freshly milled flour with oxidizing agents—now carefully controlled by federal law—to "bleach" it and give it the handling characteristics of naturally aged flour.

As flours were perfected, so were the leavenings for bread. For centuries, bakers generally relied on the frothy scrapings from brewers' vats to supply yeast for their bread, or they mixed up sourdough starters by combining flour or meal with water or milk, sugar, hops, onions or potatoes—almost any foodstuff that contained starches to nourish whatever yeast cells might descend on the mixture. But in the wake of Louis Pasteur's studies of yeast cell activity in the 1850s, European scientists rapidly mastered methods for growing yeast that would suit a baker's special needs.

The secrets of producing such yeast on a wide scale remained in Europe until 1865, when two Austrian brothers and bakers, Charles and Maximillian Fleischmann, came to America to attend their sister's wedding. They were shocked by the poor quality of the bread, which they blamed on the yeasts. In 1867, they returned to America, this time with a vial of baker's yeast tucked for warmth in Charles's breast pocket. Settling in Cincinnati, the Fleischmanns built a thriving business by growing yeast and shipping it nationwide in the form of compressed cakes—enclosed in balsa wood boxes as protection from excessive heat or cold. (Dry yeast was developed at the start of World War II to help provide the American armed forces overseas with fresh bread; it was not available to home bakers until 1945.)

Yeast and sourdough were not the only leavenings used to raise breads baked at home. One early leaven, dating back to the 18th Century, was water in which hardwood ashes had been soaked. Called pearlash, this water was a weak form of lye that produced carbon dioxide when heated. Another source of carbon dioxide was baking soda or, as it was known then, saleratus. Developed in England, saleratus soon was distributed throughout Europe and America. But because both pearlash and saleratus were alkaline, they gave bread an objectionable taste unless neutralized by an acidic ingredient.

Baking powder, which combines alkali and acid, appeared in the 1840s, when it was sold as premeasured, separate packets of baking soda and the acid salt, cream of tartar. Not until 1855 did the Boston firm of Preston and Merrill discover that the two could be combined in a single package if an inert filler such as cornstarch was added to absorb atmospheric moisture and keep the alkali and acid from reacting with each other.

Baking bread at home

The refinement of bread ingredients and the ease with which they now can be handled has been a boon for the home baker. Breads leavened with baking powder—biscuits and pancakes, for example—can be produced on even the tightest of schedules (they are rightly called "quick breads") and varied almost endlessly in flavor, texture and shape.

Yeast breads take more time, but require no special skill. The 19th Century cookery writer Eliza Acton remarked in *The English Bread-Book for Domestic Use*, "A very exaggerated idea of the difficulty and trouble of breadmaking prevails amongst people who are entirely ignorant of the process." The making of yeast breads in particular offers indubitable pleasures: the leisurely rhythm of kneading, the still-magical sight of yeast bubbling and dough rising, the delightful aroma that fills a home as bread bakes and later cools, the golden vision of a crisp crust. Breadmaking is an activity that stirs all the senses.

The most important kinds of equipment for producing yeast breads are your hands—for kneading—and your oven. All breads need even heat to rise and brown uniformly. By working with your oven, you will become familiar with its idiosyncrasies and learn how to use it best. In most cases, an oven is hotter in back; thus you may have to turn loaves around during baking.

Weather and locale may necessitate variations in the process. On humid summer days, for example, you may need to use a little less liquid; your flour will have already absorbed some atmospheric moisture. At a high altitude, dough rises faster because there is less atmospheric pressure. For yeast breads, no recipe adjustment to altitude is necessary, but keep a watchful eye on the dough: It should not be allowed to increase in volume more than the cooking instructions specify. For baking soda and baking powder breads, use a bit less leavening at high altitudes than called for. Also, at an altitude of 3,000 feet or higher, the baking temperature for bread should be increased by 25° F. [15° C.]. The extra heat is needed to set the crust faster and prevent the bread from overrising during its last surge in the oven.

Appealing as the aroma of hot, freshly baked yeast bread may be, it is generally better to let loaves cool, overnight if possible, before you eat them. The wait is necessary to let the bread's flavor mature and to allow the loaf to firm so that it can be sliced without tearing or crumbling. Small rolls will, of course, cool faster, but even they should not be served straight from the oven. Loaves or rolls baked in pans should be unmolded for cooling, and all loaves should be cooled on a wire rack. The rack will let air circulate freely around the bread, removing

steam and keeping it from spoiling the crispness of the crust.

If yeast bread is to be kept for more than 24 hours, put it in a dry, well-ventilated metal or wooden bread box, or enclose it in plastic wrap or foil and refrigerate it. The length of time bread will stay fresh is determined by its size and ingredients: Large thick loaves release moisture more slowly than small thin breads; breads rich with egg and butter—which retain moisture—keep longer than plain breads. Kept in a box, a 2-pound [1-kg.] basic loaf will stay in good condition for up to one week; an enriched loaf of the same size will keep a few days more. Refrigerated, both loaves will remain fresh for up to two weeks.

Bread freezes well if wrapped tightly in a double thickness of plastic wrap or foil. Frozen bread will keep for several months. Before you serve the bread, unwrap it and let it thaw for three to six hours or heat it, wrapped in foil, for 10 or 15 minutes in a 400° F. [200° C.] oven.

Bread can be an elemental repast, served with wine and cheese or with soup; or it can become part of a feast. Whatever role it plays in a meal, its maker will know the special satisfaction expressed with perfect simplicity in the maxim, "She who has baked a good batch of bread has done a good day's work."

Anatomy of a Wheat Kernel

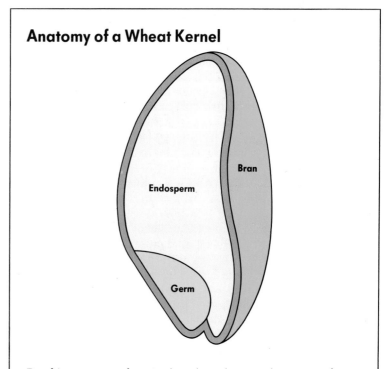

Food in a neat packet. A wheat kernel, or seed, consists of three parts: bran, germ and endosperm. Its outer coating is made up of four fibrous layers, collectively known as bran. At the stem end of the kernel is the oil-rich germ, the embryo of the future plant; it is a concentrated source of protein, iron and vitamins B and E. The bulk of the kernel—more than 80 per cent of its weight—is the endosperm, the germ's food source. It contains about 67 per cent starch and up to 11 per cent gluten-forming proteins; the remainder is made up of water and minerals.

A Spectrum of Specialty Flours

White all-purpose or bread flour is the basic ingredient of most loaves. Yet a dozen other kinds of flour—listed in the chart at right—are widely available at specialty markets, health-food stores and supermarkets, and are easily used to create yeast breads with special textures, flavors, colors and aromas.

Many of these specialty flours serve alone to produce dense-textured or flat breads. Rye flours, for example, yield a rich, moist black bread *(recipe, page 107)*, and corn flour—or *masa harina*—produces chewy tortillas *(recipe, page 141)*. However, to form light-textured risen breads, flour must have gluten-forming proteins, as well as starches to nourish yeast. And only wheat among all the cereal grains has appreciable amounts of gluten-forming proteins.

All-purpose flour is milled from a combination of high-gluten hard wheat and lower-gluten soft wheat; bread flour is milled solely from hard wheat. Not only can both be used alone in breadmaking, but they also can be mixed with other flours to bring to the loaves the starches or gluten that specialty flours may lack.

Among the specialty flours, two actually are made from wheat. Gluten flour, milled from hard wheat, is treated to remove some of its starch and concentrate its proteins so that it contains at least 70 per cent pure gluten. To make a risen loaf, gluten flour needs bolstering with all-purpose or bread flour—to provide the necessary starch. Whole-wheat flour, also made from hard wheat, includes germ and bran, which interfere with the development of its gluten; loaves baked from whole-wheat flour alone rise slowly and never attain a light, fluffy texture.

Rye flours and triticale flour—milled from a man-made hybrid of wheat and rye—contain some gluten-forming proteins, but of insufficient strength to raise loaves significantly. The rest of the flours on the chart have only traces of gluten or—in the case of soy flour, made from a bean rather than a cereal—none at all.

In spite of these variations, specialty flours can be introduced into almost any basic yeast bread recipe that calls for only all-purpose or bread flour. To combine flours successfully requires achieving a chemical balance between them.

The more low-gluten or low-starch flour is used, the more pronounced will be its effect on the flavor of the bread. But as the proportion of specialty flour increases, the ability of the dough to rise and the lightness of the finished loaf decrease. The chart at right lists ratios of specialty flour to all-purpose or bread flour that will yield loaves that are distinctive in character yet as light as ordinary white bread.

A specialty flour will vary somewhat in the amount of moisture it will absorb—depending on such factors as the exact variety of the plant from which it comes and the way the flour is milled. To achieve the proper consistency when mixing a dough, add all of the specialty flour first. Then incorporate the all-purpose or bread flour gradually, using only enough to form a firm dough that no longer sticks to the bowl or work surface.

To protect them from absorbing moisture, all flours should be stored in airtight containers. All-purpose and bread flours can be kept at room temperature for up to six months. So can gluten flour. But other specialty flours contain some of the germ of the grain, and the oils in the germ eventually turn rancid. Therefore, specialty flours should be kept in the refrigerator and used within three months if possible. Before it is used, any refrigerated flour must be allowed to warm to room temperature.

Baking with specialty flour. This chart, in ratio form, shows how much specialty flour may be substituted for part of the all-purpose or bread flour in basic yeast breads—and what characteristics the specialty will contribute to loaves. The first number of each substitution ratio indicates the proportion of specialty flour; the second number indicates the proportion of all-purpose or bread flour. Thus, for a recipe that requires 6 cups [1½ liters] of white flour, you can substitute 1 cup [¼ liter] of barley flour and 5 cups [1¼ liters] of white flour (a 1-to-5 ratio) or 3 cups [¾ liter] of dark rye flour and 3 cups of white flour (a 1-to-1 ratio).

Flour
BARLEY
BUCKWHEAT
CORN
GLUTEN
MILLET
OAT
RICE
RYE, DARK
RYE, MEDIUM
SOY
TRITICALE
WHOLE-WHEAT

Substitution Ratio	Aroma and Taste	Crust Characteristics	Interior Characteristics
1:5	Slightly malty with a pleasantly bitter aftertaste	Tan; medium hard	Grayish tan; chewy and moist
1:5	Earthy, slightly musty and full-bodied	Dark brown; soft	Dark gray; moist and fine-grained
1:5	Bland, somewhat yeasty and slightly sweet	Mottled and pale; flaky	Pale yellow; chewy and slightly dry
2:1	Bland and slightly yeasty	Dark tan to medium brown; chewy to crisp	White; fine-grained and slightly dry
1:5	Nutty and slightly sweet	Tan; smooth and chewy	White to creamy; dense and fine-grained
1:3	Slightly sweet and earthy	Uniformly pale; crunchy	Light brown; coarse-grained and crumbly
1:5	Moderately sweet	Light golden brown; delicate	Creamy white; fine-grained and slightly dry
1:1	Strongly bitter and full-bodied	Dark brown; coarse	Dark brown; coarse-grained and crumbly
2:1	Mildly bitter	Medium to dark brown; coarse	Medium brown; fine-grained and crumbly
1:5	Pleasantly musty and slightly sweet	Dark golden brown; chewy	Yellow brown; moist, firm and fine-grained
1:1	Slightly bitter	Light brown; soft	Light to medium brown; coarse- to fine-grained
1:1	Nutty	Dark brown; chewy	Light to dark brown; coarse-grained

A Guide to Yeast Leavens

Living yeast cells—the most widely used leavening for bread—grow and reproduce best in an environment that provides them with moisture and starchy nutrients such as flour, sugar or potato. As the yeast cells metabolize these nutrients—a process called yeast fermentation—they release carbon dioxide gas, alcohol and other natural by-products. The gas, trapped in a dough's developing meshwork of gluten, raises the bread. The alcohol boils off in baking. The remaining by-products contribute flavor.

Most of the yeast employed in breadmaking today is the commercially cultivated strain *Saccharomyces cerevisiae*, commonly called baker's yeast. It is sold as fresh compressed yeast cakes or as dry yeast granules. Fresh yeast should be compact and creamy-fawn in color; cakes normally will stay usable for about three weeks if left wrapped and kept refrigerated. Dry yeast also is creamy-fawn in color, but does not alter in appearance as it ages. For this reason, the envelopes or jars in which it is sold are marked with its expiration date. Dry yeast will keep in a cool, dry place for up to six months.

To prepare commercial yeasts for use, soften them with tepid liquid—water or milk are the common choices. As a rule, about ¼ cup [50 ml.] of liquid is needed to soften 1 ounce [30 g.] of fresh yeast, or ½ ounce [15 g.] of dry yeast. Ideally, the temperature of the liquid should be 100° F. [40° C.] but it can range from 80° to 110° F. [25° to 45° C.]. You can test the temperature with a rapid-response thermometer, or drop a bit of the liquid on the inside of your wrist: The liquid should feel barely warm.

Commercial yeasts impart a mild flavor to bread. For stronger flavor, some cooks prefer a home-grown yeast-and-bacteria culture called sourdough starter. Because the yeasts and bacteria give off the flavorful by-products of fermentation for a longer duration, loaves leavened with starter are pleasantly sour.

To make starter, you need only provide a medium in which yeast cells can grow and reproduce, then inoculate the medium with living yeast. Most starters are begun with a starchy ingredient, water and, in some cases, a bit of sugar. Traditionally, this medium is left to inoculate itself by picking up wild yeasts and bacteria that are in the flours and in the air *(top right; recipe, page 167)*. But wild yeasts are temperamental, and such cultures frequently do not take.

A more reliable method for starting a culture is to inoculate a medium with commercial yeast *(bottom right; recipe, page 167)*. However, the hardy commercial strain will crowd out most of the wild yeasts and, because its metabolic by-products are not as strongly flavored, the starter will not produce the distinctive results of traditional cultures.

Once established, a sourdough starter will last indefinitely if it is refrigerated and its yeasts kept supplied with nutrients and free of contaminants. After each use, but at least every two weeks, replenish the starter with flour and water.

Softening Fresh Yeast

Mashing the yeast. Pour tepid liquid into a bowl and drop in fresh yeast. With a fork, mash the yeast with the water, and stir until the liquid is smooth and cream-colored. Set the mixture in a draft-free place; as the yeast becomes active — after about 10 minutes — the mixture will begin to foam, indicating that it is ready for use.

Activating Dry Yeast

1 **Moistening the yeast.** Put tepid liquid into a bowl, sprinkle dry yeast granules over the water, and stir briefly to wet the granules. Set the mixture in a draft-free place to soften and rehydrate the yeast. After about 10 minutes, the mixture will be ready for use.

2 **Whisking the yeast.** To ensure that the yeast mixture will combine evenly when it is added to the other bread-dough ingredients, whisk it vigorously immediately before use.

Cultivating Wild Yeast

1 **Mixing the ingredients.** Boil potatoes, drain them and peel them, reserving the cooking liquid. Mash the potatoes. Put flour — in this case, rye flour — sugar, the mashed potatoes and the reserved liquid into a large bowl. Stir the ingredients together to make a thick batter.

2 **Fermenting the leaven.** Cover the bowl with plastic wrap *(above)*. To ensure a constant temperature and to protect the culture from drafts, wrap the bowl in a thick towel. Let the culture ferment in a warm place for at least three days.

3 **A ripened culture.** The leaven is ready when it is bubbly and smells strong and sour when unwrapped. Before use, stir the sourdough starter and, after use, replenish it with equal parts of flour and water.

Bolstering a Culture with Baker's Yeast

1 **Mixing flour and yeast.** In a large bowl, mix fresh or dry yeast with tepid water *(boxes, opposite)*. Whisk in enough flour to form a thick, pourable batter. The mixture need not be absolutely smooth: Any lumps will be broken down by the action of the yeast.

2 **Fermenting the mixture.** Tightly cover the bowl with plastic wrap and set the mixture aside to ferment, undisturbed, in a warm, draft-free place (70° F. [30° C.]).

3 **A matured starter.** A layer of thick bubbles on top of a fermented sourdough starter indicates that the culture is ready for use. Most starters made from commercial yeast can be used after about 24 hours of fermentation. However, for fully developed sourdough flavor, the starter must ferment for three days.

1
Basic Yeast Breads
Diverse Results from Simple Techniques

Preparing the dough
Slashing for more crust
Shaping plain and fancy loaves
Five forms for rolls
Pretzels and bread sticks

Small spheres of bread that have been baked together to keep their sides soft and moist are torn apart into individual rolls. To form the spheres, risen dough was shaped into balls that were then fitted closely into a round cake pan to join as they rose. Just before the rolls were placed in the oven, they were glazed with beaten egg and sprinkled with poppy seeds.

"All that bread wants is time and warmth," goes an old English saying. Preparing yeast bread does, in fact, depend chiefly on these two factors. With time, gluten develops in the flour, forming an elastic meshwork throughout the dough. With warmth, yeast produces carbon dioxide that inflates the gluten mesh and lightens the dough. Still, though bread-making is simple, it is an art replete with choices at every stage.

To make yeast bread, the ingredients—no more than flour, liquid and yeast are needed—must be combined, then kneaded to strengthen the gluten. One method of kneading is shown on pages 14-15, but the only real requirement is to stretch the dough repeatedly until it is smooth and elastic. If done by hand, this may take 10 to 20 minutes. You can, however, cut the time in half by using the dough-hook attachment of an electric mixer or the metal blade of a food processor.

The kneaded dough must be allowed to rise one or more times—the number depends on the qualities you want in the finished bread. Dough that is immediately shaped and left to rise just once before baking will produce a coarse-textured loaf, full of large holes. Dough that rises two or three times will yield a fine-textured loaf, with small, even holes.

The time needed for the risings may be adjusted to suit your schedule, but the slower the rise, the better will be the flavor of the finished bread. When left at warm room temperature—70° F. [20° C.] is ideal—dough usually doubles in volume in about one and one half hours. You can hasten the expansion by any of several tactics: Put the dough in a particularly warm place—up to 100° F. [40° C.]; or double the amount of yeast called for; or stir a teaspoonful [5 ml.] of sugar into the yeast solution about 10 minutes before adding it to the flour (the sugar provides extra food for the yeast organisms). On the other hand, the risings can be slowed by leaving the dough in a cool place or refrigerating it.

The choices are infinite when it comes to shaping the dough. You can form large round loaves or small cloverleaf rolls, long tapered cylinders or twisted bread sticks, loaves molded in rectangular pans or braided from strands of dough. Shaping dough is usually easy, but braids may take practice. Elizabeth David, an English authority on breadmaking, cites the case of a 19th Century baker who confessed, "I learnt plaiting on a railway journey, using the fringe of the window-strap pieces."

Mixing and Kneading

Making a yeast dough that will produce well-risen bread with a fine texture inside and a crisp brown crust requires patience: The necessary steps, shown here, take two hours or more. But the dough will be rising unattended for more than half of that time, and the balance will be spent in mixing and kneading—simple processes that call for no special skill.

Your hand is the best instrument for mixing. The only ingredients required are flour, water and yeast, with a pinch of salt for flavor (recipe, page 164). To start the yeast developing immediately, all ingredients should be at room temperature; let flour warm if it has been refrigerated, and use tepid water. Because flour varies in its absorbency, work it into the water gradually so that you can adjust the prescribed quantity to achieve a properly firm dough—one that is neither sticky nor stiff.

As soon as the flour is moistened, gluten protein begins to form. Kneading the dough then homogenizes the ingredients and strengthens the gluten mesh, increasing its ability to stretch. Kneading may be done on a bare or lightly floured surface; however, a coated surface may cause extra flour to be mixed in, stiffening the dough and toughening the bread.

When the dough finally becomes supple, smooth and glossy, it is set aside in a covered bowl to rise—or, in baker's argot, to "proof"—in a 70° F. [20° C.] place free from cooling drafts. During the rising time—which is usually about one and one half hours—the yeast cells increase their production of carbon dioxide gas, which gently infuses the dough and stretches the gluten mesh.

After the dough has risen to double its original volume, it is punched down to expel large gas bubbles. Then the dough is briefly kneaded and formed into balls before its final shaping, proofing and baking (pages 16-17). As an alternative, the dough can be left to rise again before shaping to give it a finer texture. Or it can be covered and refrigerated for up to four days. Refrigerated dough will still rise for four to five hours; knead it briefly several times as it cools. When taken from the refrigerator, it should warm for at least two hours before it is kneaded into a ball and shaped for baking.

1 Combining ingredients. Add salt to the flour. Soften active dry yeast or fresh cake yeast in a little tepid water for 10 minutes (page 10). Place the flour—in this case, all-purpose flour—in a large mixing bowl. Then pour the yeast mixture, together with additional tepid water, into the center of the bowl.

2 Mixing the dough. With one hand, hold the bowl steady. With your other hand, scoop and turn the flour and liquid until they are thoroughly combined, forming a shaggy mass.

5 Letting the dough rise. Put the dough back in the greased bowl. To keep the dough moist, cover the bowl with plastic wrap or a damp cloth. Set the bowl in a warm, draft-free place until the dough is doubled—about one and a half hours. To test the dough, press a finger into it: If the dent fills in slowly, the dough is ready.

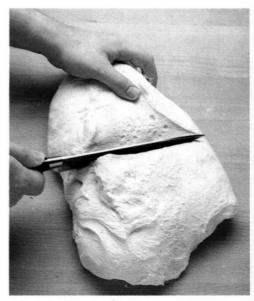

6 Dividing the dough. With your fist, punch down the risen dough to compact it in the bottom of the bowl. Then turn the dough out onto the work surface. If, as here, you have made enough for two loaves, cut the dough in half. Cover one half with plastic wrap or a damp cloth, and set it aside while you work with the other half.

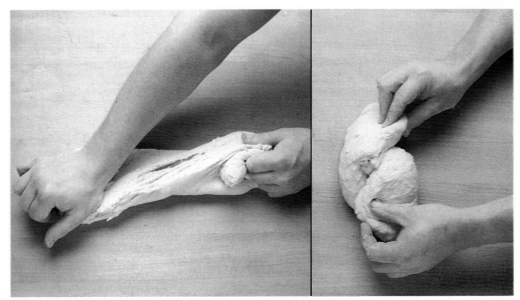

3 **Turning out the dough.** If the dough feels dry and stiff, mix in a little more tepid water; if it feels sticky and soft, work in some more flour. Empty the dough from the bowl onto a clean, dry work surface. Wash out and dry the mixing bowl, grease it lightly with soft butter or flavorless oil and set it aside.

4 **Kneading the dough.** Hold the dough with one hand. With the heel of your other hand, push the dough away in a firm, unhurried stroke *(above, left)*, taking care not to tear the mass and so break the gluten mesh. Work gently at first: The dough will be sticky and easily torn. After each stroke, fold the dough back and at the same time give it a slight turn *(right)*. Push, fold and turn the dough with a regular motion for 10 to 15 minutes. To develop the gluten further, occasionally lift up the dough and throw it down. Knead until the dough is smooth and easy to stretch.

7 **Kneading the dough into a ball.** Exerting a light pressure, push away a corner of the dough with the heel of your hand, and simultaneously give the corner a slight counterclockwise twist *(far left)* to turn the whole mass. Fold the pushed-out piece back into the middle *(center, left)*. Repeat the pushing, turning and folding *(center, right)* until the dough is rounded *(far right)*. Turn the ball so its pleats face down. Cover this ball and repeat the process with the other piece of dough. Let the dough rest — and its gluten mesh relax — for 10 minutes before shaping into loaves.

A Blueprint for Baking

After kneaded and risen bread dough has rested briefly *(page 15, Step 7)*, it is ready to be shaped into loaves and baked. A magnified cross section of the dough at this stage would reveal it to be a delicate foam composed of gas-filled gluten pockets. To protect this fragile structure, the dough should be handled as gently as possible, whether it is being shaped into the simple round loaves demonstrated here, or into the more elaborately formed loaves and rolls on pages 18-31.

Even with careful handling, some of the gluten pockets will collapse. To restore them, the shaped loaves are allowed to rise until the dough once more doubles in volume. The rising can take place on the work surface, or on a baking sheet greased with flavorless oil, unsalted butter or lard, according to taste, and perhaps dusted with cornmeal or semolina for a crisper bottom crust.

After the loaves have risen, their tops often are slashed with a razor—for practical as well as decorative reasons. Slashes let excess gas escape during baking and thus prevent the tops from splitting in the oven. Additionally, slashes let dough push up from under the surface to form secondary crusts that will be paler in color and more delicate in texture. As a further textural enhancement, the tops may be dusted with flour, which will give the loaves a powdery finish.

The loaves rise to their final size in the oven. As the interior of the loaves heats, carbon dioxide produced by the yeast rapidly expands the gluten pockets; a well-made loaf may increase in size by a third during the first few minutes of baking. This rising—so dramatic that bakers call it "oven spring"—will continue until the interior temperature reaches 140° F. [60° C.]. At this temperature the yeast cells die and the crust forms.

In a baker's oven, the last rising is given a fast start by sliding the loaves directly onto the hot oven floor. Meanwhile, steam jets humidify the air to delay the drying and setting of the crusts, thereby expanding the loaves even more.

To achieve similar results in a home oven, first allow 15 to 20 minutes for preheating it. Either bake the loaves on a shelf lined with porous quarry tiles *(box, opposite)* that will absorb moisture from beneath the loaves to ensure crunchy bottom crusts or bake them on a dark-colored, carbon-steel baking sheet that will absorb heat quickly to crisp the bottoms. In either case, humidify the oven during the first 20 minutes of baking: Place a pan of hot water on the floor of a gas oven or the bottom shelf of an electric oven when the preheating begins, and spray the oven with water from an atomizer during baking, as shown below.

3 **Slashing the loaves.** When the loaves have risen, use a single-edged razor blade in firm, decisive strokes to cut slashes ½ inch [1 cm.] deep in the tops of the loaves. Here, one loaf has been slashed in a checkerboard pattern, then dusted with flour; the other loaf is being cut with a cross.

4 **Baking the bread.** Check the water in the roasting pan; if there is less than 1 inch [2½ cm.], add boiling water. Slide the baking sheet onto the middle shelf of the oven, and spray the oven interior with water. Spray again after 10 minutes. After 20 minutes, remove the water and let the loaves brown.

1 **Shaping the dough.** Lift up a kneaded ball of risen dough with one hand, and with the other hand gently pleat any folds or tears by pinching them together *(above, left)*. Turn the ball over and place it on a work surface, with the pleats down. Lightly pat and rotate the ball with both palms *(right)*. Alternate pleating with patting the ball until it forms a smooth, round loaf.

2 **Letting the loaves rise.** Space the rounds well apart on a greased baking sheet. Cover, and set them in a warm, draft-free place for about an hour, or until the loaves double in volume. Meanwhile, place a roasting pan of hot water in the bottom of the oven and preheat the oven to 450° F. [230° C.].

5 **Serving the bread.** After baking for 45 minutes, rap the bottom of one loaf with your knuckles *(inset)*. A hollow sound means the bread is done; if you hear a dull thud, return the loaf to the oven for five minutes, then test again. Cool the bread on a wire rack for at least an hour. Slice with a serrated knife.

Tiles for a Crisper Crust

A heat-storing base. Lay scrubbed, unglazed quarry tiles side by side on the middle shelf of the oven, leaving a 2-inch [5-cm.] margin all around so that the hot air can circulate freely. Set a pan of water beneath the tiles and preheat the oven. Slide the risen loaves onto the tiles. Spray the oven with water, then spray it again in 10 minutes.

A Notched Cottage Loaf

Stacked one on top of the other, two or three simple balls of dough in various sizes can create unusual-looking tiered loaves. Tiered construction has a practical effect as well: Relative to the volume of the interior, it produces a loaf that has a high proportion of crust, which many consider the best part of any bread.

In this demonstration, two balls—one about half the size of the other—form a traditional English cottage loaf. A special joining technique ensures that the two balls will not come apart in the oven. First, each ball is indented by thrusting fingers all the way through it—a process known as bashing. The resulting rings are rested and then bashed again to re-emphasize their shape. Next, the upper piece, or topknot, is placed on the base, and together they are indented a third time to bind them. To further increase the amount of crust, the cottage loaf is then slashed vertically *(Step 3, below)*. A final bashing secures the bond between the two elements before baking.

1 Bashing. Cut risen bread dough *(page 14, Step 6)* into two pieces, one twice the size of the other. Shape them into balls. After 10 minutes, bash the larger ball by pressing three fingers and a thumb straight down through its center to the work surface. Use two fingers to bash the smaller ball.

2 Joining the rings. Let the two bashed rings rest for 15 minutes, then bash each one again. Slightly flatten the top of the large ring and the bottom of the small ring, then stack the two rings, centering their indentations. With two fingers, carefully bash the combined loaf through to the bottom.

3 Slashing. Position the loaf so that it slightly overhangs the edge of a table or board. With a single-edged razor blade, cut a gash ¼ inch [6 mm.] deep in the overhanging portion of the loaf, all the way from the top to the bottom. Rotate the dough and repeat the slashing around the loaf at intervals of about 1 inch [2½ cm.].

4 Rising. Slide the loaf onto a greased baking sheet and let it rise in a warm, draft-free place until it has almost doubled in volume—about 40 to 50 minutes. Bash the risen loaf once more.

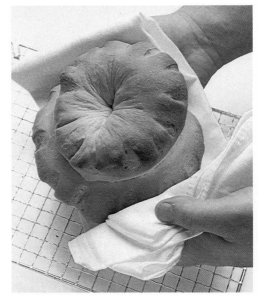

5 Baking the loaf. In a preheated and humidified 450° F. [230° C.] oven, bake the loaf for 30 to 40 minutes, spraying the oven twice *(page 16, Step 4)*. When the loaf is evenly browned and sounds hollow when rapped with your knuckles, cool it on a wire rack. To serve, slice the loaf from top to bottom or pull apart the two pieces and slice them separately.

Forming a Cylinder

A ball of dough can be molded into a cylinder—either blunt-ended, as shown here and overleaf, or tapered (page 21)—that will hold its shape well during baking. Before the molding is started, the kneaded ball must rest so that the dough loses some of its elasticity and becomes easy to handle. Then the ball can be molded in stages, each of which will bring it nearer to a cylindrical shape. Repeatedly folding and stretching the dough in different directions develops its gluten into a tight-knit mesh that will maintain the loaf's form during baking and give the interior a fine, firm texture.

Before baking the cylinder, you can decorate its surface in a number of ways. Shallow slashes made with a razor blade will open the loaf to reveal areas of paler, secondary crust (page 21), and a dusting of flour can give the crust a mottled look. For an especially striking effect, the loaf can be cut with a pair of kitchen shears, as demonstrated overleaf; the resulting notches will form a series of crusty ridges that not only have an interesting appearance but also make the loaf simple to tear into serving pieces by hand.

1 **Flattening a ball of dough.** Knead a risen basic dough into a ball (page 15, Step 7). Cover the dough with a damp cloth and let it rest for about 10 minutes. With crossed hands or a rolling pin, press down on the ball firmly to spread and flatten it into a fairly uniform round less than 1 inch [2½ cm.] thick.

2 **Rolling the dough.** Starting at the far edge of the round, roll up the dough toward you. Use your thumbs to steady the roll and maintain its shape.

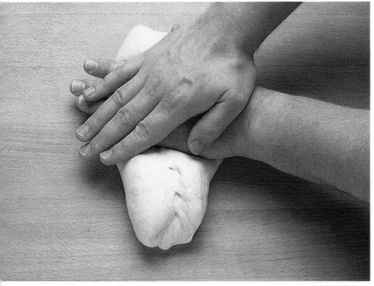

3 **Flattening the cylinder.** With crossed palms, press down one end of the roll. Move your hands along the roll and, exerting even pressure, flatten it into an oblong slightly less than 1 inch [2½ cm.] thick. Or flatten the dough with a rolling pin.

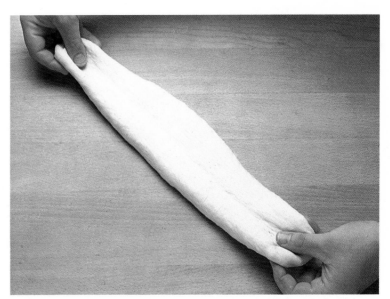

4 **Stretching the oblong.** Take one end of the flattened dough in each hand and lift both ends slightly above the work surface. Gently flap the dough up and down, at the same time pulling on the ends, until you stretch the oblong to almost twice its length. ▶

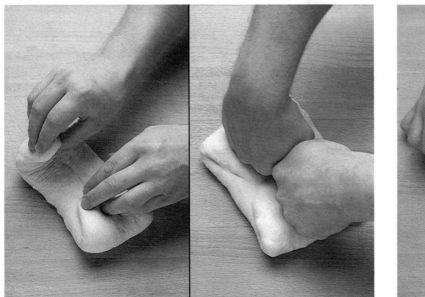

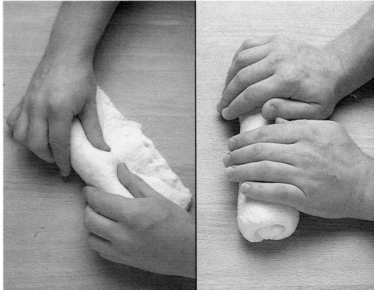

5 **Folding the dough.** Fold in both ends of the stretched oblong of dough so that they meet at the middle *(above, left)*. Working from the middle, press down firmly on the folded dough with your knuckles *(right)*. Continue until the dough is spread into a rectangle that is slightly thicker along the side farthest from you.

6 **Finishing the shaping.** Starting with the thicker side of the rectangle, roll up the dough as shown on page 19, Step 2, but this time roll it tighter, pushing in firmly with your thumbs to produce a compact cylinder *(above, left)*. To even out the surface of the cylinder, gently roll it back and forth beneath your palms *(right)*.

7 **Notching the loaf.** Place the loaf, seam side down, on a baking sheet that has been greased, or dusted with cornmeal or semolina. Sprinkle the loaf with flour. Working along the length of the loaf in a zigzag, stab a pair of open kitchen shears deep into the dough, then snip them shut to make diagonal cuts at 1½-inch [4-cm.] intervals.

8 **Baking and cooling the loaf.** Cover the loaf and let it rise for about 50 minutes, or until pressing it with a finger makes an indentation in the dough that fills in slowly. Spraying the humidified, preheated oven twice *(page 16, Step 4)*, bake the loaf at 450° F. [230° C.] for 30 to 40 minutes, until it is brown and sounds hollow when rapped. Place the loaf on a rack to cool. To serve the loaf, slice it or tear it apart between the ridges of crust.

Tapering a Cylinder's Ends

Tapering a cylinder of dough produces a bread with a generous volume of fluffy interior relative to the amount of crust. Begun in the same way as a cylindrical loaf *(pages 19-20)*, the tapered loaf takes on its particular form through a slight change in the final shaping process, as demonstrated at right. Hand pressure is used to force dough from the ends of the mass to the center; the reapportioning of mass is then further emphasized by rolling the dough over the work surface while exerting pressure only on the ends.

Tapered loaves may be left unadorned and baked with merely a few slashes embellishing their crusts, or they may be decorated with a sprinkling of aromatic seeds. Poppy seeds, used here with a light brushing of egg white to bond them to the dough, give the bread a dark-stippled, rustic look but only a light flavoring. Sesame seeds provide a slightly toasty flavor, whereas the seeds of caraway, fennel or anise contribute a distinctive licorice taste to the bread.

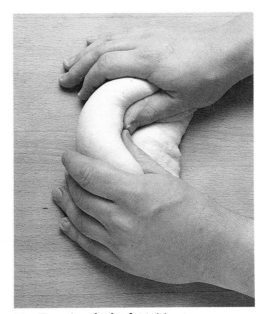

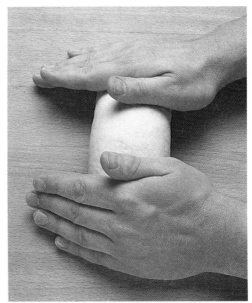

1 Tapering the loaf. Mold a risen ball of basic bread dough into a cylindrical loaf *(pages 19-20)*. As you roll up the dough for the final time *(Step 6, opposite)*, angle your hands at the ends of the roll. Exert pressure with your hands while pushing the dough toward the center with your thumbs to make a tapered, curved cylinder.

2 Completing the shaping. With your palms over the ends of the dough, gently roll the tapered cylinder backward and forward, pressing dough from the ends of the mass to fatten its midsection. Place the shaped loaf on a greased sheet, brush the loaf with lightly beaten egg white and scatter poppy seeds over its surface.

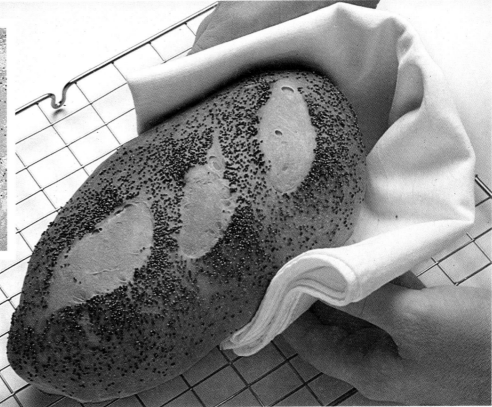

3 Finishing the loaf. Holding a razor blade almost flat, make three long, shallow cuts on the top of the loaf *(above)*. Cover with an inverted bowl or pan to avoid disturbing the seeds and let the loaf rise for about 50 minutes. Bake in a preheated, humidified 450° F. [230° C.] oven for 30 to 40 minutes, until the loaf sounds hollow when rapped. During baking, spray the oven twice *(page 16, Step 4)*. Cool on a rack *(right)*.

Multiple Uses for Elongated Dough

By repeatedly rolling a cylinder of dough, you can extend it into a thin, elongated loaf like the one demonstrated at right— a shape the French call a baguette. The loaf may be as long as you wish: The only limits are the size of your baking sheet and of your oven.

When it is further rolled into a thinner, ropelike strand, the dough can be coiled neatly to produce a spiral, turban-shaped loaf. Or the dough can be divided into several pieces and rolled out into individual strands that may then be intertwined to produce a braided loaf.

The number of strands that you may use in a braid is variable, ranging from just two for a single twist to as many as nine for an intricately patterned loaf. Three strands of dough are used in the demonstration below; the top of each braided loaf is brushed with a mixture of beaten egg yolk and water so that the crust will bake to a shiny, golden brown.

Rolling to Lengthen a Loaf

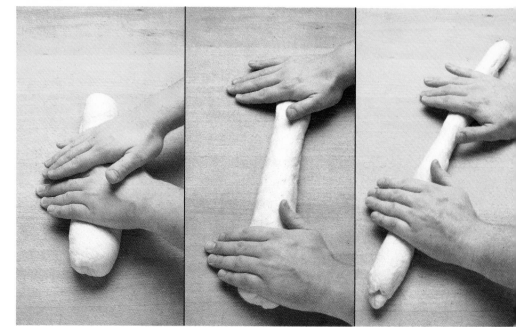

1 **Lengthening a cylinder.** Prepare basic bread dough *(pages 14-15)* and shape it into a cylinder *(pages 19-20)*. Let it rest for 10 to 15 minutes. Place your palms at the middle of the cylinder *(above, left)*, then roll it back and forth with a steady pressure, moving your hands outward as you roll *(center)*. To elongate the cylinder further, rest it for five to 10 minutes and roll it again *(right)*.

Braiding to Unite Strands

1 **Starting the braid.** Shape risen dough into three long, identical strands *(Step 1, above)*. Taper their ends and lay the strands side by side. Working from the center, lap the strands one over another to braid one end.

2 **Tapering the loaf.** To accentuate the tapering of the strands, gently pull on their tips as you braid outward from the center. At the end of the loaf, press down on the tips to stretch them.

3 **Turning over the loaf.** After braiding one half of the strands, flip the loaf upside down and away from you *(above)*. Braid the second half in the same way as the first.

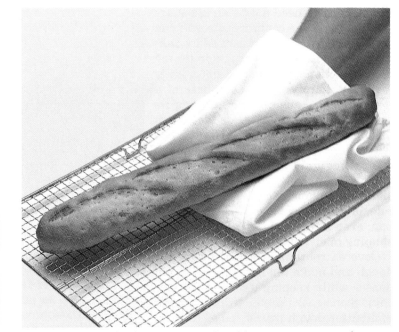

2 **Slashing the loaf.** Put the shaped loaf on a baking sheet that has been lightly greased or on one that has been sprinkled with cornmeal or, as here, semolina. Hold a single-edged razor blade almost flat against the top of the loaf and draw it along the surface: In this case, four long, shallow, overlapping cuts are made almost parallel to the length of the loaf.

3 **Baking the loaf.** Cover the loaf and let it rise in a warm place until doubled in volume — about 45 minutes. Spraying the preheated, humidified oven when the loaf is added and again after 10 minutes *(page 16, Step 4)*, bake the loaf at 450° F. [230° C.] for about 30 minutes, until the top crust is well browned. Cool the loaf on a rack. Slice the bread for serving or tear it apart by hand.

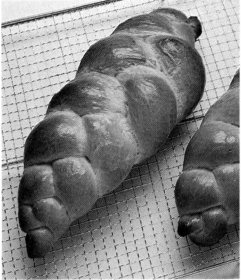

4 **Sealing the tips.** Pinch the tips of the braids together with enough pressure to join them. If they will not stay, fold the tips under the loaf so they are held by the weight of the dough.

5 **Glazing the crust.** If you make more than one loaf, place the loaves on a greased baking sheet, cover them, and let them rise until doubled — about 45 minutes. Beat an egg yolk with water and brush this glaze on the loaves.

6 **Baking and serving.** Spraying the preheated, humidified oven twice *(page 16, Step 4)*, bake the braids at 450° F. [230° C.] for 30 to 40 minutes, until brown. Cool them on a rack. To serve, slice the loaves or tear them by hand.

Rolls — Quickly Shaped and Speedily Baked

By portioning risen dough into small pieces, a cook can quickly form a dozen or more yeast rolls into any of a wide variety of shapes. The demonstrations here and on the following page show five of the options: rounds, cigars, knots, cloverleafs and those folded semicircles known as Parker House rolls, a reference to the Boston hotel where they were invented.

Any firm but malleable yeast dough can be used for rolls. Basic bread dough (pages 14-15) will produce rolls with a dense, fine-textured interior. Milk-and-butter dough (recipe, page 164) will yield a lighter, moister interior.

As with loaves, rolls should be allowed to double in volume before being baked. Because of their small size, the rising will take 20 to 30 minutes—less than half the time required for loaves.

To produce tender crusts, the shaped dough should be painted liberally with a moistening glaze before baking. An egg or egg yolk beaten with water will add a shiny, golden finish to rolls. A glaze of egg white and water will make the dough

sticky and hold seeds in place. Milk, cream or melted-butter glazes will soften crusts; salted water will add flavor.

During baking, crust formation can be further held in check by the same oven-humidifying tactics used for loaves—placing a pan of water in the oven and spraying water with an atomizer (page 17). More frequent sprayings keep roll crusts proportionately thin.

To produce firm, chewy crusts, dust the dough with flour (below) instead of applying a glaze. This will cause the surface to dry quickly. A humidifying pan is advisable, but the floured rolls should not be sprayed while they bake.

Like loaves, yeast rolls are too hot to handle or eat straight from the oven. They must be transferred to a wire rack for about 10 minutes; during this cooling period, steam from the bread will evaporate rapidly and leave the rolls dry to the touch. Then, if you want to serve the rolls warm, wrap them in napkins to preserve their heat. Otherwise, let them cool thoroughly—another 20 minutes or so.

Rounds: Molding in One Palm

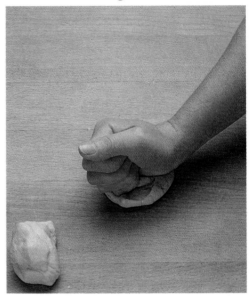

1 **Expelling air.** Mix and knead a yeast dough. Cover it with plastic wrap or a damp cloth and let it rise in a warm, draft-free place until doubled in volume. Cut the dough into pieces the size of small lemons. Press down on each piece several times with your fist to expel all large gas bubbles.

Cigars: Tapering with Finger Pressure

1 **Shaping the dough.** Divide a risen dough into equal portions the size of small lemons. Form each portion into a ball (Steps 1 and 2, above). To shape each ball into a short, broad cigar, roll the dough backward and forward under your fingers. Place the cigar-shaped rolls well apart on a greased baking sheet.

2 **Dusting with flour.** With a single-edged razor blade, cut a shallow slash along each roll. Cover the rolls with plastic wrap or a damp cloth and let them rise for 20 to 30 minutes. For a firm crust, dust the rolls with flour.

3 **Baking the rolls.** Bake the rolls in a preheated 450° F. [230° C.] oven for 15 to 20 minutes, or until they are lightly browned. Transfer them to a wire rack to cool before serving.

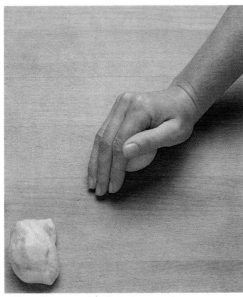

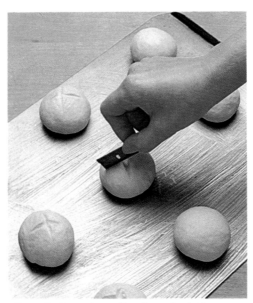

2 **Shaping the dough.** Cup the palm of your hand over the piece of dough and roll it over the work surface until it gathers into a round ball. Repeat the process with each piece.

3 **Slashing the rolls.** Place the balls of dough, spaced well apart, on a greased baking sheet. Cut a small, shallow cross on top of each roll with a single-edged razor blade. Cover the rolls with plastic wrap or a damp cloth and let them rise for 20 to 30 minutes, until they have doubled in volume.

4 **Baking the rolls.** To give the rolls a lightly seasoned crust, brush them with salted water just before placing them in a preheated oven, humidified with a pan of water. Spraying at five-minute intervals, bake the rolls at 450° F. [230° C.] for 15 to 20 minutes, until they are well browned. Cool them on a wire rack.

Knots: Tying Ropes of Dough

1 **Rolling the dough.** Divide a risen dough into equal portions, each about the size of a small lemon. Exerting an even pressure with both hands, roll each portion back and forth on the work surface to form a rope 12 to 15 inches [30 to 40 cm.] long and ½ inch [1 cm.] thick.

2 **Tying the knots.** Tie each rope of dough into a loose knot. Place the knotted rolls on a greased baking sheet, cover them with plastic wrap or a damp cloth and let them rise until doubled in volume — 20 to 30 minutes.

3 **Baking the knots.** To give the rolls a shiny crust, glaze them with a mixture of egg and water. Bake the rolls in a preheated and humidified 450° F. [230° C.] oven for 15 to 20 minutes, spraying them with an atomizer at five-minute intervals. When evenly browned, cool the rolls on a wire rack.

Parker House Rolls: Folding for a Double Crust

1 **Shaping the rolls.** Punch down a risen dough and, with a rolling pin, roll it ½ inch [1 cm.] thick. Using a floured 3½-inch [9-cm.] biscuit cutter, cut the sheet into rounds. Brush melted butter on each round and crease it across the center with a knife. Fold each roll at the crease. Gather up the trimmings, flatten them and cut more rounds.

2 **Glazing the rolls.** Place the rolls on a greased baking sheet, cover them with plastic wrap or a damp cloth and let them rise in a warm, draft-free place for 20 to 30 minutes. For a velvety finish, brush the tops with melted butter.

3 **Baking the rolls.** Spraying with water at five-minute intervals, bake the rolls in a preheated and humidified 450° F. [230° C.] oven for about 15 minutes, or until they are evenly browned. Transfer the rolls to a wire rack to cool for five minutes before serving.

Cloverleaf Rolls: Joining Small Balls of Dough

1 **Shaping the rolls.** Push up a walnut-sized portion of risen dough between your thumb and index finger and pinch the portion off. Press three such portions into each greased cup of a muffin pan. Cover, and set the pan in a warm, draft-free place; let the dough rise for 20 to 30 minutes, until it reaches just above the tops of the cups.

2 **Baking the rolls.** Bake the rolls in a preheated, humidified 450° F. [230° C.] oven for about 15 minutes, spraying regularly with water, until the tops are golden brown. To soften the crusts further and give them a lustrous sheen, brush the hot rolls with milk or cream.

3 **Cooling the rolls.** Remove the pan from the oven and set it aside until the rolls are cool enough to handle — about two to three minutes. (Leaving them longer in the pan would trap condensing steam and make them moist.) Pluck the rolls from the pan to cool further on a wire rack before serving.

A Middle Eastern Bread with a Pocket for Stuffing

When risen yeast dough is rolled or patted very thin before rising, it produces loaves of flatbread, usually no more than ½ inch [1 cm.] high, with thick crusts and chewy interiors. Among the most prized of these flatbreads is the Middle Eastern *pita* demonstrated here. As it bakes, *pita* inflates and a hollow pocket forms inside each loaf. When it cools, the *pita* loses its puff, but the pocket remains to be opened and stuffed—with meat, cheese or any sandwich or salad mixture.

For loaves that will inflate fully, *pita* is made with a variation of basic dough that includes some gluten flour for extra resilience, and olive oil to keep the bread moist *(recipe, page 96)*. To inflate the dough quickly, *pita* is baked in an oven preheated to at least 475° F. [250° C.]— some cooks prefer 550° F. [290° C.]—and the loaves are given added oven spring by starting the baking on the bottom shelf. Because the oven is so hot, the loaves rise within five minutes and cook in a total of 10 minutes; there is no need to humidify the oven or spray the bread with water.

1 **Rolling.** Shape risen dough into a 14-inch [35-cm.] cylinder and slice it into 14 rounds. Let the rounds rise until they have doubled in volume, then roll them into disks ¼ inch [6 mm.] thick. Set the disks on a baking sheet sprinkled with cornmeal or semolina; cover and let them rise until they increase in volume by about half—20 to 30 minutes.

2 **Baking.** Slide the baking sheet onto the lowest shelf of a preheated 475° F. [250° C.] oven. When the loaves inflate, after about four or five minutes, move the baking sheet to the top shelf of the oven and continue to bake the loaves until they are crisped and browned—another five minutes or so.

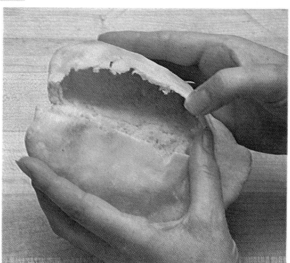

3 **Serving.** After they are baked, wrap the loaves in a dry towel, covered with a damp towel, to soften them as they cool. Serve them from a napkin-lined basket *(left)*. At the table, let each diner split his loaf open by hand *(inset)* and spread it with butter or stuff it with meat or cheese for a sandwich.

Crisp Snacks from Strips of Dough

The crispiest of breads are made from strips of dough so thin that after baking they are composed mainly of crust—and even the inside is dry and crunchy. These strips can be baked plain or fashioned into many shapes, such as the looped pretzels demonstrated at right or the twisted bread sticks shown opposite.

Traditionally, the strips of dough for pretzels are rolled out progressively from small balls (Step 1, right). So much handling may cause excess gluten to develop; if a strip becomes elastic or tears, let it relax, under a cover to prevent drying, for five to 10 minutes.

A quicker way of making strips is to roll out a thick dough sheet with a pin and then slice the sheet (Step 1, opposite). Generally, these cut, flat-sided strips are left as is or twisted into bread sticks, but they can also be used for pretzels.

Regardless of their shape, small, thin breads are commonly garnished before baking, with coarse salt or with seeds such as cumin, caraway, fennel or anise. Such piquant additions make the breads particularly suitable as snacks.

In order to achieve the dense texture that many cooks favor in these breads, the pieces are often baked just after shaping, without a final rising. For a lighter result, the shaped dough can be allowed to rise briefly—20 minutes at most. To emphasize their crunchiness, the breads are baked in a dry oven, without the humidifying pan and sprayings that most loaves or rolls require.

The Pretzel Maker's Loop

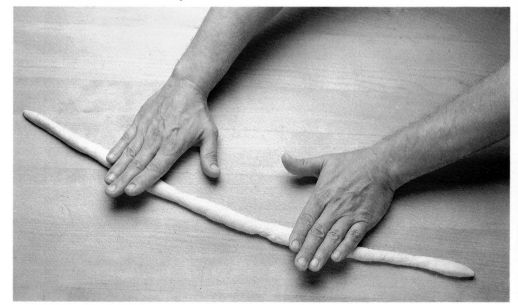

1 **Rolling out the dough.** Mix and knead basic bread dough and let it rise once (pages 14-15). Cut the dough into small pieces. Shape each piece into a ball about 2½ inches [6 cm.] in diameter. Roll each ball back and forth beneath your fingers, moving your hands along the length of the emerging cylinder to keep it even. Continue working the dough until it is about ½ inch [1 cm.] thick and 16 to 18 inches [40 to 45 cm.] long.

4 **Baking and serving.** Bake the pretzels in a preheated 450° F. [230° C.] oven for about 15 minutes, until they are golden brown. Transfer the pretzels to a wire rack to cool for at least 10 minutes; serve them either slightly warm or cooled to room temperature.

2 **Shaping the dough.** Curve each strip of dough into a broad horseshoe shape with the ends pointing toward you. Twist the ends around each other and rest them on the resulting loop of dough. Transfer the pretzel to a baking sheet that has been lightly greased, or sprinkled with cornmeal or semolina.

3 **Garnishing the dough.** For lighter-textured pretzels, cover them with a cloth and let them rise for 10 to 20 minutes. Beat an egg with a little water and brush this glaze over each pretzel. Sprinkle the pretzels with coarse salt or a light coat of aromatic seeds.

A Simple Twist for Bread Sticks

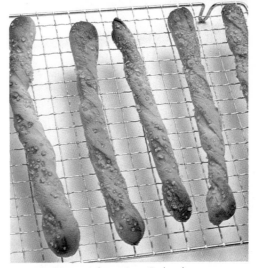

1 **Cutting dough strips.** Mix and knead basic bread dough, let it rise and knead it into a ball (pages 14-15). On a lightly floured work surface, use a rolling pin to flatten the ball gently into a 9-by-12-inch [23-by-30-cm.] oblong about ½ inch [1 cm.] thick. With a long, sharp knife, cut the dough across its width into ½-inch [1-cm.] strips.

2 **Twisting the strips.** Sprinkle the work surface with coarse salt, and lay a strip of dough on top of the salt. Place a hand at each end of the strip. Slide one hand forward and the other back simultaneously to twist the strip and coat it with salt. Place the strips on a greased baking sheet.

3 **Baking and serving.** Bake the strips in a preheated 450° F. [230° C.] oven for 10 to 15 minutes, until they are golden brown. Transfer the baked bread sticks to a wire rack and cool them for about 10 minutes. Serve them warm or fully cooled.

2
Enriched Yeast Breads
Luxurious Effects from Eggs and Butter

A sugar-dusted ring of yeast puff coffeecake is sliced for serving. To form the ring, the dough sheet was first rolled around a filling of currants and cinnamon sugar, then looped into a circle and cut deep at 1-inch [2½-cm.] intervals around its circumference. Before baking, alternate sections were flipped inward to give the coffeecake an unusual serrated look (page 51).

When eggs and butter are used as enrichments, a yeast-leavened loaf takes on cakelike qualities. Eggs make the bread taste richer and supply structure-building protein, producing a loaf that rises higher and keeps better than basic yeast bread. But egg whites tend to dry out a dough as they coagulate during baking. Butter compensates for this drying—and it also softens the gluten. This softened gluten offers less resistance as the gas produced by the yeast inflates the dough. Thus the bread doubles in volume faster than one containing no butter.

Depending on the quantities of eggs and butter used—and also on how they are incorporated—the transformations in the finished bread can range from subtle to dramatic. Even a small amount of egg and butter will endow bread with a soft crust and a moist, yellow interior. As the amounts of egg and butter increase, these characteristics become more pronounced: The peerless brioche *(pages 40-43)*, one of the crowning triumphs of French cooking, has a silken texture and an incomparable golden hue.

Because the fat in eggs and butter can inhibit the initial formation of the gluten by creating a barrier between the flour and liquid in a dough, enriched doughs are generally made in two stages: First the yeast, liquid and some of the flour are mixed and set in a warm, draft-free place to rise, then the rest of the flour and eggs and butter are added. In the case of an enriched-dough variant called yeast puff dough, however, barriers of fat play a vital role. To make yeast puff, risen dough is rolled out, then spread with butter and folded to form layers. In the oven, while the yeast inflates the dough, the butter melts to keep the layers separate, creating a light, flaky effect. Yeast puff dough is used for a host of delicate breads, including croissants *(pages 44-46)* and Danish pastries *(pages 47-51)*.

Except for yeast puff dough, most enriched doughs can be baked in pans or shaped into any of the simple loaves and rolls demonstrated in the preceding chapter. More often, however, they receive further culinary elaboration. They can be curved into rings *(pages 34-35)*, or filled with preserves for jelly doughnuts *(pages 36-37)*. And they can be rolled around nuts or cooked fruits for that cherished American breakfast treat, coffeecake, which actually is not a cake at all, but an enriched, sweetened yeast bread *(pages 38-39)*.

A Two-Stage Strategy for Mixing Dough

Whole eggs and a generous addition of butter turn a basic yeast dough into a rich bread with a tender crust and light, cakelike interior. However, the incorporation of such a large amount of fat demands special tactics for mixing. If all of the ingredients were combined in one operation, the fat from the egg yolks and butter would envelop some or all of the yeast cells, sealing them off from the flour they require for nourishment. Simultaneously, the fat would envelop the flour particles, shutting out the liquid they need to form gluten.

To allow both the yeast and the gluten to begin their development unhindered, simple egg-bread dough should be prepared in two stages, as demonstrated here *(recipe, page 164)*. In the first stage, a preliminary batter—called a sponge because of its porous texture—is made from yeast, milk and a small amount of flour. Sugar provides extra nourishment for the yeast. After it is whisked vigorously, the sponge is left to rise until doubled in volume—usually within an

hour. In the second stage—when the rising and gluten formation are well under way—eggs, butter and more flour are added to make the dough.

Because simple egg dough is considerably softer than basic bread dough, it is kneaded more gently. To keep the butter from being melted by the warmth of your hands, which would make the dough oily and difficult to handle, knead on a cool work surface—ideally, a marble slab. If the butter does begin to melt, refrigerate the dough for half an hour; then knead it until it is smooth and elastic.

After the dough has risen and has been kneaded into a ball *(page 15, Step 7)*, it can be shaped into loaves or rolls *(pages 18-28)* or formed into the ring shown here. Because of its delicacy and richness, the dough is baked at a lower temperature—usually 350° to 400° F. [180° to 200° C.]—and for a longer time than a basic dough would be. The high moisture content of egg-bread dough makes it unnecessary to humidify the oven or spray the bread with water during baking.

1 **Making the sponge.** Stir yeast and a little sugar into tepid milk in a large mixing bowl, and put the bowl aside for 10 minutes. When the yeast foams, add a few handfuls of flour and whisk vigorously to form a thick batter. Cover the bowl and let this sponge rise in a warm, draft-free place until it doubles in volume. Whisk in whole eggs.

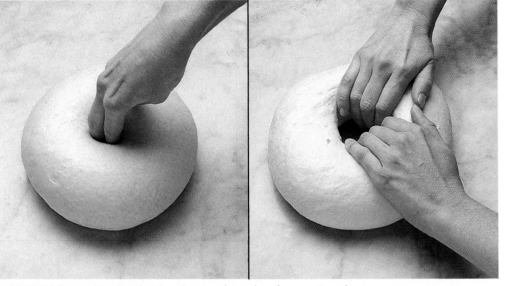

5 **Forming a ring.** Put the dough into a large bowl, cover it and set it in a warm place. Let the dough rise for at least one and one half hours, until it is three or four times its original volume. Punch down the dough and put it on a cool, lightly floured surface; knead it into a ball *(page 15, Step 7)*. Let it rest for 10 minutes. Press two fingers through the middle of the ball *(above, left)* and make gentle, circular movements to enlarge the hole. With both hands, stretch the dough from inside the hole to form a ring *(above, right)*. If the dough tears or resists stretching, cover it and let it rest for about 10 minutes before trying again.

6 **Enlarging the ring.** Supporting both sides of the ring, transfer it by hand to a lightly buttered baking sheet. Pat and stretch the dough into an even ring shape. Cover the dough with a large, inverted bowl and let it rise for about 45 minutes, until doubled in volume.

2 **Softening the butter.** To make the butter creamy enough to incorporate into the dough, place it on a cool work surface — in this case, marble — and press it with the heel of one hand. Push forward, then gather up the butter and repeat the process until it is pliable, but not soft and oily.

3 **Adding butter and flour.** Break the butter into small pieces and toss them into the sponge. Gradually add flour with one hand and mix it into the sponge with the other hand to make a fairly firm — but only roughly blended — dough. Transfer the dough to a cool, lightly floured surface.

4 **Kneading the dough.** Press the heel of one hand into the center of the dough and gently push forward. Then fold the extended section of dough back over the mass. Turn the dough slightly and begin the process again. Continue kneading until the dough is shiny and elastic — 10 to 15 minutes.

7 **Baking and serving.** Glaze the dough ring with a mixture of beaten egg and water. Bake the ring in a preheated 400° F. [200° C.] oven for 50 to 60 minutes, until the bread is evenly browned. Cool the ring on a wire rack; serve it warm or cold, in wedges.

Doughnuts: The Classic Deep-fried Bread

Simple egg-bread dough makes the most delicately textured base for yeast doughnuts. The dough is deep fried rather than baked, and the cooking is completed so rapidly that the doughnuts emerge crisp, puffed and tender—and without a trace of greasiness inside or out.

Several processes are at work during cooking. As soon as the doughnuts are plunged into hot oil, microscopic pores in their surface admit the oil to help heat the dough through quickly and stimulate the production of carbon dioxide. Within seconds the dough inflates by as much as 50 per cent. Then, as the interior reaches 160° F. [70° C.], the starches in the dough stiffen, halting its expansion while forming a firm support for the inflated bread. Simultaneously the surface dries, closing the pores, and the crust begins to brown. The change of color signals doneness.

Cooking should take only two minutes or so when both the dough and the oil are at the correct temperatures. If the dough is warmer than about 80° F. [25° C.], the oil will penetrate its pores too deeply, making the doughnuts greasy; on the other hand, cold dough will inflate slowly and burn before it cooks through.

The oil must be heated to 375° F. [190° C.] and kept at a constant temperature. If the oil cools, the dough will absorb too much before its pores close; overheated oil will burn the crusts before the dough has cooked fully. In order to maintain an even temperature when the doughnuts are added, the oil must be about 4 inches [10 cm.] deep. Monitor its temperature with a deep-frying thermometer and fry the doughnuts in batches of two or three.

To ensure rapid frying, the doughnuts should be made from dough rolled not more than ½ inch [1 cm.] thick—or ¼ inch [6 mm.] if they are formed by joining two layers. The most familiar shapes are the rings shown at right and the filled rounds demonstrated below. Other popular shapes include little balls (made from the centers of the rings and whimsically named doughnut holes), the twisted strips often called crullers and the slotted rectangles known as long johns.

For extra richness, buttermilk, sour cream or yogurt can replace the milk in the dough (recipes, pages 154-159). The flavor can be enhanced by spices, grated citrus peel or bits of nuts. With filled doughnuts, the range of variations is extended. Although jelly would melt in the heat of frying and ooze into the oil, a light egg-white wash will bind the two layers of dough together well enough to safely hold any firm, thick jam, fruit butter, marmalade or conserve.

As a finishing touch, fried and drained doughnuts of either type can be dusted with granulated or confectioners' sugar while their surfaces are still sufficiently warm to absorb, and hold, the granules.

Mass-producing Filled Spheres

1 **Marking the dough.** On a lightly floured surface, roll simple egg-bread dough into a sheet about ¼ inch [6 mm.] thick. To prevent the dough from rising while you work, prick the sheet all over with a fork. On half of the sheet, lightly imprint circles with the floured rim of a glass; do not use a cutter lest it cut through the dough.

2 **Filling.** Brush lightly beaten egg white along the edges of the imprinted circles. Spoon a heaping teaspoonful of firm jam—in this case, raspberry jam—onto the center of each circle. Carefully lift the remaining half of the dough sheet and fold it over the jam-dotted circles. The top sheet will mound clearly above each dollop of jam.

3 **Cutting.** Center the glass above each jam mound and push the rim of the glass firmly through both layers of dough. The rim will press the layers together, sealing them as it cuts. Pull away the excess dough from outside the rounds. With a spatula, put the doughnuts on a floured cloth, and let them rise until doubled—about 20 minutes.

Cutting and Cooking Rings

1 **Cutting.** On a floured surface, roll simple egg-bread dough (pages 34-35) ½ inch [1 cm.] thick. Press a floured doughnut cutter firmly through the dough to cut rings. Pick out the centers and peel away excess dough. Using a spatula, set the rings on a floured cloth to rise until doubled—about 30 minutes.

2 **Deep frying.** In a heavy pot, heat 4 inches [10 cm.] of oil to 375° F. [190° C.]. Using a skimmer dipped into the oil to prevent sticking, pick up one ring at a time and slide it into the pot. Fry the doughnuts for one and one half minutes to brown one side, then turn them and brown the other side for 45 seconds.

3 **Garnishing.** Drain the doughnuts on paper towels or on a rack set over paper towels. When the doughnuts are cool enough to touch, after about five minutes, dust them with confectioners' sugar—here, sprinkled from a dredger. Serve the doughnuts warm or cooled to room temperature.

4 **Deep frying and serving.** In a heavy pot, heat 4 inches [10 cm.] of oil to 375° F. [190° C.]. Using an oiled skimmer (Step 2, above), slide two or three doughnuts into the pot. Brown the doughnuts for about one and one half minutes on one side, 45 seconds on the other side. Drain them on paper towels for about five minutes, then roll the doughnuts in sugar.

Buns that Feature a Spiral of Sweetness

The richness and fine texture of simple egg-bread dough make it a pleasing vehicle for a sweet filling. The risen dough need only be flattened, spread with filling and rolled into a tight cylinder.

Such a cylinder can be baked as is, to produce a spiral loaf, or it can be sliced to yield buns. For the sticky buns demonstrated at right, the slices are set side by side in cake pans that have been coated with a syrup mixture *(recipe, page 130)*. During rising and baking, the slices meld together while the syrup turns to caramel, glossing and flavoring the buns. Alternatively, the slices can be further cut with kitchen shears and spread into fans *(box, below)*.

The filling must be soft enough to spread easily on the delicate dough, but dry enough so that it does not leak. Here, the buns are filled with brown sugar, raisins and cinnamon. Other combinations can be assembled from white or maple sugar, candied fruits, nuts, poppy seeds and spices such as ginger or nutmeg.

1 Spreading the filling. Punch down risen dough and set it on a lightly floured surface. Using a rolling pin, flatten the dough into a 10-by-18-inch [25-by-45-cm.] rectangle about ¼ inch [6 mm.] thick. Brush melted butter over it and sprinkle it with a mixture of brown sugar, cinnamon and raisins. Lightly roll the filling into the dough.

2 Rolling a cylinder. Lift the long edge of the rectangle with your hands and curl it over the filling. Pressing the dough tightly with both hands, roll the rectangle into a compact cylinder.

A Fan-shaped Variation

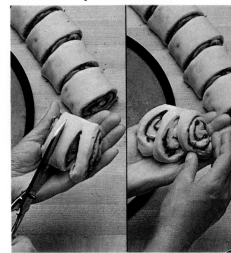

1 Cutting the dough. Cut a filled cylinder *(Step 3, above)* into slices 2¼ inches [6 cm.] thick. With kitchen shears, make two cuts in the side of each slice, snipping about two thirds of the way through the dough *(left)*. Fan out the three sections *(right)* and set the buns well apart on a buttered baking sheet.

2 Glazing the buns. Cover the fans with a damp cloth and let them rise until doubled in bulk — about 45 minutes. Using a pastry brush, glaze the buns with a mixture of egg yolk and water.

3 Baking and serving. Bake the buns in a preheated 350° F. [180° C.] oven for 15 to 20 minutes, until golden brown. With a spatula, lift the buns onto a rack to cool for at least 10 minutes; serve warm or at room temperature.

3 **Slicing.** With a sharp knife, cut the cylinder into slices about 1 inch [2½ cm.] thick. If the warmth of your kitchen has made the dough too soft to cut neatly, refrigerate the cylinder for 20 minutes.

4 **Baking.** Coat two 9-inch [23-cm.] layer-cake pans with a mixture of light corn syrup, brown sugar and melted butter. Put the dough slices edge to edge in the pans, cover, and let the slices rise until doubled — about 45 minutes. Bake in a preheated 350° F. [180° C.] oven for 25 minutes, until golden brown.

5 **Serving.** To cool the buns, first place an inverted wire rack over the pan. Holding the rack and pan together at the sides with potholders or a folded towel, flip the assembly over onto a plate. The plate will catch any dripping caramel. Lift off the pan. Let the buns cool for at least 10 minutes before serving on another plate.

The Golden Glory of Brioche

Brioche is the richest of all yeast breads: For every 4 cups [1 liter] of flour in its dough, it may include as much as 1 pound [½ kg.] of butter and six or more eggs (*demonstration, right; recipe, page 165*). Brioche also takes longer to produce than any other type of enriched bread—from 12 to 14 hours in all. However, most of this time is taken up by three long, unhurried risings, which improve the flavor of brioche and give it a silky texture that matches its richness.

As is the case with many egg-and-butter breads, the preparation of brioche begins with assembling a preliminary, butter-free dough from flour, yeast and eggs. The large number of eggs used makes the dough exceptionally soft without the addition of any other liquid. Because of its softness, the dough spreads out as it is kneaded, and a dough scraper must be used to gather it back up. When the dough is smooth and elastic, the scraper is used to fold in butter. Like most bread doughs, brioche dough is left in a warm place for its first rising. Then it is punched down to expel any large gas bubbles, ensuring a fine texture.

Refinement of texture is also one of the objects of the second (and longest) rising. During this rising, the dough is refrigerated. The cold slows down the yeast's production of carbon dioxide, so the gas stretches the dough's gluten meshwork gently. The cold also firms the dough, making it easy to shape when risen.

Brioche dough can be baked in almost any size or shape, freestanding or in a baking pan or mold. In the demonstration here and on the following pages, the dough is molded into a single, large-sized version of the traditional topknotted form known as *brioche à tête*—literally, "brioche with a head." Once shaped or put into any mold, the dough must be set aside to warm to room temperature during its third and final rising.

Brioche is best eaten warm so that its buttery flavor and fine texture can be fully appreciated. But it also may be served cold; with its moistness and high fat content, it will keep for several days.

1 **Mixing a preliminary dough.** Put flour, sugar and salt into a large mixing bowl. Mix yeast with a little tepid water (*page 10*). Make a well in the center of the flour and pour in the yeast mixture. Break eggs into the well; with your fingers, break the yolks and combine the eggs with the yeast. Stir the ingredients by hand, pulling in the flour from the sides to make a loose dough.

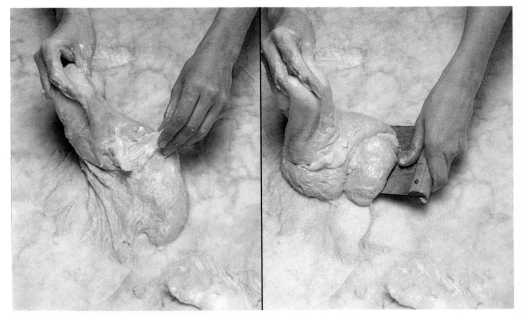

3 **Folding in butter.** Soften butter by pressing it with the heel of your hand (*page 35, Step 2*). Pull the ends of the kneaded dough slightly apart and nestle a small piece of the softened butter in the center (*above, left*). With a dough scraper, fold the butter and dough together, scraping and lifting with an up-and-over motion (*right*). Continue in this way, gradually adding small pieces of butter to the dough, until all of the butter is incorporated.

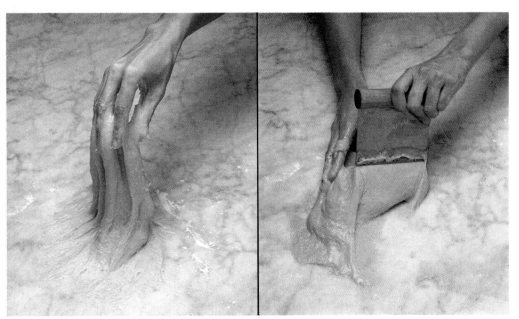

2 **Kneading the dough.** Turn the dough out onto a cool work surface — in this demonstration, a marble slab. Pull up the dough with one hand *(above, left)* and slap it back down onto the surface. Knead vigorously in this manner for about 10 minutes, until the dough is elastic and pulls freely from your hand. As the dough spreads, use a dough scraper to pull it together again *(right)*. If the dough is too loose to cohere, work in a little sifted flour.

4 **Blending.** Knead the dough with one hand until it is blended — two to three minutes — while using the dough scraper with your other hand to gather up the dough as it spreads. Put the dough into a bowl, cover, and let the dough rise at room temperature for three to four hours, until tripled in volume.

5 **Punching the dough.** With your fist, punch the dough several times to compact it in the bottom of the bowl and expel excess gas. Cover the bowl with plastic wrap and refrigerate it for six to eight hours, until the dough has doubled in volume. ▶

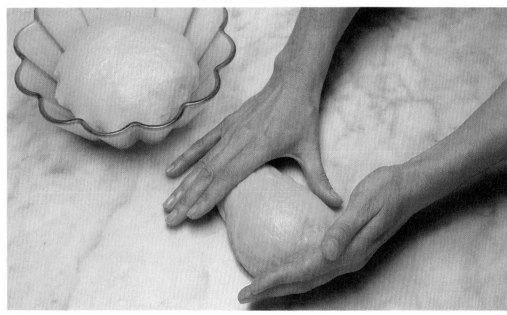

6 **Shaping the dough.** Transfer the dough to a cool, lightly floured work surface. With a knife, cut off about one quarter of the dough and set it aside. Knead the larger piece into a ball *(page 15, Step 7)* and put it into a well-buttered, fluted brioche mold with a capacity of twice the dough's volume. Shape the smaller piece of dough into a ball, then rest one side of the ball against one hand and roll the dough back and forth over the work surface with your other hand to make a tapered, teardrop shape *(above)*.

7 **Indenting the dough.** With three fingers held close together, press down into the center of the large piece of dough until your finger tips touch the bottom of the mold. Enlarge the cavity by moving your hand in a circle until the hole is slightly larger than the tapered end of the smaller piece of dough.

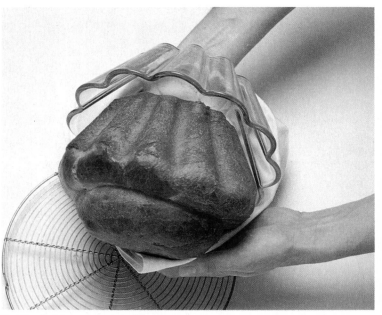

9 **Glazing the dough.** Beat an egg yolk with a little water. Brush the mixture over the surface of the dough, taking care to avoid the seam between the topknot and the base so that the topknot can rise during baking. For a pronounced and even glaze, let the surface dry for several minutes, then brush the dough a second time. Put the brioche in a preheated 425° F. [220° C.] oven.

10 **Baking and unmolding.** After 10 minutes, reduce the oven heat to 375° F. [190° C.], then bake for 30 minutes more. If the brioche browns too quickly, cover it with foil. To test for doneness, insert a wooden pick or thin metal skewer into the topknot. The pick or skewer should come out dry; if not, bake for 10 minutes more and test again. To unmold, invert the brioche onto a cloth held in your palm, then turn the brioche over onto a rack.

8 **Assembling the brioche.** Lift up the small piece of dough and lower its tapered end into the cavity *(above, left)*. Its rounded end will form a small head, or topknot, on the larger piece of dough. Pat the topknot with the fingers of both hands *(right)* to give it an even shape. Cover the filled mold with a large inverted bowl or a cloth, and let the dough rise in a warm place for about one and one half hours, until it has doubled in volume.

11 **Serving the brioche.** Let the brioche cool for 15 minutes, then put it on a slicing board, as here, or a serving plate. Cut the brioche into wedges and serve it plain or with butter.

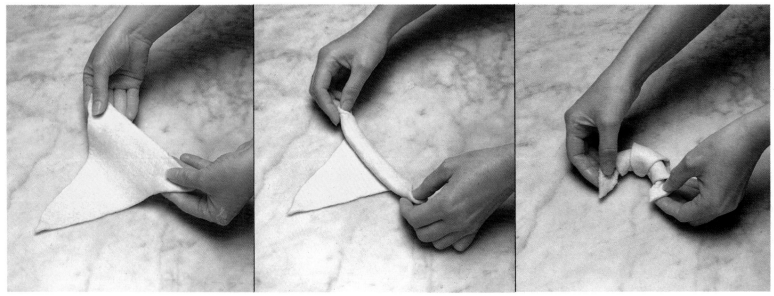

8 **Shaping the croissants.** Gently separate one triangle from the rest and place it with its base — the shortest side — toward you. Elongate the triangle slightly by rolling it away from yourself with a rolling pin. Gently stretch the corners of the base so they are well defined *(left)*. Starting at the base, roll up the triangle tightly *(center)*. Tuck the tip just under the roll: The tip will emerge during baking. Curl the ends of the roll in to form a crescent *(right)*.

9 **Glazing the croissants.** Place the croissants on a buttered baking sheet, leaving at least 1 inch [2½ cm.] between them. Cover them with a damp cloth and let them rise until they have doubled in volume — about one hour at 70° F. [30° C.] or overnight in the refrigerator. Mix a beaten egg yolk with a little water and brush this glaze over the croissants, taking care not to drip it onto the baking sheet.

10 **Baking and serving.** Place the baking sheet of croissants on the middle shelf of a preheated 425° F. [220° C.] oven; after two minutes, reduce the heat to 375° F. [190° C.] and bake for an additional 15 to 20 minutes, until the croissants turn a golden brown. Cool them on a wire rack for 10 to 15 minutes, then serve them warm in a napkin-lined basket. Pull them apart to eat them.

The Art of Shaping Danish Pastries

Fanciful shapes that are cut and folded from yeast puff dough will increase in intricacy as the paper-thin layers of dough rise and separate in the oven. Fillings, glazes and toppings add to the appeal of such breads—referred to collectively as Danish pastries *(recipe, page 133)*. The four Danish pastries demonstrated here and on the next two pages show a few of the many possibilities.

Envelopes *(right)* are formed by folding the corners of a rolled-out square over a spoonful of filling. The same squares can yield pinwheel shapes when they are cut and folded in a different way *(overleaf)*. The two other pastries demonstrated on the following pages—cockscombs and twists—are made from dough that is filled before it is shaped.

In the making of any Danish pastry, the dough is handled extensively. This tends to melt the layers of butter—and the small size of the pastries increases the hazard. To keep the layers of butter intact, the dough must stay very cold: Unless your kitchen is air-conditioned, do not make Danish pastries in the summer. And until you are adept at rolling and folding, rechill the dough frequently, even if you have to stop work on a batch of pastries that are only partially shaped. Some cooks rechill the dough in the freezer—10 minutes is usually sufficient—rather than in the refrigerator; if you use this shortcut, take care not to let the dough freeze solid.

The filling for any shape of dough can be as simple as a handful of dried currants or of grated hard cheese. Richer, moister fillings include sausage meat, almond paste *(recipe, page 165)* or a mixture of egg and soft cheese.

Both sweet and savory pastries are usually brushed before baking with a glaze of egg yolk and water. Sweet ones also may be topped after baking with a dusting of sugar, a coat of strained jam or a sprinkling of chopped nuts.

Envelopes Enclosing Almond Paste

1 Mixing an almond paste. Sift superfine and confectioners' sugar into a bowl. Add ground blanched almonds and grate in a little lemon peel. Stir the ingredients with a spoon. Beat egg whites lightly and add them to the mixture, stirring until the ingredients are amalgamated into a stiff paste.

2 Dividing the dough. Prepare a yeast puff dough *(pages 44-45, Steps 1-5)*. On a cold, lightly floured work surface, roll the dough to a thickness of about ¼ inch [6 mm.]. Trim the edges with a dough scraper or sharp knife to make a neat rectangle, and cut the rectangle into 5-inch [12-cm.] squares.

3 Shaping the envelopes. Spoon a dollop of almond paste onto the center of each square. Fold in one corner of the square to the center of the filling; fold in the opposite corner to overlap the first. Repeat these folds with the other two corners, then seal the package by pressing the center with a finger. Put the envelopes on a buttered baking sheet.

4 Baking and serving. Cover with plastic wrap or a damp cloth and let the envelopes rise until almost doubled — about one hour. Glaze the pastries with egg yolk and water; put them in a preheated 425° F. [220° C.] oven. After two minutes, lower the heat to 375° F. [190° C.]. Bake for 15 to 20 minutes, until brown. Cool, and dust with sugar.

Almond-filled Pinwheels

1 **Cutting squares.** Roll yeast puff dough into a sheet ¼ inch [6 mm.] thick and cut it into 5-inch [12-cm.] squares. With a dough scraper or a sharp knife, cut a diagonal line from each corner to about ½ inch [1 cm.] from the center of the square. Place a teaspoonful of filling — in this case, almond paste — on the uncut center of the square.

2 **Shaping the pinwheels.** Fold alternate points of dough over the filling. Lightly press the center of the pastry to stick the overlapping points together. Place the shaped pastries on a buttered baking sheet and cover them. Let them rise for about one hour, until almost doubled in volume.

3 **Baking and cooling.** Beat egg yolk with a little water, and glaze the pastries with this mixture. Bake them in a preheated 425° F. [220° C.] oven for two minutes; reduce the heat to 375° F. [190° C.] and bake the pastries for 15 to 20 minutes, until golden brown. Cool the pinwheels on a rack and dust them with confectioners' sugar before serving.

Twists of Pastry and Jam

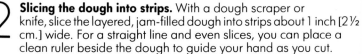

1 **Layering dough with filling.** Roll yeast puff dough to a thickness of ¼ inch [6 mm.] and, using a dough scraper or knife, trim it into rectangles about 8 by 16 inches [20 by 40 cm.]. Heat jam (this is apricot) and press it through a strainer. Spread a thin layer of the strained jam over the dough, leaving a margin of about ½ inch [1 cm.] around the edges. Fold in one third of the dough, then fold the remaining third over it.

2 **Slicing the dough into strips.** With a dough scraper or knife, slice the layered, jam-filled dough into strips about 1 inch [2½ cm.] wide. For a straight line and even slices, you can place a clean ruler beside the dough to guide your hand as you cut.

Cockscombs with a Savory Center

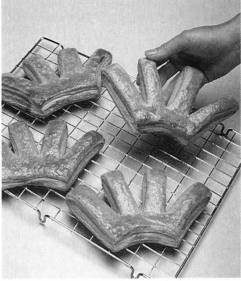

1 Filling the dough. Roll yeast puff dough into an 8-by-16-inch [20-by-40-cm.] rectangle, ¼ inch [6 mm.] thick. Spread filling — here, a cheese mixture *(recipe, page 165)* — over half the rectangle's width, leaving ½-inch [1-cm.] margins at the ends and side. Fold the uncovered half over the filling.

2 Cutting cockscombs. Using a dough scraper or sharp knife, divide the stuffed strip into four squares. Make three parallel cuts in the folded side of each square, extending each cut to within 1 inch [2½ cm.] of the opposite side. Place the pastries on a buttered baking sheet; spread their cut sections so that they resemble cockscombs.

3 Baking and cooling. Cover the pastries and let them rise for about one hour, until almost doubled in volume. Glaze them with egg yolk and water, and place them in a preheated 425° F. [220° C.] oven. After two minutes, reduce the heat to 375° F. [190° C.]. Bake for 15 to 20 minutes, until golden brown. Cool the pastries on a rack.

3 Twisting the strips. Butter a baking sheet. Give each strip a half twist as you place it on the sheet. Cover the twists with plastic wrap or a damp cloth and let them rise for about one hour, until doubled in volume. Glaze them with egg yolk beaten with water.

4 Baking and garnishing. Place the pastries in a preheated 425° F. [220° C.] oven for two minutes; reduce the heat to 375° F. [190° C.] and bake for 15 to 20 minutes, or until the twists are golden brown. Place the pastries on a rack to cool. Brush them with warm, strained jam and sprinkle with chopped walnuts.

Ingenious Constructions for Coffeecake

Yeast puff dough *(recipe, page 166)* need not be used exclusively for small breads. It also lends itself to filled coffeecakes in any of a variety of shapes, including the elaborate braid and the intricately twisted ring demonstrated at right.

To make the braid, the long sides of a rectangle of dough are cut into a diagonal fringe of narrow strips, which are then crisscrossed over a filling. To make the ring, the dough—spread with a filling—is rolled into a tight cylinder and curved into a circle. The circle is then deeply notched from the outer edge, and alternate sections are flipped inward.

The choice of filling will depend on whether or not it can be sealed within the dough. If the coffeecake has an enclosing pocket, the filling may be moist, although not so runny that it might make the dough soggy. A savory combination of ricotta and Parmesan cheeses *(recipe, page 165)* is used for the braid here. Almond-paste or poppy-seed fillings *(recipes, page 165)* and thick fruit butters or marmalades are other possibilities.

With a little extra effort, you also may create a filling from firm fresh fruits— whole cranberries or blueberries, sliced apples, peaches or pears—or from dried prunes or apricots. Simmer the fruit until tender in a sugar syrup made with one and one half parts sugar to one part water. Lift out the fruit and boil the syrup down to a thick glaze; then firm the glaze with a solution of cornstarch or arrowroot and water, and pour the glaze over the fruit. Like any cooked filling, the glazed fruit must be cooled thoroughly before it is used.

For a coffeecake in which the filling is exposed along cut edges of dough, as in the ring, the mixture must be a relatively dry one. To fill the ring, the dough is slathered with softened butter and sprinkled with white sugar, cinnamon and dried currants. Brown sugar could be used instead of white sugar, and the cinnamon and currants might be replaced by nutmeg or allspice and chopped nuts or grated fresh orange peel.

A Plait Stuffed with Cheese

1 Filling and cutting. Roll yeast puff dough into a rectangle ¼ inch [6 mm.] thick. Spread filling—in this case, cheese—down the middle third of the rectangle, leaving 2-inch [5-cm.] margins at the ends. Cut out the corners and make slanting cuts to within ½ inch [1 cm.] of the filling at 1-inch [2½-cm.] intervals down the long sides.

2 Shaping the ends. Completely remove the corners that were cut away in Step 1. Using both hands and working gently, fold the rectangular end flaps up and over the filling.

A Fruit and Spice Wreath

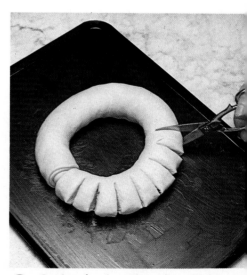

1 Filling the dough. Roll out and trim yeast puff dough into a rectangle ¼ inch [6 mm.] thick *(page 45)*. Spread a thin layer of filling over the dough with a spatula, leaving an uncovered margin of ½ inch [1 cm.] all around. Sprinkle dried fruits on the filling. Tightly roll the dough lengthwise into a cylinder.

2 Cutting the ring. Place the cylinder on a buttered baking sheet, curving the dough into a ring as you set it down. With a pair of scissors, cut into the outside edge of the ring at 1-inch [2½-cm.] intervals, cutting to within ½ inch [1 cm.] of the inner edge.

3 **Braiding the tart.** Starting at one end, fold one diagonal strip of dough over the filling. Cross the opposite strip over the first. Continue to bring strips from alternate sides over the filling, forming a braid down the length of the cake. Tuck the loose ends of the last pair of strips under the coffeecake.

4 **Baking.** Place the coffeecake on a buttered baking sheet and cover it. Allow it to rise for about one and a half hours. Brush an egg-yolk-and-water glaze over the cake. Bake in a preheated 425° F. [220° C.] oven for two minutes; reduce the heat to 375° F. [190° C.] and bake for 20 to 30 minutes longer, or until golden brown. Cool on a rack, then move the cake to a board for slicing.

3 **Shaping the ring.** Working around the ring, flip alternate slices inward with one hand while using your other hand to steady the preceding slice. Cover the twisted ring with a large inverted bowl. Let the ring rest for about one and a half hours.

4 **Baking and serving.** Glaze the top of the ring with egg yolk beaten with a little water. Place in a preheated 425° F. [220° C.] oven; after two minutes, reduce the heat to 375° F. [190° C.] and bake the coffeecake for 20 to 30 minutes, until golden brown. Place the coffeecake on a wire rack to cool. Let it rest for 30 minutes if you want to serve it warm, longer if you prefer it cool. Garnish the ring with a liberal dusting of confectioners' sugar.

3
Special Yeast Breads
Elaborations Subtle and Substantial

Yeast dough—either basic or enriched—can be embellished and manipulated in myriad ways to change its flavor, alter its color, modify its texture, incorporate other foodstuffs into it and dress it up for the holidays. The various breadmaking strategies of this kind, so wide-ranging they defy any neat classification, are the subject of this chapter.

The subtlest, and simplest, methods of modifying dough are to change its basic ingredients—flour, leavening and liquid—or its cooking process. Tangy sourdough loaves, for example, are produced by using sourdough starter for baker's yeast or, for especially light loaves, by supplementing yeast with starter *(page 11)*. If yeast is augmented with baking soda and the dough is thinned into a batter that can be cooked on a griddle, the result is breads with a honeycomb texture *(pages 56-57)*. Poaching dough before baking it imparts the fine texture characteristic of bagels *(pages 58-59)*. And using extra liquid in a dough also makes it possible to produce French loaves with a moist interior *(page 61)*.

More far-reaching effects are achieved by adding sweet or pungent foodstuffs—as diverse as cheese and molasses—to dough mixtures or risen doughs. The proper moment for incorporating these ingredients depends on their consistency and bulkiness. Fresh cheeses and puréed vegetables or fruits will disperse readily through the dough to color and flavor it evenly. They will also supply some or all of the necessary liquid and, therefore, must be added to the flour and yeast when mixing starts *(pages 62-63)*. Syrupy liquids such as melted chocolate and molasses are difficult to distribute smoothly; in the dark bread demonstrated on pages 64-65, the problem is solved by blending these flavorings into a warm cornmeal paste before adding them to the flour mixture. Light, dry ingredients—chopped herbs or grated Parmesan cheese, for example—can likewise be added at the start, but their effect will be more pronounced if they are kneaded into risen dough *(pages 66-67)*.

When introducing a large quantity of dry, bulky ingredients such as the fruits and nuts in the Scotch bun opposite, one approach is to knead them in after the dough has risen once; if added earlier, such ingredients would hinder the leavening action of the yeast. Alternatively, the risen dough can be treated like a platform on which to display sausages, whole eggs and the like with a dramatic flourish *(pages 70-71)*.

A ball of yeast-leavened dough, scented with spices and packed with chopped almonds, citrus peels, raisins and currants, is wrapped in a sheet of plain dough large enough to enclose it completely *(demonstration, pages 68-69)*. The dough wrapper helps to keep the rich interior of the bun moist during baking and hides it teasingly until the moment of slicing.

The Double Cooking of Bagels

When a yeast-leavened dough is poached briefly in boiling water before baking, the resulting bread will have a dense, tender interior and a soft, chewy crust. The most familiar embodiment of such a transformation is the bagel, which is shaped as a ring to increase the area of the special crust.

Bagels can be made from virtually any yeast dough. In the demonstration here, a light enrichment of butter and egg white is added to a basic dough to accentuate the softness of the interior *(recipe, page 103);* milk is used as the liquid to help retard crisping of the crust during baking. To achieve the full textural density that marks a good bagel, the dough's first rising is limited to an hour and, once shaped, the dough is left to rise again only briefly before cooking.

Shaping perfect rings is a straightforward process: Divide the dough into balls and use your finger to make and enlarge a hole in the center of each ball *(Step 4)*.

The bagels are poached for only about 15 seconds. Poaching moistens the outer dough and keeps the bagels from crisping when they are subsequently baked. Before baking, the bagels can be brushed with an egg glaze and, if you like, sprinkled with coarse salt, poppy, sesame or caraway seeds or chopped, lightly sautéed onion. Bagels are traditionally eaten with cream cheese and smoked salmon for a hearty breakfast, or split in half, toasted and buttered for a lighter one.

1 **Stirring in butter.** In a small, heavy pan, heat milk until it boils. Remove the pan from the heat, and add sugar and butter. Stir until the sugar dissolves and the butter melts.

2 **Adding egg white.** Pour the milk mixture into a large bowl and let it cool until tepid. Stir yeast into tepid water, add it to the milk, and leave the mixture for about 10 minutes, until it is frothy. Separate an egg; reserve the yolk to use in the glaze and add the white to the milk. Stir the mixture vigorously until the ingredients are well combined.

5 **Poaching the bagels.** Heat a large pot of water until it boils; reduce the heat to maintain a gentle boil. Using a perforated skimmer, carefully lower a few bagels into the water. Poach each batch, uncovered, for about 15 seconds, until the bagels begin to puff up. Lift them out, drain them and transfer them to a greased baking sheet.

3 **Mixing in flour.** Stir salt into the milk mixture. Add flour a handful at a time, stirring after each addition. When the dough is cohesive but still soft, turn it out onto a work surface and knead it *(page 15, Steps 3 and 4)*. Put the dough into a bowl, cover it and let it rise in a warm place for about 40 minutes, until it has increased in volume by half.

4 **Shaping the dough.** Cut the dough into pieces about the size of small lemons and shape each piece into a neat ball *(pages 26-27)*. To form a ring, first poke your floured forefinger into the center of a ball *(above, left)* and work your finger through the dough until it touches the work surface; move your finger in a circle to widen the hole. Twirl the ring until the hole is about one third of the bagel's diameter *(right)*. Place the bagels on a sheet, cover them with a damp cloth and let them rise for about 10 minutes.

6 **Baking the bagels.** Beat the reserved egg yolk with a little cold water, and brush the mixture over the bagels *(inset)*. Bake them in a preheated, humidified 400° F. [200° C.] oven for about 20 minutes, until golden brown. With a spatula, transfer the bagels to a wire rack to cool for at least 10 minutes.

An Amalgam of Elements in a Rich, Dark Loaf

Unlike a vegetable or fruit bread, which takes its special characteristics from the incorporation of a single ingredient, a dark bread owes its rich taste, dense, moist texture and depth of color to a combination of many different flavorings. Strong-flavored flours and meals are a natural starting point. Traditional German pumpernickel loaves, for example, are made entirely from rye flour, but the American version of pumpernickel shown here—one better suited to the tastes of people accustomed to lighter, softer breads—contains a mixture of rye and whole-wheat flours and cornmeal (recipe, page 107).

To add more flavor and further intensify the color of dark breads, the flour is blended with sweet, syrupy or malty ingredients such as molasses, unsweetened chocolate or beer. The mixture may be scented with spices and citrus peel. Potato is often added for body and moistness.

Combining so many different ingredients with varying consistencies and textures requires patience and a methodical approach. In the demonstration at right, the cornmeal is heated in water to soften it. The hot paste that results serves as a convenient medium in which to melt and blend chocolate and molasses (Step 1); without this paste, the flavorings would have to be melted gently in a heavy pan set in a water bath. The flavored mixture is cooled until tepid: Too much heat kills yeast. Cooled mashed potato and yeast are then incorporated.

Only at this stage are the flours introduced—first stirred in, then worked in by hand (Steps 3 and 4). Because the resulting dough is very stiff and sticky, it needs more energetic kneading than usual to develop its gluten and give it the necessary smoothness and elasticity. Because it is much heavier than ordinary, unflavored dough, the dark dough is simply patted into loaf shapes.

Dark breads should be prepared and baked at least one day before serving. During the interim period, their flavors mingle and mature, and the slight staling makes the loaves easier to cut into the thin slices that best suit their richness. Dark bread retains moisture well because of its density, and will keep for several weeks if wrapped tightly in foil.

1 Blending in flavorings. Sprinkle yellow cornmeal into a pan of boiling water, stirring all the time with a wooden spoon (inset). Reduce the heat and stir until the mixture forms a light paste — two to three minutes. Remove the pan from the heat and add flavorings — in this case, molasses (above), small pieces of unsweetened baking chocolate, butter, sugar, salt and caraway seeds. Stir until the chocolate and butter melt and the mixture is well combined.

5 Kneading. Turn the dough out onto a surface dusted with whole-wheat flour, and sprinkle more flour on the dough. Press the dough down and spread it out with the heel of your hand; gather it together — using a dough scraper, if necessary — give it a slight turn, and repeat. Knead until it is no longer sticky — 10 to 15 minutes.

6 Shaping the loaves. Put the kneaded dough into a greased bowl and cover it with plastic wrap or a damp cloth. Let the dough rise in a warm place until it has increased in volume by half — about one hour. Turn the dough out onto a floured surface and cut it in two. Knead each piece for a few minutes, then pat each piece into a smooth round.

2 **Adding mashed potato.** Transfer the flavored cornmeal to a large mixing bowl; let the mixture cool until it is lukewarm. Add lukewarm mashed potatoes. Mix yeast in a little tepid water and stir it thoroughly into the mixture.

3 **Adding the flours.** A little at a time, sprinkle the flours — rye and whole-wheat are used in this demonstration — into the flavored cornmeal-and-potato mixture. Stir briefly with a wooden spoon after each addition.

4 **Mixing the dough.** Continue to add the flours to the dough until the mixture becomes too stiff to stir. Coat your hands lightly with oil to prevent sticking, and use them to work in the remaining flour.

7 **Glazing the loaves.** Set the loaves on a baking sheet dusted with cornmeal or semolina. Cover them with inverted bowls, and let them rise again until they have increased in volume by half — about 30 minutes. Glaze the tops of the loaves with a lightly beaten mixture of egg white and water.

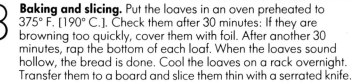

8 **Baking and slicing.** Put the loaves in an oven preheated to 375° F. [190° C.]. Check them after 30 minutes: If they are browning too quickly, cover them with foil. After another 30 minutes, rap the bottom of each loaf. When the loaves sound hollow, the bread is done. Cool the loaves on a rack overnight. Transfer them to a board and slice them thin with a serrated knife.

A Loaf that Offers a Whole Meal

With a bit of artistry on the part of the cook, bread can serve as a spectacular platform for foodstuffs too bulky to be integrated by kneading. As seen in the picnic loaf demonstrated at right *(recipe, page 113)*, the foods are simply set in place on the surface of the loaf, held secure with ropes or lids of dough, and baked along with the bread.

The foods chosen for such a festive creation must be relatively dry, lest they exude copious juices and inhibit rising and crust formation. The picnic loaf here, for example, holds sausage, eggs and cheese. The sausage is smoked—in this case, Polish kielbasa sausage—and it needs only heating to be ready to eat. The eggs are raw, their shells pricked with a needle at one end to keep them from cracking as they bake.

The cheese selected is firm Muenster, shredded so that it will melt evenly in the oven's heat and lidded with dough so that its molten flow is contained. The Muenster could be replaced by such other firm cheeses as provolone, Cheddar, Gruyère, Gouda or Cantal, or by a small disk of soft Brie, Camembert or Boursault.

Similarly, the sausage and eggs could be supplemented or replaced by slices of ham, anchovy fillets or sardines, wedges of raw onion, pitted ripe or green olives, or roasted sweet red peppers. Improvisation—even an element of whimsy—is the essence of breads that are used in such a showcase role.

1 Forming the base. Mix basic yeast dough *(page 14)* and let it rise once. Punch down the dough and divide it into two pieces, one slightly larger than the other. On a greased pizza pan, press the larger piece into a disk about ½ inch [1 cm.] thick and 14 inches [35 cm.] in diameter.

2 Covering the cheese. Pat shredded cheese —here, Muenster — into a ball and center it on the dough base. Press the remaining dough flat, cut off half of it and press this portion into a 7-inch [18-cm.] disk. Use this disk as a lid for the cheese. Brush water on the edge of the lid, then seal it to the base.

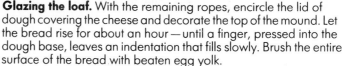

5 Glazing the loaf. With the remaining ropes, encircle the lid of dough covering the cheese and decorate the top of the mound. Let the bread rise for about an hour —until a finger, pressed into the dough base, leaves an indentation that fills slowly. Brush the entire surface of the bread with beaten egg yolk.

3 **Arranging the eggs and sausages.** Place whole uncooked eggs and segments of sausages alternately around the circumference of the base; in this instance, two eggs alternate with each sausage segment. Divide the remaining dough into small pieces, mold each into a ball and roll it under your hands *(page 27)* to form it into a rope about as thick as a pencil.

4 **Anchoring the toppings.** Cross a pair of ropes over each of the sausage segments. Moisten both ends of each rope with water and press the ends firmly into the dough base. Drape a rope over each egg and moisten the rope ends to secure the egg to the base.

6 **Baking and serving.** Spraying the preheated, humidified oven twice *(page 16, Step 4)*, bake the bread at 400° F. [200° C.] for 25 minutes, then at 350° F. [180° C.] for an additional 25 minutes. Cool the loaf on a rack. To serve, slice the loaf into wedges by cutting between the eggs and through the middle of each sausage segment.

4

Breads without Yeast
Alternative Ways to Lighten Batters and Doughs

Breads that are made without yeast vary remarkably. They range from flat, thin disks and soufflé-light puffs raised only by steam to tender, cakelike loaves and crisp waffles leavened by baking powder.

Although such breads lack the fine texture and the keeping qualities of most yeast-leavened breads, they possess certain distinct advantages. Nonyeast doughs require little, if any, of the kneading that develops the gluten network necessary to trap gas slowly given off by yeast. Whereas yeast must have time to act on dough before baking, other leavens rise quickly and need only moisture and the oven's heat to do their work. And because nonyeast leavens do not rely on gluten, you can use flours and meals that have little or no gluten-forming potential—barley, oats and cornmeal, for example.

Heat alone, without a leavening agent, is enough to raise light batters and soft, flattened doughs. In the case of the flour-and-water blend used to make the Indian flatbreads called *chappatis,* for example, moisture in the dough is converted to steam that puffs up the bread, as demonstrated on pages 74-75.

With popovers *(pages 78-79),* more dramatic puffing results from a higher proportion of liquid and the use of eggs in the batter. When subjected to the oven's heat, the egg proteins combine with those of the flour to stiffen the gluten meshwork. The steam created by the batter's liquid is trapped in this meshwork, causing maximum expansion.

The most popular nonyeast leavens utilize baking soda in one form or another. Moistened and subjected to heat, the soda releases carbon dioxide, which raises the bread mixture. However, the alkaline soda will give bread a soapy taste unless it is neutralized by the addition of some acidic element. (The acid also speeds the production of gas.) Breads leavened by baking soda *(pages 78-79)* are often made with some type of soured milk to supply the necessary acidity.

Such precautions are not necessary when the soda used is in the form of baking powder, which includes its own acid—usually cream of tartar. When moistened, the two chemicals instantly begin to act on each other. Therefore, baking powder also contains a little starch—in most cases, cornstarch—which keeps the mixture so dry that the soda and acid cannot react while in storage.

A loaf of golden-hued banana bread is cut into thick slabs for serving. Made from a batter leavened with baking powder and flavored with puréed bananas, chopped nuts and raisins, the bread has a moistness and a tenderness typical of nonyeast loaves.

Puffing Up an Unleavened Dough

In many parts of the world, the daily bread is no more than a soft dough of flour and water, shaped into thin rounds and—more often than not—cooked on a griddle or in a pan. Such a flatbread usually is made with flours that contain little or no gluten: barley, millet, oat, rye, corn or whole-wheat are all used. Nonetheless, the dough must be kneaded and rested. Kneading—accomplished in only a few minutes—distributes the liquid evenly, thus softening the flour and permitting its starches and proteins to bind the dough together. Resting the dough tenderizes it by relaxing any gluten present in the flour.

Elemental though they are, flatbreads can be surprisingly varied in texture. The light, airy quality of the Indian *chappatis* demonstrated at right *(recipe, page 139)* is obtained by cooking the dough in two stages. First, each thin disk is browned lightly in a preheated pan. Then the bread is held for a few seconds over an open flame—a lighted gas burner as here or, using tongs, a barbecue or camp-fire. The direct heat quickly turns the dough's moisture to steam, puffing up the bread while the cooking is completed.

For a crisper effect, the disks can be cooked through in the pan or on a griddle, so that the steam leavens the bread minimally. For a denser, softer bread, the disks may be made slightly thicker, then wrapped in foil and baked in an oven.

Different flavorings further extend the range of unleavened breads. At the very least, the dough mixture should be seasoned with salt, while ground spices or chopped herbs can make exciting additions. If you like, substitute milk for some or all of the water to enrich the dough slightly.

You can produce flaky bread that is richer still by repeatedly brushing each round of dough with melted butter, folding it and then rolling it out again—a technique used for Indian *parathas (box, below; recipe, page 140)*. For a more substantial result, you can stuff the dough with puréed vegetables before cooking *(recipe, page 144)*.

1 **Mixing the dough.** Combine flour—in this case, whole-wheat flour—and salt in a large bowl or on a work surface. With your hand, mix in water to make a soft, slightly sticky dough. On a lightly floured surface, knead the dough for five to 10 minutes, until it is supple. Cover the dough with plastic wrap or a damp cloth.

A Textural Change from Melted Butter

1 **Buttering the dough.** Prepare thin disks of unleavened, whole-wheat dough *(Steps 1-3, above)*, replacing half of the water with milk. Brush the top of each disk lightly with melted butter.

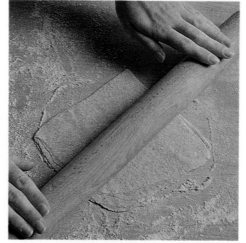

2 **Folding and rolling.** Fold each disk of dough in half, then fold it again into a quarter circle. With a rolling pin, roll out the dough as evenly as possible to re-form a rough circle. Butter, fold and roll the dough three more times.

3 **Cooking and serving.** Butter a seasoned griddle lightly and preheat it over low to medium heat. Cook each disk for three to five minutes, until its underside is well browned. With a spatula, flip the bread, then cook it for three to five minutes. Stack the breads on a napkin-lined plate and serve at once.

3 **Greasi...** well-se... heat. Le... drops o... surface... few se... generou... melted...

2 **Dividing the dough.** Let the dough rest for 30 minutes. Then, keeping the bulk of the dough covered, pull off two or three walnut-sized pieces. Flour your hands and roll each piece between your palms to shape it into an even ball. On a floured surface, press each ball firmly to form a flat round.

3 **Rolling out the dough.** Sprinkle each round of dough with flour. Push a rolling pin back and forth over the dough with one hand and turn the dough with the other hand to make an even disk. Keep rolling and turning until the disk is about 1/16 inch [2 mm.] thick.

4 **Browning the bread.** Preheat a seasoned, cast-iron griddle or skillet *(box, page 76)* over medium heat. Put a disk of dough on it. When bubbles appear on the surface — after about three minutes — carefully turn the disk over with your finger tips or a spatula. Cook the bread for another minute, until its underside begins to brown.

2 **Forming...** griddle... water, fli... instantly... hands wi... of dough... With you... balls and... about 1/2...

5 **Completing the cooking.** To puff up the bread, lift it with a spatula, tongs or a skimmer and hold it over an open flame. After a few seconds, when the bread puffs up *(left)*, remove it from the heat. Place the breads in a napkin-lined dish; *chappatis* should be eaten hot, torn apart by hand *(inset)*.

Two Old-fashioned Leavening Methods

Before the invention of modern baking powder in the 1850s *(page 7)*, bakers used a variety of stratagems to raise nonyeast breads. Among the most successful were those developed for popovers *(top demonstration)* and Irish soda bread *(bottom demonstration)*.

Popovers rely on the simplest of natural leavenings: steam. The batter for popovers is thin—it contains as much milk as flour—and is enriched with butter and eggs *(recipe, page 142)*. As the batter's liquid turns to steam in the heat of the oven, the proteins of the flour and eggs coagulate to form an elastic shell that traps the steam inside. For maximum expansion, popovers are baked in a hot oven until fully risen, then the heat is reduced to firm their crusts. While the popovers are rising, they are very fragile. The oven door must not be opened, lest a draft cause the popovers to collapse.

Popovers will rise highest if baked in small molds: The batter can only expand upward. The cups of an old-fashioned cast-iron pan are set close together so that the ballooning popovers will press against each other and spread irregularly *(Step 4, top)*. For more even tops, popovers can be baked in individual soufflé dishes or custard cups. Preheating the molds will help to set the undersides of the popovers and speed rising.

Steam is not an adequate leavening to lighten thick batters or heavy doughs. But more than two centuries ago, cooks learned to raise weightier breads with baking soda, which rapidly releases carbon dioxide when it is moistened and heated. Soda alone is not enough: Its saltiness must be balanced by an acid food such as the buttermilk used in the Irish soda bread at right.

Classic Irish soda bread is made either with all-white flour *(recipe, page 136)* or, for a pale brown loaf with an agreeably coarse texture, with equal parts of white and whole-wheat flours. Traditionally, soda bread is baked in a container—here, a cast-iron pot. During the first part of baking, the container is covered to trap moisture, thus delaying the formation of crust and allowing the dough to rise to its fullest extent. Then the lid is removed to let the surface of the bread brown.

Popovers: Light and Puffy

1 Mixing the batter. Sift flour and salt together into a large mixing bowl. In a saucepan, heat milk and butter just until the butter melts. Make a well in the center of the dry ingredients and gradually pour in the milk and butter, stirring with a fork or whisk until the batter is smooth and free of lumps.

2 Beating in eggs. Break eggs one at a time and stir them into the batter with a whisk. Whisk the mixture until the eggs are thoroughly combined with the other ingredients and the batter has the consistency of heavy cream.

Soda Bread: Crusty and Robust

1 Stirring in the liquid. Place all of the dry ingredients — in this case, white flour, whole-wheat flour, baking soda and salt — in a large mixing bowl and stir them. Make a well in the center and gradually pour in the liquid — buttermilk, here — while stirring with a fork.

2 Kneading the dough. Continue stirring, working outward from the center of the bowl, until a cohesive dough forms. Flour your hands and gather together the dough; turn it out onto a floured work surface. Knead the dough lightly and swiftly for two to three minutes. Pat the dough into a ball.

3 **Filling the molds.** Preheat a seasoned popover pan for 10 minutes in a 425° F. [220° C.] oven. Brush the cups of the pan with butter. Immediately ladle the batter into the cups, filling each no more than two thirds full to allow room for the batter to expand.

4 **Baking and serving.** Quickly return the pan to the oven and bake the popovers for 30 minutes — without opening the oven door. Reduce the heat to 350° F. [180° C.] and bake for five to 10 minutes longer until the popovers are firm and well browned. Serve the popovers at once; if left to cool, they will deflate.

3 **Scoring the dough.** Oil a seasoned cast-iron pot *(box, page 76)* and preheat it for 10 minutes in a 400° F. [200° C.] oven. Flatten the dough into a round and place it in the pot. With a sharp, floured knife, score a deep cross in the dough, taking care not to cut to the edges of the round. Cover the pot with its lid.

4 **Baking the bread.** Return the pot to the oven and bake the bread for 30 minutes. Remove the lid and bake for 10 minutes to brown the crust. Protecting your hands with a potholder, tip the bread out of the pot *(inset)* and cool it on a rack for about 45 minutes. To serve, break the bread along the scored lines.

The Speed and Versatility of Baking Powder

When a bread is leavened with baking powder—baking soda mixed by the manufacturer with an acid, such as cream of tartar—the liquid in the dough or batter triggers the reaction between the soda and acid so that they begin to release carbon dioxide even before the bread is baked. The oven's heat then speeds up the reaction to inflate the dough or batter fully. The result is moist, fluffy bread such as the baking powder biscuits and blueberry muffins demonstrated at right (*recipes, pages 136 and 146*).

Baking powder will raise batters and soft doughs based on any flour or combination of flour and meal; it is generally used in the ratio of 1½ teaspoons [7 ml.] of baking powder to 1 cup [¼ liter] of flour or meal. Quick and gentle handling of the mixture is essential to avoid dissipating the carbon dioxide before the batter or dough is baked. Working fast also prevents excessive development of gluten, which would toughen the bread.

To make airy baking powder biscuits, for example, dry ingredients are combined only lightly with fat. You can do this most easily by gently chopping them with a pastry blender as shown at top right. The fat may be lard, vegetable shortening or a mixture of half lard and half butter, and it must be soft enough to be readily incorporated.

To moisten the dough, milk is stirred in quickly; then the dough is turned out, kneaded very gently, and patted—not rolled—flat. The biscuits are cut out at once and baked. In all, the process should take only about 10 minutes.

For tender muffins, based on a thick batter rather than a dough, the ingredients are stirred only until the mixture is roughly blended, as shown at bottom right. Stirring the batter to smoothness would toughen the bread, and would not serve a useful purpose: Small lumps left in the batter disappear during baking.

Both biscuits and muffins can be made plain or seasoned with herbs and spices. The muffin batter will support heavy additions as well. Blueberries are used here, but cranberries, raisins, nuts or bits of crisply fried bacon can be substituted. To prevent large morsels from sinking during baking, they should be dusted with flour before they are added.

Biscuits Stamped from a Sheet of Dough

1 **Cutting in the fat.** Let the fat—in this case, lard—warm at room temperature until it is soft but not oily. In a large mixing bowl, sift together flour, baking powder and salt. Add the fat and, using a light chopping motion, cut through the ingredients repeatedly with a pastry blender just until the mixture has the consistency of cornmeal.

2 **Stirring in milk.** Add milk, and stir the mixture lightly with a fork until the ingredients cohere in a loose, soft mass. Do not overstir. Turn the dough out onto a lightly floured work surface.

Muffins Brimming with Berries

1 **Mixing the batter.** Sift together flour, salt and baking powder into a mixing bowl; if you like sweeter muffins, add a little sugar. In a separate bowl, whisk eggs and milk until they are thoroughly blended. Stir melted butter into the liquid. Pour the liquid into the flour and stir briefly, until the ingredients are roughly blended.

2 **Adding the fruit.** Wash fresh blueberries and drain them on a towel. Put the berries in a strainer. Hold the strainer over a plate and sprinkle the berries with flour, tapping the strainer so that excess flour falls through. Add the floured berries to the muffin batter and stir them in with a few swift strokes.

 Working the dough. Knead the dough briefly — just seven or eight times — until it holds together. Pat it lightly into a sheet ½ inch [1 cm.] thick. Do not overwork the dough by trying to pat the top perfectly smooth.

4 **Cutting out the biscuits.** Dip a biscuit cutter into flour to prevent sticking, and push it straight down through the dough; twisting the cutter would produce lopsided biscuits. Pull the cutter straight up and out. Place the biscuits on an ungreased baking sheet, either close together or with space between them to brown the sides.

5 **Baking and serving.** Bake the biscuits in a preheated 450° F. [230° C.] oven until lightly browned — 10 to 15 minutes. Transfer the biscuits directly to a serving dish and serve them hot, accompanied by butter and — if desired — honey, jelly or jam.

 Filling the muffin pan. Spoon the batter into generously buttered cups of a muffin pan, filling each two thirds full. Bake the muffins in a preheated 400° F. [200° C.] oven for 20 to 25 minutes, until they are fully risen and light brown.

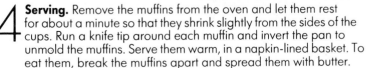 **Serving.** Remove the muffins from the oven and let them rest for about a minute so that they shrink slightly from the sides of the cups. Run a knife tip around each muffin and invert the pan to unmold the muffins. Serve them warm, in a napkin-lined basket. To eat them, break the muffins apart and spread them with butter.

Puréed Fruit for a Cakelike Interior

A baking powder batter thickened with puréed fruit yields a mildly sweet bread with a moist, tender interior. To combine easily with the other ingredients, the fruit purée must be fairly smooth. Soft fruits can be puréed raw: For example, the ripe bananas used in this demonstration *(recipe, page 146)* are simply peeled and mashed. The same treatment would apply to avocados or persimmons. Firmer fruits such as apricots, apples or pumpkins must be cooked and then puréed.

The ingredients should be combined in a sequence that does not require persistent beating of the flour, which would develop its gluten and make the bread tough. First, the butter and the sugar are creamed together—beaten until the mixture is soft, fluffy and almost white. This process may take 30 minutes by hand, or 10 minutes with an electric mixer, but it aerates the butter-sugar mixture to such an extent that the mixture almost triples in volume and constitutes an additional lightener for the bread. The sugar used here has been flavored by leaving a whole vanilla bean in a covered jar of sugar for a few days; this scented sugar contributes a more subtle vanilla taste than vanilla extract, although extract can be used if preferred.

Next, the creamed mixture is enriched with an egg. Then, in alternate spoonfuls, the puréed fruit and dry ingredients—flour, baking powder, salt and nutmeg—are stirred in. Blending the ingredients in small batches ensures that no lumps form. Any solid elements—in this case, nuts and dried fruits—are folded in at the very end, before the batter is put into a pan and baked.

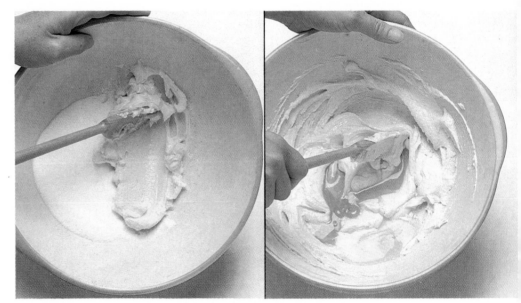

1 **Starting the batter.** In a large mixing bowl, cream softened unsalted butter and vanilla-flavored sugar together with an electric mixer or, as here, by beating the mixture vigorously against the sides of the bowl with a wooden spoon. When the mixture forms a fluffy, white blend, add a raw egg and stir *(right)* until smooth.

4 **Adding nuts and raisins.** Chop nuts coarse—in this case, pecans. Toss raisins in a sieve with a spoonful of flour; the flour will keep the raisins separate by coating their moist surfaces and will prevent them from sinking to the bottom of the bread. Add the raisins and the pecans to the batter and stir briefly to mix them in.

5 **Filling the loaf pan.** Butter and flour a loaf pan that is twice the volume of the batter. Scrape the batter from the bowl into the pan, then level the batter with the spoon or a spatula.

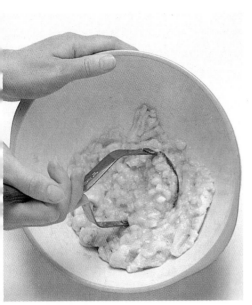

2 **Mashing the bananas.** Peel large, ripe bananas, cut them into rough chunks and put them in a bowl. Using a fork or, as above, a potato masher, mash the bananas to a smooth pulp.

3 **Adding dry ingredients and fruit.** In a separate bowl, sift together flour, salt, baking powder and grated nutmeg. A spoonful at a time, add the flour mixture *(above, left)* and the banana purée *(right)* alternately to the creamed mixture, stirring after each addition so that the ingredients blend thoroughly.

6 **Baking the bread.** Bake the bread in a preheated 350° F. [180° C.] oven for an hour. To test for doneness, push a skewer into the center of the loaf; if the skewer comes out clean, the bread is ready; if not, bake the loaf for 10 minutes more and test again. Unmold the bread and cool it on a wire rack. Transfer the bread to a board for slicing.

Pancakes — The Staple Breakfast Bread

Savory or sweet, a pancake is no more than a cooked disk of leavened batter, but the elements in pancake batters are subject to extensive variation and elaboration *(recipes, pages 159-162)*. The batter can be based on almost any flour or combination of flours—such as the mixture of buckwheat and all-purpose flours used for the pancakes demonstrated on these pages. The liquid for the batter can be milk, cream or fruit juice—combined, if you like, with cottage or farmer cheese, sour cream, fruit or vegetable purées, or liqueurs. For richness, almost all pancake batters contain butter and eggs. In some pancakes, the eggs provide the only leavening; however, most pancakes are also lightened by yeast, sourdough starter or, as here, baking powder.

Depending on the batter's proportions of liquid and flour, pancakes can range from plump to almost transparently thin. Whatever the formulation, the batter will blend more evenly if the dry ingredients and the liquids are first separately mixed, then combined. If the batter contains melted butter, cool the butter a little before adding it, and be sure that the other liquids are at room temperature—otherwise, the butter will congeal. In blending liquids and flour, stir only until the mixture is evenly moist and fairly smooth: Too much stirring overdevelops the gluten in the flour, yielding tough pancakes. As added insurance against toughness, you can let the batter rest for five to 10 minutes to relax the gluten.

Pancakes should be cooked on a heavy griddle or pan so well seasoned *(box, page 76)* that it requires minimal greasing. In correct culinary parlance, pancakes are baked, not fried—a term that means "cooking food in a fat or oil." Preheat the griddle or pan until it is hot enough to set the batter instantly, but not so hot that the pancakes burn *(Step 3, top)*.

To shape simple pancakes, ladle pools of batter onto the hot griddle. For more elaborate effects, dribble the batter in decorative patterns; these can be used in conjunction with simple disks, as in the bottom demonstration. Always serve the pancakes immediately to prevent drying—garnished with fruit, maple syrup, jam or honey, or with sweetened whipped or sour cream.

Simple Disks Quickly Cooked

1 **Mixing batter.** Sift buckwheat flour, all-purpose flour, salt, sugar and baking powder into a mixing bowl. Separate egg yolks from the whites. In another bowl or a pitcher, stir together milk and cooled melted butter, then stir in the egg yolks. Lightly whisk the liquids into the dry ingredients to make a fluid but slightly lumpy batter.

2 **Adding egg whites.** With a clean whisk, beat the egg whites until they form stiff peaks. Whisk a spoonful of egg white into the batter to lighten it. Pour the rest of the whites onto the batter and, using a rubber spatula, gently fold in the whites until the mixture is light and no trace of white is visible. Do not overmix, lest the whites deflate.

A Filigree Frame for a Jam Topping

1 **Forming the base.** Make pancake batter *(Steps 1 and 2, top)*. Coat a heated griddle *(Step 3, top)* with a film of butter. Ladle on enough batter to make a large pancake. When bubbles appear on its surface, turn the pancake and finish cooking *(Step 4, top)*. Transfer the pancake to a heated plate.

2 **Cooking the filigree top.** With a large spoon, dribble ribbons of pancake batter onto the hot griddle to make an openwork pattern approximately the same size as the pancake base *(above, left)*. When the first bubbles break on top, carefully turn the filigree pancake *(right)*, then finish cooking. Slide the pancake onto a plate.

3 **Forming pancakes.** Set a heavy griddle over medium heat and heat it until drops of water thrown on the surface dance for a moment, then evaporate. Immediately brush the griddle with a film of butter or vegetable oil. Using a pitcher or — as here — a ladle, pour the batter into disks of the desired size, spaced well apart.

4 **Finishing the cooking.** Bake the pancakes for one to two minutes, until bubbles form all over their surfaces. As soon as the first bubbles break, use a large metal spatula to flip the pancakes over. After 15 to 30 seconds, lift the edge of a pancake with the spatula. If the underside is golden brown, the pancake is done.

5 **Serving the pancakes.** With the spatula, transfer the pancakes to heated plates, piling two or three pancakes together for each serving. Top the stack of pancakes with a knob of butter, and pour on maple syrup *(above)* or a fruit sauce or honey.

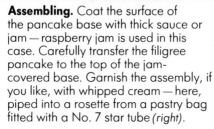

3 **Assembling.** Coat the surface of the pancake base with thick sauce or jam — raspberry jam is used in this case. Carefully transfer the filigree pancake to the top of the jam-covered base. Garnish the assembly, if you like, with whipped cream — here, piped into a rosette from a pastry bag fitted with a No. 7 star tube *(right)*.

A Range of Effects for Waffles

The same batters that produce soft pancakes *(pages 84-85)* yield crisp waffles: The different effect is achieved by sandwiching the batter between the hinged, checkered grids of a waffle iron to bake.

Most waffle irons used today are electrically heated *(right);* however, some specialty shops sell old-fashioned irons that are used over direct heat *(below).* Either type must be handled in a way that keeps the batter from sticking. The grids of old-fashioned irons and some modern ones are made of cast iron; these must be seasoned *(box, page 76)* before use. (Electric irons with coated, nonstick grids do not require seasoning.) Preheat all grids until they are hot enough to set the batter instantly. To ensure perfect results, test any iron as described in Step 2 at right. As soon as an iron is hot, brush it lightly with melted butter.

In both demonstrations here, the batter is flavored—in one case with molasses and spices, in the other with apricot purée *(recipes, page 166).* The handling of eggs follows pancake-batter practice: Egg whites are beaten separately before they are added. However, because waffle batter is fully enclosed during baking and cannot rise much, many cooks whisk in eggs whole.

How much batter you use for each waffle depends on the texture you want: A thin layer produces crisp results; a thicker layer makes a softer waffle. Texture also is determined by cooking time. If cooked just until steam ceases to issue from the iron, the waffle will be tender and light-colored. Longer cooking makes the waffle darker and crisper.

Like pancakes, waffles are fine vehicles for garnishes. Attractive toppings for savory waffles include cheese sauce or creamed chipped beef or chicken. Sugars, syrups, jams, fruits and ice cream all are excellent garnishes for sweet waffles.

Ginger-accented Squares

1 **Making batter.** Separate eggs and beat the whites stiff. Whisk the yolks with milk, molasses and melted butter. Stir this mixture into a sifted blend of flour, sugar, baking powder, salt, ginger and allspice. Fold in the whites.

Apricot-flavored Hearts

1 **Pouring on batter.** Heat the iron for about four minutes on each side — until water sprinkled on the grids steams briefly and disappears. Brush the grids with butter. Ladle batter—here, apricot batter—onto the bottom grid *(above)* and close the iron. After a minute, gently turn the iron over *(right).*

2 **Serving.** Cook for about a minute more, until no steam appears at the edges of the iron. Open the iron slightly; if the waffle sticks to the top grid, close the iron and cook for a few moments more. Open the iron, lift off the waffle, trim away rough edges, garnish as desired, and serve.

2 **Preparing the iron.** Heat an electric waffle iron until a few drops of water sprinkled on the bottom grid steam for a second, then vanish. Immediately brush both grids very lightly with melted butter.

3 **Cooking the batter.** Ladle enough batter onto the center of the bottom grid to almost cover it; you may have to experiment to find the amount of batter needed. Close the iron immediately and leave it closed for at least three minutes, until no steam appears at its edges.

4 **Removing the waffle.** Lift the top of the iron slightly; if the waffle seems to stick to the top grid, close the iron and cook for a few moments more. When the waffle is done, slide wooden spatulas under it to lift it intact from the iron.

5 **Serving.** Trim any rough edges from the waffle, slice it into sections, and transfer the sections to heated plates. Sandwich sour cream between the sections; if you like, top with more sour cream and sprinkle with brown sugar.

Corn Bread in a Fitting Form

Corn breads, sweet and golden, are made much like other quick breads: Cornmeal —often mixed with all-purpose flour and usually leavened by baking powder—is combined with liquids such as milk or buttermilk, as well as with eggs, butter and flavoring ingredients, and the resulting batter is baked (recipes, pages 150-153). The batter can be molded into a single loaf or cake (the traditional mold is a cast-iron skillet) or, for individual portions, into smaller shapes such as muffins or the corn sticks shown here.

Corn sticks call for a cast-iron pan with troughs molded like little ears of corn. These pans are obtainable from kitchen-equipment shops and should be well seasoned, as described in the box on page 76, to help prevent the batter from sticking. Even so, before being used the corn-stick pan should be liberally coated with butter—melted so that it can be brushed into every part of the molds—to ensure that the corn sticks will set without sticking and develop crisp, golden crusts.

1 **Making the batter.** Lightly whisk eggs, then whisk in buttermilk. Into a separate bowl, sift cornmeal, flour, baking powder and salt. Stir the liquid ingredients into the dry ones just until the batter is evenly blended.

2 **Preparing the pan.** Using a clean paintbrush or, as here, a pastry brush, generously coat the corn-stick molds of the baking pan with melted butter. To make the crispiest crusts, allow a tablespoonful of butter for each mold.

3 **Baking.** Spoon the batter into each corn-stick mold to within ¼ inch [6 mm.] of its rim. Place the pan in a 350° F. [180° C.] oven and bake the corn sticks for 25 to 30 minutes, until golden and shrinking from the sides of the molds.

4 **Serving.** Use a fork to ease the fragile corn sticks from the mold, and tongs to transfer them to a serving dish. Serve warm or cool. For a second batch, butter the molds again; the hot pan will make these corn sticks cook faster.

Anthology of Recipes

Drawing upon the cooking literature of more than 23 countries, the editors and consultants for this volume have selected 201 published recipes for the Anthology that follows. The selections range from the familiar to the fanciful—from bran muffins and Boston brown bread to croissants filled with almond cream and topped with icing and almond slivers.

Many of the recipes were written by world-renowned exponents of the culinary art, but the Anthology also includes selections from rare and out-of-print books and from works that have never been published in English. Whatever the sources, the emphasis in these recipes is always on techniques that are practical for the home cook and that do justice to fine ingredients.

Since many early recipe writers did not specify amounts of ingredients, sizes of pans or even cooking times and temperatures, the missing information has been judiciously added. In some cases, instructions have been expanded. Where appropriate, clarifying introductory notes have also been supplied; they are printed in italics. Modern terms have been substituted for archaic language; but to preserve the character of the original recipes and to create a true anthology, the authors' texts have been changed as little as possible.

Recipes for standard preparations—basic bread dough and sourdough starters among them—appear at the end of the Anthology. Unfamiliar cooking terms and uncommon ingredients are explained in the combined General Index and Glossary.

Most of the recipes for yeast breads have been standardized to give quantities for both active dry yeast and fresh cake yeast; the only exceptions occur where an author's method for incorporating yeast requires a particular type. Wherever the kind of flour is not specified, all-purpose flour can be used; if the recipe is for a basic yeast bread, bread flour can also be used.

Apart from the primary components—flour, meal and leavening—all ingredients are listed within each recipe in order of use, with both the customary United States measurements and the metric measurements provided. All quantities reflect the American practice of measuring such solid ingredients as flour or sugar by volume rather than by weight, as is done in Europe.

To make the quantities simpler to measure, many of the figures have been rounded off to correspond to the gradations on U.S. metric spoons and cups. (One cup, for example, equals 237 milliliters; however, wherever practicable in these recipes, a cup's equivalent appears as a more readily measured 250 milliliters—¼ liter.) Similarly, the weight, temperature and linear metric equivalents have been rounded off slightly. Thus the American and metric figures do not precisely match, but using one set or the other will produce the same good results.

Basic Yeast Breads

Recipes for basic bread dough and milk-and-butter dough appear in Standard Preparations, page 164.

Monsieur Montfort's French Bread

The author of this recipe, Yves Montfort, runs his own bakery in the resort town of Bénodet, in Brittany, France.

To make two 10-inch [25-cm.] round or
four 18-by-2-inch [45-by-5-cm.]
cylindrical loaves

7 to 8 cups	flour	1¾ to 2 liters
two ¼ oz.	packages active dry yeast	two 7½ g.
4 tsp.	salt	20 ml.
3 cups	tepid water	¾ liter

Into a large bowl, measure 7 cups [1¾ liters] of flour and stir in the yeast and salt. Form a well in the flour and pour in the water. With a wooden spoon, slowly pull the flour into the liquid until it is fully absorbed. Work the dough into a ball by hand and put it on a lightly floured work surface.

The dough should be tacky. Begin turning and folding the dough with a pastry scraper or putty knife. Sprinkle small amounts of flour on the work surface and your hands if you must, but do so sparingly. Continue to lift, fold and turn the dough for 10 minutes. Throw the dough down against the work surface to break the lift-fold-turn rhythm. The dough will become elastic but will continue to stick to your moist fingers unless they are powdered with flour.

Wash the large bowl, grease it and place the dough in it. Cover tightly with plastic wrap and set in a warm—70° F. [21° C.]—place. Allow the dough to expand fully to double its volume—about one and one half to two hours. Punch down the dough, re-cover the bowl and let the dough double in volume again.

Turn the dough onto the floured work surface, punch it down and knead briefly to press out the air bubbles. Divide the dough, which will weigh about 3¾ pounds [1¾ kg.], into as many loaves as you wish to make. Form the divided dough into balls and let them rest for five minutes before shaping the loaves. For a long loaf, flatten the ball into an oval. Fold it over lengthwise, flatten with the side of your open hand, fold again and roll the dough with the palms of your hands. If the dough resists, let it rest for another three or four minutes while preparing the other pieces. Return to the partially formed length and continue to roll under the palms of your hands until it is shaped. The seam will disappear.

The long pieces of dough can be placed directly on greased baking sheets to rise, although they will slump somewhat because the dough lacks stiffness. They can also be placed in long bread baskets lined with cloth and liberally sprinkled with flour. The baskets will direct the dough upward during the rise period.

Third and perhaps the best way to let long loaves rise is to place them in half-cylindrical, French-type metal bread-baking pans. Round loaves can be placed on baking sheets to rise, but because of the softness of this particular dough it is better to use round cloth-lined baskets. Place the shaped dough in the warm place and drape wax paper, supported on water glasses, above the loaves. Leave until the loaves are fully doubled. More rising, rather than less, is desirable. The longer the dough is allowed to rise, the larger the cell structure will be in the baked loaf.

Preheat the oven to 425° F. [220° C.] approximately 20 minutes before putting the dough in it. Place a broiler pan or a similar vessel on the lowest shelf. Five minutes before baking, pour 1½ cups [375 ml.] of hot tap water into the pan. If the loaves rose in a basket, tip each of them onto your hand and lower them gently onto baking sheets. With a razor blade, slash the tops of the round loaves in a tick-tack-toe design. Hold the blade at a 45-degree angle as you make the cuts. For the long loaves, make a series of diagonal cuts.

Brush or spray the loaves with water as you place them in the hot oven. At three-minute intervals during the first 15 minutes, spray the loaves. Do this from the oven door. Do not pull out the loaves or the moist hot air will be lost. The loaves will be fully ovenproof (expanded) in about 18 minutes, at which time color will begin to tinge the crusts. If water remains in the pan, empty it. Midway through the baking period and again near the end of it, shift the loaves to expose them equally to the temperature variations in the oven.

Bake the loaves until golden brown—after a total time of 25 to 30 minutes. Turn over one loaf and rap the bottom crust with your forefinger. A hard hollow sound indicates that the bread is baked.

Take the bread from the oven. Put the loaves on a wire rack to cool. The French baker stands his loaves on end so cool air freely circulates around them. For a bright, shiny crust, brush the loaves lightly with slightly salted water.

BERNARD CLAYTON JR.
THE COMPLETE BOOK OF BREADS

Oat Flour Bread

Kauraleipä

To make two 8-inch [20-cm.] round loaves

3 cups	oat flour	¾ liter
2¼ cups	gluten flour	550 ml.
two ¼ oz.	packages active dry yeast or two ⅗ oz. [18 g.] cakes fresh yeast	two 7½ g.
2 cups	tepid water, whey or vegetable stock	½ liter
1 tbsp.	honey	15 ml.
1½ tsp.	sea salt	7 ml.

Mix the yeast with the liquid. Stir in the gluten flour. Beat well until the mixture thickens. Then add the honey, salt and as much oat flour as necessary to make an elastic, soft and silky dough. Knead the dough for about 20 minutes.

Put the dough into a bowl, cover it and let it rise in a warm place until it has doubled in bulk, about one hour. Punch down the dough, divide it in half and shape it into two round loaves. Place the loaves on baking sheets and prick the loaves all over with a fork. Cover and let them rise until almost doubled in bulk, about 30 minutes. Bake the loaves in a preheated 425° F. [220° C.] oven for 25 to 30 minutes. For a crisp crust, let them cool on a wire rack. It is best to eat the bread when fresh as it does not keep well.

ULLA KÄKÖNEN
NATURAL COOKING THE FINNISH WAY

Blanche Frankehauser's Old-fashioned Oatmeal Bread

To make two 8½-by-4½-inch [21-by-11-cm.] loaves

5½ cups	sifted flour	1½ liters
1 cup	rolled oats	¼ liter
two ¼ oz.	packages active dry yeast	two 7½ g.
2 cups	boiling water	½ liter
5 tbsp.	butter	75 ml.
½ cup	light molasses	125 ml.
4 tsp.	salt	20 ml.
2	eggs, lightly beaten	2

Combine the boiling water with the oats, butter, molasses and salt. Cool the mixture to tepid, then add the yeast and mix well. Blend in the eggs and stir in the flour. The dough will be softer than a kneaded dough. Place the dough in a buttered bowl, cover it and store it in the refrigerator for at least two hours, or until needed.

Remove the chilled dough and knead it about five times (this helps to remove the air). Shape it into two loaves on a well-floured surface, place the loaves in buttered 8½-by-4½-inch [21-by-11-cm.] loaf pans and cover them with a cloth. Let the loaves rise in a warm place until they double in bulk, about two hours.

Bake in a preheated 375° F. [190° C.] oven for one hour, or until the loaves sound hollow when rapped on the bottom.

BETTY GROFF AND JOSÉ WILSON
GOOD EARTH AND COUNTRY COOKING

Anadama Bread

Anadama bread originated in New England. The name is said to come from a Gloucester fisherman whose wife Anna refused to bake bread; he devised his own and named it "Anna, damn her."

To make two 8½-by-4½-inch [21-by-11-cm.] loaves

about 5 cups	flour	about 1¼ liters
½ cup	cornmeal	125 ml.
¼ oz.	package active dry yeast or ⅗ oz. [18 g.] cake fresh yeast	7½ g.
2½ cups	water	625 ml.
1 tsp.	salt	5 ml.
2 tbsp.	butter	30 ml.
½ cup	molasses	125 ml.

Stir 1 cup [¼ liter] of cold water into the cornmeal. Bring another cup of water to a rolling boil in a saucepan. Stirring constantly, pour in the cornmeal mixture. Stirring from time to time, cook the mixture until it is very thick—about 10 minutes. Add the salt, butter and molasses. Let the mixture cool to tepid.

Warm the remaining water until it is tepid, and stir the yeast into it. Add this mixture to the cooled cornmeal and gradually stir in about 4½ cups [about 1 liter] of the flour, kneading to make a stiff dough. Knead well for about 10 minutes until the dough is springy; if it remains too sticky, it may be necessary to add more flour. Shape the dough into a ball, put it into a buttered bowl, cover and let the dough rise in a warm place for about one and one half hours, or until doubled in bulk.

Punch down the dough and divide it into two pieces. Shape each piece into a loaf and put the loaves in buttered 8½-by-4½-inch [21-by-11-cm.] loaf pans. Cover the pans with a cloth and leave them in a warm place until the dough has doubled in bulk again, about 30 minutes. Bake the loaves in a preheated 350° F. [180° C.] oven for one hour, or until the loaves sound hollow if rapped on the bottom.

MARIA CHAMBERLIN-HELLMAN (EDITOR)
FOOD NOTES

Wheat-Germ-Millet Bread

To make two 9-by-5-inch [23-by-13-cm.] loaves

3 to 4 cups	whole-wheat flour	¾ to 1 liter
1 cup	coarsely cracked millet	¼ liter
½ cup	wheat germ	125 ml.
¼ oz.	package active dry yeast or ⅗ oz. [18 g.] cake fresh yeast	7½ g.
1¾ cups	boiling water, ¼ cup [50 ml.] cooled to tepid	425 ml.
¼ cup	honey	50 ml.
2 tsp.	salt	10 ml.
2 tbsp.	oil	30 ml.

Combine the millet and wheat germ in a large bowl; pour 1½ cups [375 ml.] of boiling water over them and set aside. Mix the yeast into ¼ cup [50 ml.] of tepid water and set aside. Add the honey, salt and oil to the millet-and-wheat-germ mixture. When this mixture has cooled to tepid, add the yeast and 1½ cups of the flour. Beat vigorously to develop the gluten in the flour; add enough of the remaining flour to make the dough smooth and workable; knead well. Set the dough aside in an oiled bowl, covered with a damp cloth, to rise for one hour, or until doubled in bulk.

Punch down the dough, shape it into two loaves, and place the loaves in two 9-by-5-inch [23-by-13-cm.] loaf pans or on a baking sheet. Let the dough rise once more, for about one hour, then bake in a preheated 375° F. [190° C.] oven for 50 minutes. Remove the loaves from the pans or the baking sheet immediately, and let them cool slightly on a wire rack before slicing them.

MARLENE ANNE BUMGARNER
THE BOOK OF WHOLE GRAINS

Swedish Tin Loaves

To make two 9-by-5-inch [23-by-13-cm.] loaves

3½ cups	all-purpose flour	875 ml.
7 cups	dark rye flour	1¾ liters
two ¼ oz.	packages active dry yeast or two ⅗ oz. [18 g.] cakes fresh yeast	two 7½ g.
4 cups	milk, ½ cup [125 ml.] warmed to tepid	1 liter
2 tsp.	salt	10 ml.
2 tbsp.	fennel seeds, pounded in a mortar (optional)	30 ml.
1 cup	light corn syrup	¼ liter

Mix the yeast with the ½ cup [125 ml.] of tepid milk. Sift the all-purpose and rye flours, salt and pounded fennel seeds, if using. Add the cold milk and work the mixture into a smooth dough. Add the yeast mixture and the corn syrup, and keep on kneading the dough. When it is smooth and glossy, cover it with a cloth and let it rise in a warm place for 24 hours.

Knead the dough again for about five minutes, and divide it in half. Put the dough into two 9-by-5-inch [23-by-13-cm.] loaf pans, making sure the pans are no more than half-full. Stand the pans in a warm place until the dough rises to the rims of the pans. Bake the loaves in a preheated 400° F. [200° C.] oven for 15 minutes, then reduce the temperature to 375° F. [190° C.] for the rest of the baking time, about 30 minutes. Test the loaves with a skewer to see if they are done: If they are, the skewer will come out clean. Remove the loaves from the oven, then brush the surfaces lightly with tepid water, and turn them out onto a wire rack to cool. Wrap them in a cloth until they are cold, to prevent them from becoming too crusty.

INGA NORBERG
GOOD FOOD FROM SWEDEN

Homemade Italian Milk Bread

Pane al Latte Fatto in Casa

To make two 8-inch [20-cm.] round loaves or 20 rolls

4 cups	flour	1 liter
2½ cups	whole-wheat flour	625 ml.
two ¼ oz.	packages active dry yeast or two ⅗ oz. [18 g.] cakes fresh yeast	two 7½ g.
1 tsp.	sugar	5 ml.
1½ cups	tepid milk, mixed with 1½ cups [375 ml.] tepid water	375 ml.
2 tsp.	salt	10 ml.

In a large bowl, combine the yeast and sugar with 6 tablespoons [90 ml.] of the tepid milk-and-water mixture. Stir well, leave in a warm place until the yeast foams, then add the remaining liquid. Stir in the flours and the salt, and knead to make a fairly soft dough, adding more tepid water if necessary. Turn the dough onto a work surface sprinkled with additional all-purpose flour and knead the dough for 10 minutes, or until it is smooth and elastic. Divide and shape the dough into 20 balls or into two large round loaves, and place them on buttered baking sheets. Cover the rolls or loaves with a cloth and let them rise in a warm place for about one and a half hours, or until a floured finger poked into the dough leaves a dent that does not spring back immediately. Glaze the rolls or loaves with milk, if you like.

Bake the bread in a preheated 425° F. [220° C.] oven— about 25 to 30 minutes for the rolls or 50 minutes to one hour for the loaves. Both the rolls and loaves should be golden brown and should sound slightly hollow when rapped on the bottom. Cool them on wire racks.

MARIÙ SALVATORI DE ZULIANI
LA CUCINA DI VERSILIA E GARFAGNANA

Dutch Brown Bread

Bruin Brood

To make one 9-by-5-inch [23-by-13-cm.] loaf

3 cups	whole-wheat flour	¾ liter
1¼ cups	all-purpose flour	300 ml.
¼ oz.	package active dry yeast, plus 1 tsp. [5 ml.] sugar, or ⅗ oz. [18 g.] cake fresh yeast	7½ g.
about 1¼ cups	tepid milk or water	about 300 ml.
1 tsp.	salt	5 ml.
1 tbsp.	butter, softened (optional)	15 ml.

Mix the yeast and sugar, if using, with the tepid milk or water and let stand for 10 minutes. Combine the whole-wheat and all-purpose flours in a mixing bowl and make a well in the center. Pour the yeast mixture into the well. Gradually work in the flours, add the salt and finally the butter, if using. Knead the dough thoroughly for 10 minutes, or until it is smooth and elastic. Cover the bowl with a damp cloth and let the dough rise in a warm place for at least one and a half hours, or until it has doubled in bulk.

On a floured board, form the risen dough into a ball. Place the dough on a buttered baking sheet, cover it with a cloth and let it rise for about 20 minutes. To test whether the dough is well risen, push two finger tips into the top of it; if the impressions remain in the dough, it is ready.

Put the dough on a floured board. Punch it down and knead it for about five minutes. Form it into a ball again, return it to the baking sheet and let it rise for 10 minutes. Remove the dough to the floured board, punch it down again and roll it out into an elongated oval shape. Fold the ends toward the center and shape the dough into a rectangle. Roll out the dough again, shape it into a loaf and place it in a buttered 9-by-5-inch [23-by-13-cm.] loaf pan. Cover, and let it rise for 25 minutes.

Uncover the pan and bake the loaf in a preheated 450° F. [220° C.] oven for 30 to 40 minutes, or until the surface is brown and crisp. The loaf should sound hollow when it is unmolded and rapped underneath. Let it cool on a wire rack.

C. A. H. HAITSMA MULIER-VAN BEUSEKOM (EDITOR)
CULINAIRE ENCYCLOPEDIE

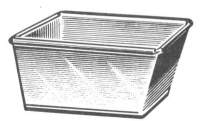

Pinwheel Bread

To make three 7½-by-3½-inch [19-by-9-cm.] loaves

about 10 cups	unbleached all-purpose flour, sifted	about 2½ liters
2½ cups	whole-wheat flour	625 ml.
two ¼ oz.	packages active dry yeast or two ⅗ oz. [18 g.] cakes fresh yeast	two 7½ g.
2 cups	milk	½ liter
8 tbsp.	vegetable shortening	120 ml.
½ cup	sugar	125 ml.
2 tbsp.	salt	30 ml.
2 cups	water, 1 cup [¼ liter] heated to tepid	½ liter
¼ cup	molasses	50 ml.

Scald the milk in a saucepan. Mix together the shortening, sugar and salt, and blend in the milk. Add 1 cup [¼ liter] of cold water and cool the mixture to tepid. Mix the yeast with 1 cup of tepid water and add to the milk mixture. Blend the mixture well. Add 4 cups [1 liter] of the all-purpose flour and beat until smooth (with an electric mixer, one minute at medium speed). Cover the dough with a dish towel and allow it to rise in a warm, draft-free place until light and doubled in bulk (approximately one hour).

Divide the dough into two equal portions. Place each in a separate bowl. Blend 3½ to 4 cups [¾ to 1 liter] of the all-purpose flour into one portion to form a stiff dough. Stir the molasses into the second portion, and add the whole-wheat flour and as much of the remaining all-purpose flour as is necessary to form a dough that doesn't stick to your fingers.

Knead the light and dark doughs separately on a floured board until smooth and elastic (approximately five to seven minutes each). Place the doughs in two large greased bowls, turning them over once to grease the tops. Cover each bowl with a dish towel and allow the doughs to rise in a warm, draft-free place for one and one half hours, or until they have doubled in bulk. If the whole-wheat dough has not risen sufficiently by this time, let it rise a little longer and proceed to shape the white dough.

Divide each dough into three parts. Roll out each part on a lightly floured board to a 12-by-8-inch [30-by-20-cm.] rectangle. Place one dark rectangle on top of one light rectangle and roll them up tight like a jelly roll, beginning at the 8-inch [20-cm.] end. Press both doughs together firmly and tuck the ends of the loaf under. Repeat the process with the remaining dough. Place each loaf in a well-greased 7½-by-3½-inch [19-by-9-cm.] loaf pan. Cover the loaves with a dish towel and let them rise in a warm place until doubled in bulk (approximately one hour). Bake the loaves in a preheated 375° F. [190° C.] oven for 45 to 50 minutes, or until they sound hollow when the bottoms are rapped.

YVONNE YOUNG TARR
THE NEW YORK TIMES BREAD AND SOUP COOKBOOK

Fried Flatbread

Bortellina Bettolese

To make about twenty 4-inch [10-cm.] round flatbreads

8 cups	flour	2 liters
two ¼ oz.	packages active dry yeast or two ⅗ oz. [18 g.] cakes fresh yeast	two 7½ g.
about 2½ cups	tepid water	about 625 ml.
	salt	
7 tbsp.	lard	105 ml.

Mix half of the yeast with ¼ cup [50 ml.] of tepid water. Stir in 1 cup [¼ liter] of the flour and 1 cup of tepid water. Leave this sponge for 30 minutes, or until foaming.

Put the rest of the flour into a bowl. Add the yeast sponge, salt and the rest of the yeast, if using fresh yeast. If using active dry yeast, mix the rest of the yeast with 3 tablespoons [45 ml.] of tepid water, then add to the sponge and dry ingredients. Mix the ingredients together, gradually incorporating enough additional tepid water to make a firm dough. Knead the dough until it forms a smooth, soft ball.

Let the dough rest for 10 minutes, then divide it into small pieces and flatten them into rounds about 4 inches [10 cm.] in diameter.

In a heavy cast-iron skillet, melt the lard over medium heat. Fry the rounds in several batches until they are golden brown, about eight to 10 minutes on each side.

CARMEN ARTOCCHINI
400 RICETTE DELLA CUCINA PIACENTINA

❖

Middle Eastern Pocket Bread

Pita

To make fourteen 6-inch [15-cm.] flatbreads

about 4½ cups	all-purpose flour'	about 1 liter
1 cup	gluten flour	¼ liter
¼ oz.	package active dry yeast or ⅗ oz. [18 g.] cake fresh yeast	7½ g.
2¼ cups	tepid water	550 ml.
1 tsp.	sugar	5 ml.
1 tsp.	olive oil	5 ml.
2 tsp.	salt	10 ml.
	cornmeal	

Combine ¼ cup [50 ml.] of tepid water, the sugar and yeast in a large mixing bowl and let stand until very foamy, about 10 minutes. Beat in the remaining warm water, the olive oil and salt. Beat in the gluten flour and beat vigorously for two or three minutes. Gradually add all-purpose flour until the mixture is too stiff to beat, then turn the dough out onto a floured work surface and knead well, adding enough additional all-purpose flour to make an elastic, nonsticky but not-too-stiff dough. Form the dough into a cylinder about 14 inches [35 cm.] long and cut it into 14 slices. Lay the slices 2 or 3 inches [5 or 8 cm.] apart on a floured towel. Cover with a dry cloth, then with a well-dampened one, and let the slices rise until doubled, about one hour.

On a floured surface, roll each piece of dough into a round about 6 inches [15 cm.] in diameter. Lay the rounds on baking sheets sprinkled with cornmeal, spacing the rounds at least 2 inches apart. (You will need four or more baking sheets for this quantity of dough.) Cover with dry cloths topped with damp ones and let the loaves rise for 30 minutes: The dough should be not quite doubled.

While the loaves are rising, preheat the oven to 475° F. [250° C.]. If yours is a gas oven, put one baking sheet directly on the oven floor and bake the loaves for four and one half minutes (they will balloon), then transfer the pan to the top shelf, at the same time putting another baking sheet of *pita* on the oven floor. At the end of the second four-and-a-half-minute period, remove the upper sheet from the oven, move the lower sheet to the upper shelf and put the third sheet on the bottom, proceeding in this way until all of the loaves are baked. If yours is an electric oven, follow the same leapfrog method, but bake the loaves first on a shelf placed as close as possible to the bottom of the oven before transferring them to the upper shelf.

As the bread is removed from the oven, stack the rounds and wrap them in a dry towel, then in a damp one. Keep adding to the stack and rewrapping it, then allow all the loaves to cool thoroughly (unless you want to serve some of the bread right away). The loaves will deflate, but the pockets will remain. Store in plastic bags, or freeze. Before serving, rewarm the *pita*.

HELEN WITTY AND ELIZABETH SCHNEIDER COLCHIE
BETTER THAN STORE-BOUGHT

❖

Yemenite Pita or Flapjack Bread

Lakhoach or Khubs

Lakhoach, Yemenite bread, looks like an American flapjack before it is turned over: brown on one side and doughy-dry and bubbly on the other. The same ingredients (but double the amount of flour) make *khubs,* or Yemenite *pita. Lakhoach* is made on a heavy pan or griddle (the Yemenites bake it just as the Bedouins do—on a rounded iron over embers); *khubs* are baked as they were in Biblical times, on the wall of a "tannour," a primitive oven heated with embers and with the fire put out before the baking. *Khubs* stick to the wall of the oven and, when ready, are lifted off with a kind of spatula. *Lakhoach* and *khubs* are eaten rolled up and dipped into *hibeh* and *schoog*—spicy Yemenite condiments—or into the gravy of the Yemenites' soupy stews.

	To make about ten to twelve 8-inch [20-cm.] round flatbreads	
3 cups	flour for *lakhoach*, or 6 cups [1½ liters] for *khubs*	¾ liter
¼ oz.	package active dry yeast or ⅗ oz. [18 g.] cake fresh yeast	7½ g.
3 cups	tepid water	¾ liter
1 tsp.	salt	5 ml.

Mix the yeast with ¼ cup [50 ml.] of the water. Then mix all of the ingredients together and set the batter or dough aside to rise for two or more hours. For *lakhoach*, ladle out ½ cup [125 ml.] of batter at a time onto a heavy cast-iron pan or griddle, and cook until the bubbles on the top are set and the surrounding area is cooked—about three minutes. Remove from the griddle and serve hot or cold.

For *khubs*, divide the dough into 12 balls, roll out each ball as thin as possible and bake for about five minutes in a preheated 450° F. [230° C.] oven.

MOLLY LYONS BAR-DAVID
THE ISRAELI COOK BOOK

Crumpets

The technique of making crumpets is shown on pages 56-57.

	To make 8 to 10 crumpets	
4 cups	flour	1 liter
⅗ oz.	cake fresh yeast	18 g.
2½ cups	tepid milk	625 ml.
1 tsp.	salt	5 ml.
1 tsp.	baking soda	5 ml.
about ¼ cup	tepid water	about 50 ml.
	melted lard	

Warm the flour in a bowl by setting it over the pilot light of a gas stove or in a 200° F. [100° C.] oven. Combine the yeast with ⅓ cup [75 ml.] of the milk and use a fork to crumble the yeast. It will soon cream and swell into frothiness.

Make a well in the center of the flour and pour in both the yeast mixture and the rest of the tepid milk. Beat for a good five minutes. Cover the bowl and let the batter rise in a warm place for an hour. Dissolve the baking soda in the tepid water, add it to the mixture, beating it in thoroughly, then let the batter rise for another hour.

Grease a griddle with the lard and grease the crumpet rings. Place the rings on the griddle and heat the griddle.

Pour spoonfuls of batter to half-fill the rings, and let the crumpets cook for about five minutes. Turn over each crumpet when the surface loses its liquid appearance, and cook for a further 30 seconds. Remove the crumpets from the griddle, ease off the rings and start again with some more batter.

Eat these crumpets with plenty of butter. They make good bases for fried eggs, or scrambled eggs with anchovies. Some people like them with syrup as well as butter.

JANE GRIGSON
ENGLISH FOOD

Burger Buns

	To make 20 buns	
5½ to 6½ cups	flour	1½ to 1¾ liters
two ¼ oz.	packages active dry yeast	two 7½ g.
⅓ cup	instant nonfat dry milk	75 ml.
¼ cup	sugar	50 ml.
1 tbsp.	salt	15 ml.
5 tbsp.	butter, softened	75 ml.
1½ cups	hot water (120° to 130° F. [49° to 54° C.])	375 ml.

Combine the dry milk, sugar, yeast, salt and 2 cups [½ liter] of the flour in a large mixing bowl. Cut in the softened butter. Stir the hot water slowly into the mixture, blending well. Beat for two minutes at the medium speed of an electric mixer, scraping the bowl from time to time. Blend in ¾ cup [175 ml.] of the remaining flour and beat for two minutes at high speed, stopping occasionally to scrape the bowl.

Make a stiff dough by blending in as much of the remaining flour as necessary. Knead the dough on a lightly floured board for eight to 10 minutes, or until it becomes elastic and smooth. Grease a large bowl and set the dough in it, turning the dough over to grease the top. Allow the dough to rise, covered, in a warm, draft-free place until it doubles in volume (approximately 45 minutes).

Using your fist, punch down the dough. Cover it and allow it to rise again for only 20 minutes. Before the dough doubles in size, cut it into two equal parts and divide each part into 10 pieces of equal size. Shape each piece into a ball. Flatten the balls into bun shapes and place them about 2 inches [5 cm.] apart on greased baking sheets.

Let the buns rise once more, covered, in a warm, draft-free place until doubled in volume. This should take approximately one hour. Preheat the oven to 375° F. [190° C.] and bake the buns for 15 or 20 minutes. Slide the buns off the baking sheets and cool them on wire racks.

YVONNE YOUNG TARR
THE NEW YORK TIMES BREAD AND SOUP COOKBOOK

Split Rolls

Les Pistolets

These split rolls—small, round milk rolls with a distinctive indentation across the top—are a specialty of eastern France. The groove is usually made with an oiled stick. The stick may also be used dry, provided the tops of the rolls have been moistened with a little oil.

To make about 40 rolls

9 cups	flour	2¼ liters
¼ oz.	package active dry yeast or ⅗ oz. [18 g.] cake fresh yeast	7½ g.
2 tbsp.	unflavored malt extract	30 ml.
2 to 3 cups	tepid water	½ to ¾ liter
2 tsp.	salt	10 ml.
3 tbsp.	sugar	45 ml.
⅓ cup	nonfat dry milk	75 ml.
7 tbsp.	butter, softened	105 ml.
	oil	
	rye flour	

Mix the yeast with ⅓ cup [75 ml.] of tepid water and the malt extract. Leave it until it is foaming, about 10 minutes. Sift the flour, salt, sugar and dry milk into a bowl and make a well in the center. Pour in the yeast mixture and 1⅔ cups [400 ml.] of tepid water. Mix, adding more water if necessary, to form a firm dough.

Turn the dough out onto a floured board and knead it well for about 10 minutes, or until it is smooth and elastic, then let it rest for 15 minutes. Mix in the softened butter and knead vigorously for a further five minutes: The dough should be fairly firm. Put the dough into a bowl, cover it with a cloth or plastic wrap and let it rise at warm room temperature for about three hours, or overnight in the refrigerator, until more than tripled in bulk.

Punch down the dough, turn it over and cover the bowl. Let the dough rise again until doubled in bulk, about two hours. Punch down the dough again and divide it into about 40 equal-sized pieces. Shape each piece into a ball about 1½ inches [3 cm.] in diameter. Make a deep groove with an oiled stick across each ball, and dust the surface with rye flour to prevent the two halves of the roll from sticking together during baking. Transfer the rolls, grooves downward, to a floured surface and let them rise again for 30 minutes.

Preheat the oven to 425° F. [220° C.]. Twenty minutes before baking, put a pan of hot water on the floor or bottom shelf of the oven. Transfer the rolls with the grooves upward to floured baking sheets. Bake the rolls for 25 to 30 minutes, or until they are golden brown and feel hard and hollow.

RAYMOND CALVEL
LA BOULANGERIE MODERNE

Huffkins

To make ten 3-inch [8-cm.] rolls

4 cups	flour	1 liter
¼ oz.	package active dry yeast or ⅗ oz. [18 g.] cake fresh yeast	7½ g.
1 tsp.	sugar	5 ml.
1¼ cups	tepid water	300 ml.
1 tsp.	salt	5 ml.

In a cup, mix the yeast with the sugar and half of the water. Leave the mixture in a warm place until it is frothy, about 10 minutes. Sift the flour and salt together, mix in the yeast and the rest of the water. Knead the dough for about 10 minutes, or until it is smooth and elastic; let it rise in a warm place for one and a half hours, or until it has doubled in bulk.

Shape the dough into 10 balls, and press a hole in the center of each with your finger. Place the huffkins on a large baking sheet and let them rise in a warm place for 20 minutes, or until well risen again. Bake them in a preheated 400° F. [200° C.] oven for 15 minutes, or until golden brown. Eat them on the day they are baked.

FLORENCE WHITE
GOOD ENGLISH FOOD

Soft Pretzels

The techniques of shaping pretzels appear on pages 30-31.

To make 12 pretzels

about 3 cups	all-purpose flour	about ¾ liter
¾ cup	gluten flour	175 ml.
¼ oz.	package active dry yeast	7½ g.
1½ cups	tepid water	375 ml.
4 tsp.	sugar	20 ml.
1 tsp.	table salt	5 ml.
3 tbsp.	baking soda	45 ml.
1 tbsp.	coarse salt, preferably sea salt	15 ml.

In a small bowl, combine ½ cup [125 ml.] of tepid water with 1 teaspoon [5 ml.] of the sugar and the yeast. Let rise until fluffy, about 10 minutes. Combine 1 cup [¼ liter] of tepid water, the table salt, the gluten flour and 1 cup of the all-purpose flour in the large bowl of an electric mixer; beat these ingredients until well blended. Add the yeast mixture and beat on medium-low speed for four or five minutes. Stir in 1½ cups [375 ml.] more flour.

Turn the dough onto a floured work surface and knead until very smooth and shiny, adding about ½ cup of flour as you knead. Form the dough into a ball and place it in an ungreased bowl. Cover the bowl with plastic wrap and let the dough rise until doubled in bulk, one hour or more.

Punch down the dough, cut it into 12 equal pieces, and cover them with plastic wrap. Roll each piece to form a long rope about 16 to 18 inches [40 to 45 cm.] long, with tapered ends. Form each into a pretzel shape and lay it on a lightly floured board. Let the pretzels rise until not quite doubled, about 30 minutes.

In a 9-inch [23-cm.] enameled or stainless-steel skillet, combine 1 quart [1 liter] of water, the baking soda and the remaining sugar. Bring to a simmer. Slide three pretzels at a time into this bath; keep it at a bare simmer and cook the pretzels for 20 seconds on each side, flipping them gently with a skimmer. Then remove the pretzels with the skimmer, draining them onto a large parchment-covered baking sheet with their original topsides up. Sprinkle the pretzels sparingly with the coarse salt.

Bake the pretzels in the center of a preheated 425° F. [220° C.] oven for 15 minutes, or until nicely browned. Cool the pretzels to lukewarm and eat them fresh, or wrap and freeze them after they have cooled completely.

HELEN WITTY AND ELIZABETH SCHNEIDER COLCHIE
BETTER THAN STORE-BOUGHT

Salted Pretzels

Salzbrezeln

The technique of shaping pretzels appears on pages 30-31; boiling dough before baking it is shown on pages 58-59.

	To make 15 large pretzels	
4 cups	flour	1 liter
¼ oz.	package active dry yeast or ⅗ oz. [18 g.] cake fresh yeast	7½ g.
about ¾ cup	tepid water	about 175 ml.
	sugar	
	salt	
1½ tbsp.	butter	22 ml.
⅔ cup	milk	150 ml.
	coarse salt	

Mix the yeast and a pinch of sugar with 2 tablespoons [30 ml.] of tepid water and leave until foaming, about 10 min-

utes. Sift the flour and 1 teaspoon [5 ml.] of salt into a bowl. Make a well in the center and pour in the yeast mixture. Add ¼ cup [50 ml.] of tepid water to the well and stir it into the yeast mixture, drawing in a little of the flour from the edge of the well. Cover the bowl and leave it in a warm place for 10 minutes, or until the yeasty liquid begins to foam.

Add the butter to the milk and heat them in a small pan until the butter melts. Cool this mixture to tepid and pour it into the well. Add ½ cup [125 ml.] of tepid water. Then incorporate the flour gradually into the yeast mixture, and beat until the dough comes away easily from the sides of the bowl. Knead the dough on a floured board and let it rise for 30 minutes, or until doubled in bulk.

Knead the dough again for about 10 minutes and divide it into 15 pieces. Roll each piece until it forms a cylinder that is the thickness of a pencil and about 12 inches [30 cm.] long; taper the cylinder at both ends. Flour the working surface with additional flour if the dough sticks to it. Shape each cylinder of dough into a pretzel ring by forming a loop and folding the two ends over the loop. Cover the pretzels with cloth towels and let them rise for 10 minutes. Preheat the oven to 450° F. [230° C.].

Fill a saucepan with 3 quarts [3 liters] of water, add 2 tablespoons of salt, and bring to a boil. Using a slotted spoon, lower each pretzel into the boiling water and remove it with the spoon as soon as it rises to the surface—this will happen almost immediately. Drain the pretzels on cloth towels.

With a sharp knife, make a notch in the thickest part of each pretzel and sprinkle the notch with coarse salt. Transfer the pretzels to floured baking sheets. Just before putting them in the oven, sprinkle tepid water on the oven floor and shut the door quickly to create steam. Reduce the oven temperature to 400° F. [200° C.] and bake the pretzels for 30 minutes, or until well browned. Serve cold.

EVA AND ULRICH KLEVER
SELBER BROT BACKEN

Old Maids

To make about twenty-five 3-inch [8-cm.] cakes

5¾ cups	flour	1½ liters
¼ oz.	package active dry yeast or ⅗ oz. [18 g.] cake fresh yeast	7½ g.
½ cup	tepid water	125 ml.
1 tsp.	sugar	5 ml.
1 cup	tepid milk	¼ liter
2 tbsp.	butter, softened	30 ml.
1 tsp.	salt	5 ml.
3	eggs, beaten	3
about 1½ cups	cornmeal	about 375 ml.

Mix the yeast with the water and sugar and let the mixture stand for five minutes, or until it is frothy. Add the milk, butter and salt. Stir in the beaten eggs and 4 cups [1 liter] of the flour to make a moist dough. Turn the dough onto a floured board and knead in the remaining flour. Beat and knead the dough until its surface glows and it becomes elastic—about 20 minutes. Roll out the dough ½ inch [1 cm.] thick and cut it into round cakes with a coffee cup. Sprinkle the cornmeal on the board and press both sides of each cake into the meal to give an interesting gritty surface. Let the cakes rise for one hour, then fry them on a lightly greased griddle or heavy frying pan over medium-low heat until they are straw-colored and ringed with brown on both sides.

GRACE FIRTH
STILLROOM COOKERY

Yorkshire Cakes

These cakes must be buttered hot out of the oven, or cut in two when cold, toasted brown and buttered.

To make ten to fifteen 6-inch [15-cm.] square cakes

8 cups	flour	2 liters
two ¼ oz.	packages active dry yeast or two ⅗ oz. [18 g.] cakes fresh yeast	two 7½ g.
8 tbsp.	butter	120 ml.
2½ cups	milk	625 ml.
2	eggs, beaten	2

In a saucepan, warm the butter and milk together until the butter melts. Remove from the heat and let cool, until the milk is tepid. Then add the eggs and yeast and let the mixture stand for 10 minutes, or until the yeast begins to foam. Stir the mixture into the flour. Mix well together; knead the

dough for 10 minutes and then let rise in a warm place for one hour, or until doubled in bulk.

Knead the mixture thoroughly, then break off pieces of dough and shape them into cakes about ¾ inch [2 cm.] thick and 6 inches [15 cm.] square. Put the cakes on a baking sheet, and leave in a warm place for one hour, or until slightly less than doubled in bulk. Bake in a preheated 350° F. [180° C.] oven for 30 to 40 minutes, or until browned on top.

DUNCAN MACDONALD
THE NEW LONDON FAMILY COOK

Rusks

Zwieback

Rusks made without salt, as in this recipe, and stored in an airtight container will keep for months. Salt should not be added to the dough because it absorbs moisture from the atmosphere, making the rusks soften more quickly.

To make about 72 rusks

8 to 9 cups	flour	2 to 2¼ liters
two ¼ oz.	packages active dry yeast or two ⅗ oz. [18 g.] cakes fresh yeast	two 7½ g.
3 cups	tepid milk	¾ liter
½ cup	sugar	125 ml.
3	egg yolks	3
8 tbsp.	butter, melted and cooled	120 ml.

Cream the yeast with ½ cup [125 ml.] of the milk and 1 teaspoon [5 ml.] of the sugar. Leave it in a warm place until foaming, about 15 minutes. Then add it to 2 cups [½ liter] of the flour. Mix thoroughly, gradually adding ⅔ cup [150 ml.] of the remaining milk, to make a yeast sponge. Let it rise in a warm place until it has doubled in bulk, about one and one half hours.

Stir into the sponge the egg yolks, remaining sugar, butter and the rest of the flour and milk. Blend the mixture into a dough. Turn the dough out onto a floured surface and knead it thoroughly for about 15 minutes, or until it is smooth and elastic. Cover the dough with a damp cloth and let it rise for 30 minutes in a warm place.

Shape the dough into three 12-inch [30-cm.] cylindrical loaves. Sprinkle the tops with a few drops of tepid water. Place the loaves on buttered baking sheets, let them rise for about 45 minutes, then bake them in a preheated 400° F. [200° C.] oven for 50 minutes, or until light brown.

The next day, cut the loaves into thin slices with a very sharp knife. Place the slices on buttered baking sheets and bake them in a preheated 325° F. [170° C.] oven for 30 minutes, turning them after 15 minutes. When finished, they should be dry and evenly browned.

ELEK MAGYAR
KOCHBUCH FÜR FEINSCHMECKER

Flavored Yeast Breads

Pumpernickel Bread

The technique of making pumpernickel bread is demonstrated on pages 64-65.

To make one 12-inch [30-cm.] round loaf or two 8-inch [20-cm.] round loaves

½ cup	cornmeal	125 ml.
3 cups	rye flour	¾ liter
about 1 cup	whole-wheat flour	about ¼ liter
¼ oz.	package active dry yeast or ⅗ oz. [18 g.] cake fresh yeast	7½ g.
1¾ cups	water	425 ml.
¾ cup	molasses	175 ml.
1 tbsp.	butter	15 ml.
1 tbsp.	salt	15 ml.
2 tsp.	sugar	10 ml.
1½ tsp.	caraway seeds, slightly crushed	7 ml.
½ oz.	unsweetened baking chocolate, broken into small pieces	15 g.
2	medium-sized potatoes, boiled, peeled and mashed (about 1 cup [¼ liter])	2
	oil	
1	egg white, mixed with 1 tbsp. [15 ml.] cold water	1

Combine 1½ cups [375 ml.] of the water with the cornmeal in a medium-sized saucepan and cook the mixture over low heat, stirring with a wooden spoon until it is thickened—about five minutes. Remove the pan from the heat and add the molasses, butter, salt, sugar, caraway seeds and chocolate. Stir until the mixture is well blended, pour it into a large bowl and set it aside until it has cooled to tepid.

Meanwhile, slightly warm the remaining ¼ cup [50 ml.] of water, stir the yeast into it and let it stand for 10 minutes.

Add the yeast and the mashed potatoes to the mixture in the bowl. Blend them well and stir in the rye flour and 1 cup [¼ liter] of the whole-wheat flour. The dough should be stiff and sticky. Turn the mixture out onto a work surface liberally sprinkled with additional whole-wheat flour. Put a little oil on your hands before you start to knead, and keep the surface of the dough powdered with whole-wheat flour. Have a scraper handy to remove the dough that accumulates on the work surface. The dough will require a lot of kneading before it begins to come away cleanly from the work surface and from your fingers. Knead it until it is elastic, though stiff—about 15 minutes.

Place the dough in a buttered bowl, cover it with a towel or plastic wrap and put it in a warm place to rise for about one hour, or until the dough has doubled in bulk. Punch down the dough, knead out the air bubbles for 30 seconds and form the dough into one or two round, smooth balls. Place the bread on one or two buttered baking sheets dusted with cornmeal or flour. Cover the bread with wax paper and return it to a warm, draft-free place for 30 minutes to double in bulk. Brush the dough with the egg white and water, and bake it in a preheated 375° F. [190° C.] oven for 50 minutes, or until rapping on the bottom crust yields a hard, hollow sound.

BERNARD CLAYTON JR.
THE COMPLETE BOOK OF BREADS

Beer Bread

Øllebrød

To make 1 large loaf or 3 small loaves

5 cups	rye flour	1¼ liters
about 5 cups	all-purpose flour	about 1¼ liters
two ¼ oz.	packages active dry yeast or two ⅗ oz. [18 g.] cakes fresh yeast	two 7½ g.
2 cups	tepid water	½ liter
1½ cups	beer	375 ml.
⅔ cup	molasses, warmed to tepid	150 ml.
2 tsp.	salt	10 ml.

Mix all but ½ cup [125 ml.] of the tepid water with the beer and molasses. Mix the yeast with the remaining water, then add this to the mixture. Add the rye and all-purpose flours and the salt. Mix well. Let the dough rise in a warm place until doubled in bulk—about one and one half hours. Knead on a floured board, using additional all-purpose flour, if necessary, to make a stiff dough—about 10 minutes.

To make one large loaf, place the dough in a floured cloth in a large bowl and let it rise again until doubled in bulk. For three loaves, divide the dough into three equal parts and let them rise separately. Turn the dough upside down into one buttered 11-by-7-by-2-inch [28-by-18-by-5-cm.] pan or three buttered 7¾-by-3⅝-by-2½-inch [20-by-9-by-6-cm.] pans. Bake the single loaf in a preheated 400° F. [200° C.] oven for 10 minutes, then at 325° F. [170° C.] for 50 minutes. If you are making three small loaves, bake them for 10 minutes at 400° F. and at 325° F. for 35 to 40 minutes.

INGEBORG DAHL JENSEN
WONDERFUL, WONDERFUL DANISH COOKING

Molasses Triticale Bread

To make two 9-by-5-inch [23-by-13-cm.] loaves

3 cups	triticale flour	¾ liter
3 cups	whole-wheat flour	¾ liter
½ cup	whole-grain cornmeal	125 ml.
two ¼ oz.	packages active dry yeast or two ⅗ oz. [18 g.] cakes fresh yeast	two 7½ g.
2 cups	dark beer	½ liter
2 tbsp.	butter	30 ml.
¾ cup	molasses	175 ml.
1 tbsp.	salt	15 ml.
½ cup	tepid water	125 ml.

Heat the beer in a medium-sized saucepan until just about boiling; stir in the cornmeal, butter, molasses and salt. Stir until the butter is melted, then pour the mixture into a large bowl and let it cool until tepid. In the cup used to measure the molasses, mix the yeast with the tepid water. When the cornmeal mixture has cooled, pour into it the yeast mixture, which should have bubbled considerably, and stir in the whole-wheat flour. Stir vigorously for five minutes to develop the gluten in the flour; add the remaining flour, stirring and kneading until the dough is flexible and smooth. Then set the bowl aside, covered, for about 20 minutes.

Divide the dough into two parts, shape into loaves, put into two 9-by-5-inch [23-by-13-cm.] loaf pans or on a baking sheet, and place in a warm location to rise for one hour. Put the loaves into a preheated 450° F. [230° C.] oven and immediately reduce the temperature to 375° F. [190° C.]. Bake for 50 to 55 minutes—or until the loaves, when unmolded briefly and rapped on the bottom, sound hollow. Remove the bread from the pans and let it cool slightly before slicing it.

MARLENE ANNE BUMGARNER
THE BOOK OF WHOLE GRAINS

Sourdough English Muffins

You may cook the muffins on a griddle set over medium heat.

To make twelve 3-inch [8-cm.] muffins

2¾ cups	flour	675 ml.
½ cup	sourdough starter *(recipe, page 167)*	125 ml.
½ tsp.	baking soda	2 ml.
1 cup	milk	¼ liter
2 tbsp.	sugar	30 ml.
¾ tsp.	salt	4 ml.
2 to 3 tbsp.	cornmeal	30 to 45 ml.

Combine the starter, milk and 2 cups [½ liter] of the flour in a large pottery bowl. Mix, cover with a tea towel, and let the dough stand at room temperature for eight hours or overnight. Mix ½ cup [125 ml.] of flour, the soda, sugar and salt, and add them to the dough. Turn the dough out onto a board sprinkled with the remaining ¼ cup [50 ml.] of flour. Knead the dough for three to five minutes until smooth, adding more flour if necessary. Roll the dough ¾ inch [2 cm.] thick. Cut out twelve 3-inch [8-cm.] square or round muffins. Place the muffins on wax paper that has been sprinkled with half of the cornmeal. Sprinkle the remaining cornmeal on top of the muffins. Cover, and let the muffins rise in a warm place for 45 minutes. On a lightly greased electric griddle preheated to 275° F. [140° C.], cook the muffins for about 10 minutes on each side, or until lightly browned.

THE JUNIOR LEAGUE OF LITTLE ROCK
LITTLE ROCK COOKS

Sourdough Bread

Pain au Levain

When using a new starter, I add half water, half beer as liquid to increase sourness.

To make one 10-inch [25-cm.] round or 16-inch [40-cm.] cylindrical loaf

about 6½ cups	all-purpose flour	about 1½ liters
2 tbsp.	rye flour	30 ml.
1 tbsp.	buckwheat flour	15 ml.
1 tbsp.	bran	30 ml.
¼ oz.	package active dry yeast or ⅗ oz. [18 g.] cake fresh yeast	7½ g.
2 cups	sourdough starter *(recipe, page 167)*	½ liter
2¾ cups	tepid water	675 ml.
2 tbsp.	sesame seeds, toasted in a 350° F. [180° C.] oven for 20 minutes, then pounded in a mortar	30 ml.
1 tbsp.	unflavored powdered malt extract	15 ml.
2 tsp.	salt	10 ml.

To make the yeast sponge, empty the starter into a mixing bowl. Stir in 1 cup [¼ liter] of tepid water and 1¼ cups [300 ml.] of the all-purpose flour. Cover the sponge with a towel, place it in a warm spot and leave it for 24 to 36 hours. At the end of this time, stir down the yeast sponge and put half of it back into the starter container for your next baking.

To make the bread, mix the yeast with 1½ cups [375 ml.] of tepid water. Stir this into the sponge and add the rye and buckwheat flours, sesame seeds, bran, malt extract and salt. Add enough all-purpose flour to form a soft dough, then turn it out onto a floured work surface and knead it. Sprinkle more flour on the work surface as needed and work the dough for 12 minutes, or until it feels firm and elastic. Add the minimum amount of flour required to reach this point.

Place the dough in a lightly oiled bowl, cover it with a towel and let it rise until doubled in bulk. Remove it from the bowl, punch it down and shape the dough into a 10-inch [25-cm.] round loaf or a 16-inch [40-cm.] cylindrical loaf.

Let the loaf rise, towel-covered, in a warm place until it has reached almost full size. This rising can be slowed by placing the bread in a cooler spot, and it is often desirable to do so because it allows the flavoring essences to develop more fully. It will take a good hour at the very least for the bread to rise and expand enough, even in a warm place.

Bake the bread in a preheated 375° to 400° F. [190° to 200° C.] oven for 15 minutes, then reduce the heat to 350° F. [180° C.] for 20 minutes, and reduce the heat again to 325° F. [170° C.] until the bread is done, another 15 to 25 minutes, depending on the shape of the loaf. (This lessening heat progression attempts to duplicate the falling heat in a wood-fired baker's oven.) Remove the bread from the oven. Test doneness by knocking on the bottom. If the sound is hollow, the bread is finished. Let it cool, propped at a tilt or on a rack so the bottom crust does not become moist and soft.

JUDITH OLNEY
COMFORTING FOOD

Buckwheat Flatbread

Tattarleipä

To make one 8-inch [20-cm.] round flatbread

2 cups	buckwheat flour	½ liter
1 cup	gluten flour	¼ liter
¼ oz.	package active dry yeast or ⅗ oz. [18 g.] cake fresh yeast	7½ g.
2	medium-sized baking potatoes, scrubbed	2
3 cups	water	¾ liter
2 tsp.	sea salt	10 ml.
½ cup	buttermilk	125 ml.
1	egg, beaten, or 1 tbsp. [15 ml.] melted butter (optional)	1

To make the starter, boil the potatoes in their skins in the water with half a teaspoon [2 ml.] of the salt until they are soft. Drain them and reserve the cooking liquid. Peel and mash the potatoes while still warm, and stir in 2 cups [½ liter] of the cooking liquid. Pour the potato mixture through a strainer into a bowl. Let it cool.

Mix the yeast with 3 tablespoons [45 ml.] of the potato cooking liquid when it has cooled to tepid. Let the mixture stand for 10 minutes, until the yeast begins to foam. Then stir the yeast into the potato mixture. Add 1 cup [¼ liter] of the buckwheat flour. Cover, and leave in a warm place overnight. The dough should become bubbly.

The next day, add the buttermilk and the rest of the buckwheat flour to the potato starter. Stir in the gluten flour and the rest of the salt. Mix well until the dough has the consistency of thick porridge. Butter a deep, 8-inch [20-cm.] circular baking dish, and pour in the dough, spreading it evenly. Bake the flatbread in a preheated 450° F. [230° C.] oven for 20 to 30 minutes. After it has cooked for 10 to 15 minutes, the bread may be brushed with beaten egg or butter. When it is finished, cut it in pieces and serve it warm.

ULLA KÄKÖNEN
NATURAL COOKING THE FINNISH WAY

German Household Bread

Hausmannsbrot

If you prefer to make two or three smaller loaves, bake them at 375° F. [190° C.] for 45 or 50 minutes.

To make one 14-inch [35-cm.] cylindrical loaf

1¼ cups	rye flour	300 ml.
4 to 5 cups	all-purpose flour	1 to 1¼ liters
2 cups	whole-wheat flour	½ liter
two ¼ oz.	packages active dry yeast or two ⅗ oz. [18 g.] cakes fresh yeast	two 7½ g.
¼ cup	rye sourdough starter *(recipe, page 167)*	50 ml.
1¼ cups	tepid water	300 ml.
1 tsp.	sugar	5 ml.
1⅓ cups	buttermilk, at room temperature	325 ml.
1 tbsp.	salt	15 ml.

Blend the starter with ¾ cup [200 ml.] of tepid water and the rye flour. Cover; leave overnight at room temperature.

Sift 4 cups [1 liter] of the all-purpose flour and all of the whole-wheat flour into a bowl and make a well in the center. Mix the yeast with ½ cup [125 ml.] of tepid water and pour it into the well with the sugar. Stir together about 6 tablespoons [90 ml.] of flour from the edges and mix with the liquid to form a yeast sponge. Cover the bowl with a cloth and let the yeast sponge rise for 20 to 30 minutes or until it bubbles. Add the sourdough starter, all but 2 tablespoons [30 ml.] of the buttermilk, and the salt. Mix the sponge into the rest of the flour with the other ingredients, and knead well—adding more all-purpose flour if the dough is sticky—for about 10 minutes, or until the dough is smooth and elastic. Cover the bowl with a cloth and let the dough rise in a warm place for two hours or until doubled in bulk.

Knead the dough again for 10 minutes, then form a cylindrical loaf. Place the loaf on a buttered baking sheet and, with a sharp knife or razor blade, make a shallow, lengthwise gash. Cover and let rise in a warm place for two hours.

Brush the loaf with the rest of the buttermilk and bake it in the center of a preheated 425° F. [220° C.] oven for 50 to 60 minutes, or until the bottom sounds hollow when rapped.

MARGRET UHLE AND ANNE BRAKEMEIER
EIGENBRÖTLERS BROTBACKBUCH

Sourdough French Bread

The author of this recipe is a food technologist at the University of California, Davis, and has done extensive research on sourdough starter cultures.

To make two 12-inch [30-cm.] cylindrical
or 8-inch [20-cm.] round loaves

about 7 cups	flour	about 1¾ liters
¼ oz.	package active dry yeast or ⅗ oz. [18 g.] cake fresh yeast	7½ g.
2 cups	tepid water	½ liter
2 tsp.	salt	10 ml.
2 tsp.	sugar	10 ml.
1 tsp.	cornstarch, dissolved in ½ cup [125 ml.] cold water	5 ml.
	Yogurt sourdough starter	
2 tbsp.	plain yogurt	30 ml.
1 cup	milk	¼ liter
1 cup	flour	¼ liter

Prepare the starter three to six days in advance.

First heat the milk to tepid—90° to 100° F. [32° to 38° C.]—and put it in a clean, warm pint or quart jar. Add the yogurt. (Nonfat milk and low-fat yogurt give the tangiest flavor.) Cover the jar tightly and let the starter stand in a warm—80° to 100° F. [25° to 38° C.]—place for 18 to 24 hours. If a clear liquid rises to the top of the milk during this time, stir it back into the mixture. However, if the liquid develops a light pink color, the milk is breaking down; discard the culture and start again.

When the starter is the consistency of yogurt—a curd that does not flow easily when the container is tilted—gradually stir in the flour until it is smoothly blended. Cover the container tightly and let it stand in a warm place until the mixture is full of bubbles and has a good, sour smell—from two to five days. The starter is now ready to use; there will be about 1¾ cups [425 ml.]. If you prefer, the starter can be refrigerated safely for up to two weeks.

Each time you use 1 cup [¼ liter] of starter, replenish the remainder with 1 cup of tepid milk. Let the starter stand in a warm place overnight or until it is bubbly. Then refrigerate it. Before using it again, allow the starter to warm to room temperature. Then add 1 cup of flour to the starter and let the mixture stand for several hours at room temperature before making the bread. If you do not use the starter regularly, discard half of it every two weeks and replenish it.

To make the bread, combine 2 cups [½ liter] of tepid water with 1 cup of starter, the yeast and 4 cups [1 liter] of flour. Place this sponge in a bowl and cover the bowl with plastic wrap or a clean dish towel, and allow it to stand in a warm place for six to eight hours or overnight. The sponge will be very thick and full of bubbles.

Work the salt, sugar and about 3 cups [¾ liter] of flour into the sponge. Turn the dough out onto a floured board and knead it until it is smooth and elastic—10 to 15 minutes. Add flour as needed to prevent the dough from sticking. Place the dough in a greased bowl and turn the dough over once to grease the top and sides. Cover the bowl and let the dough rise in a warm place until it has doubled in bulk—one and one half to two hours.

Punch down the dough and divide it in half; shape each half into a loaf. Place the loaves on a pastry board sprinkled with cornmeal. Cover the loaves with plastic wrap or a clean cloth and let them rise for one and one half to two hours. Using a sharp knife or razor blade, make diagonal slashes for long loaves or crisscross slashes for round loaves.

Bring the dissolved cornstarch mixture to a boil. Cool it slightly and brush it over the top and sides of the loaves. Place the oven shelves on the two lowest levels in the oven. Put a pan with ¼ inch [6 mm.] of water in it on the bottom shelf. Preheat the oven to 400° F. [200° C.].

Slide the bread onto baking sheets and place them in the heated oven. After baking for 10 minutes, brush the bread again with the cornstarch-and-water solution. Continue to bake for 20 to 25 minutes more, or until the loaves are golden brown. Cool on a wire rack.

GEORGE K. YORK

Sourdough Onion Bread

Sauerteig-Zwiebelbrot

To make two 14-inch [35-cm.] cylindrical loaves

7 cups	rye flour	1¾ liters
1¼ cups	rolled oats	300 ml.
1 cup	rye sourdough starter (recipe, page 167)	¼ liter
1 to 1½ cups	tepid water	250 to 375 ml.
5	onions, finely chopped	5
½ cup	finely cut fresh chives	125 ml.
2 tbsp.	olive oil	30 ml.
3½ tsp.	salt	17 ml.
1 tsp.	freshly ground white pepper	5 ml.
2 tbsp.	whole-wheat flour	30 ml.

The night before, stir together the rye sourdough starter, ¾ cup [175 ml.] of tepid water and 1¾ cups [425 ml.] of the rye flour until the mixture is smooth. Cover it with a cloth and leave overnight in a warm place.

Put ¼ cup [50 ml.] of the onions in a heatproof dish and toast them under the broiler until they are brown. Mix the remaining onions with the chives and fry them gently in the olive oil until they are transparent—about 10 minutes. Sea-son with ½ teaspoon [2 ml.] of the salt and the pepper, and let the mixture cool.

To the starter mixture add the remaining rye flour, the rolled oats, the onion-and-chive mixture and the rest of the salt. Mix them, adding just enough tepid water to make a firm dough. Knead the dough for 15 minutes, or until smooth and fairly elastic. Cover the dough and let it rest in a warm place for two hours, or until it doubles in bulk.

Knead the dough again for 10 minutes, then divide it in half and shape it into two long, thin loaves. With a sharp knife or a razor blade, cut a few shallow, diagonal slashes in the tops of the loaves. Place the loaves on a greased and lightly floured baking sheet, cover them with a towel and let them rise in a warm place for two hours.

With your fingers, lightly press the toasted onions into the tops of the loaves. Sprinkle the loaves with the whole-wheat flour and bake in the center of a preheated 425° F. [220° C.] oven for 35 to 45 minutes, or until the loaves sound hollow when rapped on the bottom.

MARGRET UHLE AND ANNE BRAKEMEIER
EIGENBRÖTLERS BROTBACKBUCH

Black Rye Bread

Schwarzbrot

This bread can also be made without a sourdough starter, in which case the yeast should be increased to three ⅗ oz. [18 g.] cakes or three ¼ oz. [7½ g.] packages.

To make six 8 ½-by-4 ½-inch [21-by-11-cm.] loaves

4 cups	rye flour	1 liter
20 cups	whole-wheat flour (5 lb. [2½ kg.])	5 liters
¼ oz.	package active dry yeast or ⅗ oz. [18 g.] cake fresh yeast	7½ g.
¼ cup	rye sourdough starter *(recipe, page 167)*	50 ml.
6 cups	tepid water	1½ liters
1 tbsp.	salt	15 ml.
1 or 2 tbsp.	caraway seeds (optional)	15 or 30 ml.
4 or 5	small potatoes, boiled, peeled and mashed (optional)	4 or 5

Mix the yeast with ½ cup [125 ml.] of tepid water. Add 1½ cups [375 ml.] of the whole-wheat flour to make a sponge and let it rise overnight.

The next day, mix the remaining whole-wheat flour and the rye flour together with the sponge, the sourdough starter, 5½ cups [1¼ liters] of tepid water, the salt, and the caraway seeds and mashed potatoes if you are using them. Knead the resulting stiff dough until it comes away from your hands easily and contains air bubbles—after about 10 minutes. Then sprinkle the dough with flour, cover and leave it

for four hours in a warm, but not too warm, place—the dough must rise slowly—until it doubles in bulk.

Divide the dough into six pieces and shape them into ovals. Butter six 8½-by-4½-inch [21-by-11-cm.] loaf pans and half-fill them with the dough; let the loaves rise in a warm place for 20 to 30 minutes so that they rise to the tops of the pans, then brush the tops with tepid water.

Bake the loaves for one hour in a preheated 400° F. [200° C.] oven, or until they are well browned. Brush them with tepid water again, while they are still hot, to give them a soft crust. Let them cool.

HERMINE KIEHNLE AND MARIA HÄDECKE
DAS GROSSE KIEHNLE-KOCHBUCH

Cheese Bread

To make two 8 ½-by-4 ½-inch [21-by-11-cm.] loaves

4½ cups	flour	1 liter
two ¼ oz.	packages active dry yeast or two ⅗ oz. [18 g.] cakes fresh yeast	two 7½ g.
1 cup	milk, scalded	¼ liter
3 tbsp.	sugar	45 ml.
1 tbsp.	salt	15 ml.
3 tbsp.	butter, melted	45 ml.
¼ tsp.	ground ginger (optional)	1 ml.
1 cup	tepid water	¼ liter
1 cup	grated Cheddar cheese	¼ liter

To the scalded milk, add the sugar, salt, 2 tablespoons [30 ml.] of the butter and, if you wish, the ground ginger. Cool to tepid. Meanwhile, put the water into a large mixing bowl, add the yeast and let it stand for at least five minutes. Add the milk mixture, the cheese and the flour, then beat with an electric mixer for two minutes or with a large wooden spoon for about 300 strokes. This is too soft a dough to be kneaded.

Allow the dough to rise, covered, until it is more than doubled in bulk—45 to 60 minutes. Stir the dough down, then beat it for approximately half a minute. Put the dough in two buttered, 8½-by-4½-inch [21-by-11-cm.] ovenproof-glass loaf pans. Let the bread rise until it comes almost to the tops of the pans, about 30 minutes. Bake in a preheated 350° F. [180° C.] oven for about 30 to 40 minutes, until the bottoms of the loaves sound hollow when rapped. If the tops brown too quickly, cover them with foil. Remove the loaves from the oven. Melt the remaining butter and use it to brush the tops of the loaves. Turn them out of the pans immediately. Let the loaves cool on a wire rack before cutting them.

ANNE ROE ROBBINS
THE SEVEN-INGREDIENTS COOKBOOK

Pepper Cheese Loaf

To make two 7 ½-by-3 ½-inch [19-by-9-cm.] rectangular or 6-inch [15-cm.] cylindrical loaves

2½ to 3 cups	all-purpose or bread flour	625 to 750 ml.
¼ oz.	package active dry yeast	7½ g.
2 tbsp.	sugar	30 ml.
1 tsp.	salt	5 ml.
2 tsp.	freshly ground black pepper	10 ml.
1 cup	tepid water	¼ liter
1 tbsp.	vegetable oil	15 ml.
2 cups	coarsely grated sharp Cheddar cheese	½ liter

In a mixer bowl blend 1 cup [¼ liter] of flour, the yeast, sugar, salt and ground pepper. Add the water and oil. Beat with an electric mixer at low speed for 30 seconds, scraping the bowl once or twice. Then, at high speed, beat for three minutes. With a wooden spoon stir in additional flour, a half cup [125 ml.] at a time, to form a soft dough that is elastic. Turn out on a floured work surface and knead with a strong push-turn-fold action, adding more flour if necessary to control the stickiness. Alternatively, knead for about five minutes with a dough hook.

Place the ball of dough in a lightly greased bowl, cover the bowl tightly with plastic wrap and put it in a warm place until the dough has doubled in bulk. Punch down the dough and work it briefly under your hands to press out the bubbles. Spread half of the cheese on the dough and fold it in. Knead for one minute, sprinkle on the rest of the cheese and continue kneading until the dough has absorbed it.

With a sharp knife, divide the dough in half. Shape the pieces into balls, and let them rise under a towel for three or four minutes. Press each ball of dough into a greased 1-pound coffee can. One ball should fill a coffee can about halfway, no more. If using loaf pans, form the dough by pressing each ball into a flat oval, roughly the length of a 7½-by-3½-inch [19-by-9-cm.] loaf pan. Fold the oval in half lengthwise, pinch the seam tightly to seal, tuck under the ends, and place in the greased loaf pan, seam under.

Place the containers in a warm place, cover with wax paper and leave them until the centers of the dough have risen to the rims of the coffee cans or 1 inch [2½ cm.] above the rims of the loaf pans.

Preheat the oven to 400° F. [200° C.]. Bake the loaves until the crust is a deep brown and the loaves test done—30 to 35 minutes. Turn out one loaf from its can or pan and tap the bottom crust with a forefinger. A hard hollow sound means the bread is baked.

Place the loaves on wire racks to cool. Serve either warm from the oven or reheated later. This bread freezes especially well and will keep for six months or longer.

BERNARD CLAYTON JR.
THE COMPLETE BOOK OF BREADS

Italian Easter Bread with Cheese

Crescia di Pasqua col Formaggio

To make four 9-by-5-inch [23-by-13-cm.] loaves

1 lb.	basic bread dough *(recipe, page 164)*	½ kg.
8 cups	flour	2 liters
two ¼ oz.	packages active dry yeast or two ⅗ oz. [18 g.] cakes fresh yeast	two 7½ g.
1 cup	tepid water	¼ liter
2 cups	tepid milk	½ liter
10	eggs	10
3¼ cups	freshly grated Parmesan cheese (about 10 oz. [300 g.])	800 ml.
1 cup	diced Gruyère cheese	¼ liter
10 tbsp.	butter, softened	150 ml.
4 tbsp.	lard, softened	60 ml.
1 tbsp.	salt	15 ml.

On the evening before making the bread, prepare a sourdough leaven by mixing the bread dough with 1 cup [¼ liter] of tepid water and 1 cup of tepid milk. Then sift the flour onto a work surface and make a well in the center. Pour the softened bread dough into the well and gradually work the flour into the dough, kneading for about 10 minutes, to make a firm, elastic dough. Form the dough into a ball. With a sharp knife, make two cuts in the shape of a cross on the surface of the ball of dough, to help the rising process. Cover and leave the dough in a warm place overnight.

The next day, stir the yeast into 1 cup of tepid milk, and set aside for about 10 minutes. In a large bowl, beat the eggs and add the Parmesan and Gruyère cheeses, the butter, lard and salt. Mix them all together thoroughly. Knead the yeast mixture into the sourdough, then work in the egg-and-cheese mixture, kneading until the mixture is soft and smooth, about 10 minutes.

Butter four 9-by-5-inch [23-by-13-cm.] loaf pans. Divide the dough into four portions, shape the portions into loaves and put them into the pans. The dough should reach no higher than halfway up the sides of the pans. Let the loaves rise in a warm place for 30 minutes, or until the dough has risen to about ½ inch [1 cm.] above the rims of the pans. Bake the loaves in a preheated 400° F. [200° C.] oven for 50 minutes, or until the loaves are golden brown and sound hollow when they are rapped.

PIERO LUIGI MENICHETTI AND LUCIANA MENICHETTI PANFILI
VECCHIA CUCINA EUGUBINA

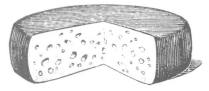

Cheese Brioche

Brioche au Fromage

If the brioche is to be eaten at midday, prepare the dough the night before; if it is to be used for the evening meal, prepare the dough at midday.

	To make one 8-inch [20-cm.] brioche	
½ lb.	rich egg-bread dough (recipe, page 165)	¼ kg.
3½ oz.	Gruyère cheese, 2 oz. [60 g.] finely shredded (about ½ cup [125 ml.]), and the rest diced	100 g.
	salt and pepper	
1	egg, beaten	1

Prepare the dough in the usual way. Let it rise, then punch it down, and mix in the shredded and diced Gruyère cheese and a pinch each of salt and pepper. Let the dough rise again until it is double in bulk, about one hour. Butter an 8-inch [20-cm.] brioche or savarin mold, or a baking sheet. Put the dough into the mold, or shape it into a ring if you are baking it on a sheet. With a sharp knife or razor knife, make two or three shallow diagonal incisions—spacing them well apart—in the dough.

Glaze the brioche with the beaten egg and bake it in a preheated 400° F. [200° C.] oven for 30 minutes, or until it is well risen and golden brown.

PIERRE ANDROUET
LA CUISINE AU FROMAGE

Sheep's-Milk Cheese Bread

Schafskäsebrot

Any soft sheep's-milk cheese—obtainable from cheese specialty stores—can be used. If it is not available, substitute farmer cheese.

	To make one 12-inch [30-cm.] oval loaf	
8 cups	flour	2 liters
two ¼ oz.	packages active dry yeast or two ⅗ oz. [18 g.] cakes fresh yeast	two 7½ g.
2 cups	tepid water	½ liter
1 tsp.	sugar	5 ml.
½ lb.	sheep's-milk cheese	¼ kg.
1 tsp.	salt	5 ml.
3	medium-sized onions, chopped	3
1 tbsp.	oil	15 ml.

Mix the yeast with the sugar and all but 3 tablespoons [45 ml.] of the tepid water. Leave the mixture in a warm place until it is foaming, about 10 minutes. Mix together the cheese and remaining water. Sift the flour and salt into a warmed mixing bowl and add the onions. Stir in the cheese and yeast mixtures and knead the dough thoroughly for about 10 minutes. Cover the bowl and let the dough rise in a warm place for about one and one half hours, or until the dough has doubled in bulk.

Punch down the dough and knead it again for about five minutes, dusting it with additional flour if it sticks to your fingers. Shape the dough into an oval 12 inches [30 cm.] long and set it on a buttered baking sheet to rise for about 30 minutes, or until it has doubled in bulk again. With a very sharp knife, make three shallow diagonal slashes in the top of the loaf. Brush the loaf with the oil, but do not brush the oil into the gashes. Bake the loaf in a preheated 400° F. [200° C.] oven for 45 minutes to one hour.

JUTTA KÜRTZ
DAS BROT BACKBUCH

A Picnic Loaf

The technique of making this bread appears on pages 70-71.

	To make one 14-inch [35-cm.] round loaf	
2 lb.	basic bread dough (recipe, page 164)	1 kg.
10 oz.	Gruyère cheese, coarsely grated or sliced	300 g.
4	eggs, in the shell	4
1 lb.	Polish sausage (kielbasa), cut into 4 pieces and pricked with a fork	½ kg.
1	egg yolk, beaten	1

Let the dough rise once in a bowl. Divide it into two equal portions and roll one portion into a circle 14 inches [35 cm.] in diameter. Place the circle of dough on an oiled baking sheet. Pile the cheese in the middle in a neat, round heap 6 inches [15 cm.] wide. Roll out half of the remaining dough into a circle just large enough to cover the cheese topping. Lay this circle of dough on top of the cheese, sealing it on with a little water at the edges. Space the eggs and sections of sausage alternately around the edge of the large dough circle. Roll the remaining dough into narrow strips the width of a pencil and use them in a crisscross pattern to bind the eggs and sausage to the bread base. Moisten the ends of the dough strips to help them stick. Let the loaf rise in a warm place for about one hour.

Glaze the loaf with the egg yolk and bake it in a preheated 400° F. [200° C.] oven for 25 minutes. Then lower the heat to 350° F. [180° C.] and bake the loaf for another 25 minutes. The eggs will cook, the sausage render its juices and the cheese melt succulently into the bread.

JUDITH OLNEY
SUMMER FOOD

Neapolitan Rustic Brioche

Brioche Rustica

To make one 10-inch [25-cm.] brioche

1 lb.	rich egg-bread dough (recipe, page 165)	½ kg.
3½ oz.	prosciutto, coarsely chopped	100 g.
5 oz.	provolone cheese, diced	150 g.
5 oz.	Bel Paese or butter cheese, diced	150 g.
¼ to ½ tsp.	freshly ground pepper	1 to 2 ml.
1 cup	freshly grated Parmesan cheese	¼ liter

Prepare the dough in the usual way, but after the second rising, knead in the prosciutto, diced cheeses, pepper and grated Parmesan. Put the dough into a fluted 10-inch [25-cm.] brioche mold with a center tube; the dough should only half-fill the mold. Let the dough rise in a warm place for one hour, or until doubled in bulk.

Put the brioche into a preheated 300° F. [150° C.] oven. Bake it for about 45 minutes, or until it is well risen and golden brown. Let the brioche rest for 10 minutes after removing it from the oven, then turn it out onto a serving dish.

JEANNE CARÒLA FRANCESCONI
LA CUCINA NAPOLETANA

Country Flatbread

Pizza Rustica

Pecorino cheese is Italian sheep's-milk cheese, obtainable at cheese specialty stores. If it is not available, Gruyère or sharp Cheddar cheese may be substituted.

To make one 10-inch [25-cm.] round flatbread

1 lb.	basic bread dough (recipe, page 164), risen once	½ kg.
2	eggs, beaten	2
3½ oz.	prosciutto, diced	100 g.
¼ cup	finely diced pecorino cheese	50 ml.
1 cup	freshly grated Parmesan cheese	¼ liter
¼ cup	olive oil	50 ml.
	salt and freshly ground black pepper	

Mix the eggs, prosciutto, cheeses, oil and a pinch each of salt and pepper with the dough, and knead the mixture well for about five minutes. Then, with your hands or a rolling pin, roll out the dough into a round about 10 inches [25 cm.] in diameter and ¼ inch [6 mm.] thick. Place the dough on a well-oiled baking sheet and let it rest in a warm place, protected from drafts, for one hour, or until it is light and puffy.

Prick the surface of the dough thoroughly with a fork and bake it in a preheated 425° F. [220° C.] oven for about 20 minutes, or until it is golden brown.

GUGLIELMA CORSI
UN SECOLO DI CUCINA UMBRA

No-Knead Dill Bread

To make one 8-inch [20-cm.] round loaf

2¼ to 2½ cups	flour	550 to 625 ml.
¼ oz.	package active dry yeast or ⅗ oz. [18 g.] cake fresh yeast	7½ g.
¼ tsp.	baking soda	1 ml.
¼ cup	tepid water	50 ml.
1 cup	small-curd cottage cheese	¼ liter
2 tbsp.	butter	30 ml.
2 tbsp.	honey	30 ml.
2 tsp.	dried dillweed	10 ml.
1 tsp.	salt	5 ml.
1	egg, beaten	1

In a large mixing bowl, mix the yeast with the tepid water. In a saucepan, heat the cottage cheese, 1 tablespoon [15 ml.] of the butter, and the honey until they are lukewarm. Add to the cottage-cheese mixture the baking soda, dillweed, salt and egg. Stir to blend all of the flavorings.

Scrape the cottage-cheese mixture into the yeast and water, and stir together. Add enough flour to make a firm ball of dough; stir the mixture with a wooden spoon but do not knead. Soak a cloth with hot water, wring it out, and place it over the mixing bowl. Let the dough rise in a warm place until it has doubled in bulk, about one hour.

Stir down the dough, and put it in a well-buttered, 8-inch [20-cm.] round cake pan, patting the dough to smooth it a little. Let the dough rise for about 45 minutes.

Bake in a preheated 350° F. [180° C.] oven for 40 to 50 minutes, or until the top is nicely browned. Cool the bread slightly, then remove it to a rack. To achieve a shiny crust, melt the remaining butter and brush it over the top.

THE GREAT COOKS' GUIDE TO BREADS

Italian Flatbread with Butter

Schiacciata col Burro

To make one 10-inch [25-cm.] flatbread

1 lb.	basic bread dough *(recipe, page 164)*	½ kg.
8 tbsp.	butter, softened	120 ml.
2 tsp.	salt	10 ml.
10	fresh basil leaves	10
2 tbsp.	olive oil	30 ml.

Knead the dough thoroughly, then incorporate the butter and knead for a further five minutes. Let the dough rise in a warm place for 30 minutes.

Roll out the dough to fit into an oiled, 10-inch [25-cm.] pizza pan, and dimple the surface by pressing it here and there with your finger. Sprinkle the dough generously with salt, then distribute the basil leaves evenly over the surface. Sprinkle the dough with the olive oil.

Bake the flatbread in a preheated 425° F. [220° C.] oven for about 30 minutes, or until golden. Before serving, discard the basil leaves, which only flavor the bread. Serve hot.

MARIÙ SALVATORI DE ZULIANI
LA CUCINA DI VERSILIA E GARFAGNANA

Crustless Caraway Bread

Kümmelbrot (Ohne Rinde)

*To make one 10-by-4-inch
[25-by-10-cm.] loaf*

3¼ cups	flour	800 ml.
¼ oz.	package active dry yeast or ⅗ oz. [18 g.] cake fresh yeast	7½ g.
½ cup	tepid milk	125 ml.
½ tsp.	salt	2 ml.
1 tbsp.	caraway seeds	15 ml.
2 tbsp.	butter or lard	30 ml.

Stir the yeast into the tepid milk and set aside for about 10 minutes, or until foaming. Sift the flour into a bowl, make a well in the middle, and pour in the yeast mixture. Mix together to make a dough, and leave for 30 minutes to rise about half as much again. Then mix in the salt, caraway seeds, and butter or lard, and knead well to form a soft dough—about 10 minutes. Leave the dough in a warm place until it has doubled in bulk—approximately one and one half to two hours.

Butter a *pain de mie* pan or a 1½-quart [1½-liter] baking pan with a tightly fitting lid. Knead the dough well and place it in the pan; the dough should only half-fill the pan.

Cover the pan tightly and set it on a trivet in a large pot of gently simmering water. Cover the pot and cook the bread for one and one half hours, or until it is firm to the touch and sounds hollow when rapped. Turn the bread out of the pan, cool, and store in a dry place until you are ready to use it.

HERMINE KIEHNLE AND MARIA HÄDECKE
DAS GROSSE KIEHNLE-KOCHBUCH

Swedish Salt Sticks

Saltstänger

The author of this famous Swedish cookbook ran a cooking school in Stockholm in the 1930s. The book is dedicated to her three most illustrious pupils: Princess Margaretha of Denmark, Crown Princess Märtha of Norway and Crown Princess Astrid of Belgium.

To make about 30 sticks

2 cups	flour	½ liter
⅗ oz.	cake fresh yeast	18 g.
2 tbsp.	butter, cut into small pieces	30 ml.
½ tsp.	salt	2 ml.
1 tsp.	sugar	5 ml.
2 or 3	whole cardamoms, husks removed and seeds pounded to a powder in a mortar	2 or 3
¾ cup	milk	175 ml.
Salt topping		
¼ cup	milk	50 ml.
1 tbsp.	coarse salt	15 ml.
1 tbsp.	caraway seeds (optional)	15 ml.

Put the butter, flour and salt into a bowl. With your finger tips, rub the butter into the flour. Stir together the yeast, sugar and pounded cardamom seeds. Make a well in the center of the flour and pour in the yeast mixture and the milk; mix thoroughly to make a firm dough.

Divide the dough into 30 small pieces, and roll each piece into a stick the thickness of a finger and about 3 inches [8 cm.] long. Put the sticks onto buttered-and-floured baking sheets. Take a sharp knife or razor blade and make two or three diagonal slits in each stick. For the topping, brush the sticks with the milk and sprinkle the coarse salt—mixed with caraway seeds if you like—over them.

Let the sticks rise in a warm place until they have doubled in volume—about 30 minutes. Bake them in a preheated 350° F. [180° C.] oven for 20 minutes, or until they are lightly browned.

JENNY ÅKERSTRÖM
PRINSESSORNAS KOKBOK

Saffron Christmas Wreath

To make one 14-inch [35-cm.] wreath

about 4 cups	flour	about 1 liter
¼ oz.	package active dry yeast or ⅗ oz. [18 g.] cake fresh yeast	7½ g.
¼ cup	tepid water	50 ml.
1 cup	milk or half-and-half cream	¼ liter
8 tbsp.	butter, softened	120 ml.
1 tbsp.	ground saffron	15 ml.
1	egg, beaten	1
¼ cup	sugar	50 ml.
1 cup	raisins, soaked in hot water for 15 minutes and drained	¼ liter
1 tsp.	salt	5 ml.
1	egg, beaten with 1 tbsp. [15 ml.] milk	1

Almond and cherry topping

½ cup	almonds, blanched and slivered	125 ml.
3 tbsp.	sugar	45 ml.
3	candied cherries, halved	3

Stir the yeast into the water and set it aside. In a saucepan, warm the milk or half-and-half cream with the butter; when the butter has melted, remove the pan from the heat and cool the mixture to tepid. Stir in the saffron.

Pour the milk mixture and the yeast mixture into a large bowl and stir in the egg, the sugar and half of the flour. Mix well. Add the raisins, and continue to stir vigorously until the dough is thick and glossy.

Cover the bowl with plastic wrap, and let the dough rise in a warm place until it has doubled in bulk, about one hour. Add the rest of the flour and the salt, and knead them in to make a firm dough. Turn the dough out onto a floured board, and continue kneading until the dough is firm and elastic, about 10 minutes.

Roll and press the dough into a 27-inch [70-cm.] cylinder. Cut off a 3-inch [8-cm.] piece and reserve it for the center of the wreath. On an oiled baking sheet, fashion the cylinder into a large ring by joining the ends and pinching them firmly together. With scissors, cut the ring at ½-inch [1-cm.] intervals—cutting about two thirds of the way through the cylinder—and turn the slices alternately to the left and to the right. Pat the ring into shape. The center space should be about 6 inches [15 cm.] across. Roll the 3-inch reserved piece of dough into a ball and place it in the center space. Flatten the ball slightly, but be certain there is clear space between the ring and the ball because both will expand during the rising and baking processes.

Brush the ring and the ball with the egg-and-milk mixture, sprinkle them with the almonds and sugar, and place the cherries at intervals around the ring. Cover the wreath carefully with wax paper and place it in a warm spot until the dough has doubled in size, about one hour.

Bake the wreath in a preheated 375° F. [190° C.] oven for 45 minutes, or until a wooden toothpick inserted into the wreath comes out clean. Remove the wreath and ball from the oven, and cool them on the baking sheet for 15 minutes before transferring them to a wire rack for further cooling. Slip them off the baking sheet gently so the wreath does not break. When the wreath and ball are cool and firm, place them on a circular cake board.

BERNARD CLAYTON JR.
THE COMPLETE BOOK OF BREADS

Christmas Bread

Vörtlimpor

The original version of this recipe calls for Swedish malt beer, a beverage similar to stout, an easily obtainable substitute.

To make three 10-inch [25-cm.] cylindrical loaves

6 cups	rye flour	1½ liters
3 cups	all-purpose flour	¾ liter
three ⅗ oz.	cakes fresh yeast	three 18 g.
4 tbsp.	tepid water	60 ml.
1 tbsp.	sugar	15 ml.
4 tbsp.	lard or butter	60 ml.
3 cups	stout	¾ liter
1 cup plus 2 tbsp.	molasses	280 ml.
1 tsp.	salt	5 ml.
2 cups	chopped candied orange peel	½ liter
2 tbsp.	ground anise seeds or fennel seeds	30 ml.

Mix the yeast with 2 tablespoons [30 ml.] of the water and the sugar. Melt the fat, add the stout and heat them to lukewarm. Pour the fat and stout into a bowl, add 1 cup [¼ liter] of the molasses and half of each of the flours. Mix well. Then add the yeast mixture, salt, candied peel, ground seeds, the rest of the rye flour and all but 1 cup of the all-purpose flour. Beat the dough until smooth and firm. Cover it with a towel and let it rise in a warm place until almost doubled in bulk.

Put the dough on a floured pastry board and knead it with the reserved all-purpose flour until firm and glossy. Shape the dough into three cylindrical loaves. Place them on buttered baking sheets and cover with a cloth. Let them rise for about 30 minutes. Prick the loaves with a toothpick and bake at 350° F. [180° C.] for 30 to 40 minutes, or until golden brown. When they are half-done, brush them with a glaze made by mixing the remaining water and molasses. Brush the loaves again with the glaze when they are done. Place them between cloths while cooling to keep the crusts soft.

SAM WIDENFELT (EDITOR)
FAVORITE SWEDISH RECIPES

Bremen Christmas Bread

Bremer Klaben

This bread is a variety of the German sweet loaf called a stollen, popular from Alsace to Czechoslovakia.

To make one 14-inch [35-cm.] loaf

9 cups	flour	2¼ liters
three ¼ oz.	packages active dry yeast or three ⅗ oz. [18 g.] cakes fresh yeast	three 7½ g.
½ tsp.	salt	2 ml.
2 cups	tepid milk	½ liter
20 tbsp.	butter, melted and cooled to tepid	300 ml.
3 cups	raisins, soaked in hot water for 15 minutes and drained	¾ liter
2¼ cups	dried currants, soaked in hot water for 15 minutes and drained	550 ml.
1 cup	chopped candied citrus peel	¼ liter
2 tsp.	grated lemon peel	10 ml.
½ tsp.	ground cinnamon	2 ml.
½ tsp.	ground cloves	2 ml.
½ tsp.	ground cardamom	2 ml.
½ tsp.	ground mace	2 ml.
	semolina	

Mix the yeast with ⅔ cup [150 ml.] of the milk. Put the flour and salt in a large mixing bowl. Make a well in the center, pour in the yeast mixture and the remaining milk and mix to make a dough. Knead the dough for 10 minutes, then leave it in a warm place to rise until it has doubled in bulk, about one and a half hours. Knead the butter gradually into the dough, work in the remaining ingredients except the semolina, and knead for about five minutes. Let the dough rise again for two to three hours, until doubled in bulk.

Flatten the dough with your hands to make a thick rectangle about 14 by 12 inches [35 by 30 cm.]. Seal the ends firmly and taper them to make the traditional stollen shape.

Dust a baking sheet with semolina, place the loaf on it and let it rise for about 30 minutes, until doubled in bulk. Bake in a preheated 350° F. [180° C.] oven for 50 minutes to one hour, or until the loaf sounds hollow when rapped.

MARIA ELISABETH STRAUB
GRÖNEN AAL UND RODE GRÜTT

Viennese Braided Loaf

Striezel

The technique of braiding a loaf is demonstrated on pages 22-23. Coarse sugar is obtainable from bakery-supply stores and some gourmet-food specialty stores.

To make one 10-inch [25-cm.] braided loaf

4 cups	flour	1 liter
¼ oz.	package active dry yeast or ⅗ oz. [18 g.] cake fresh yeast	7½ g.
⅓ cup	sugar	75 ml.
1¼ cups	tepid milk	300 ml.
¼ tsp.	salt	1 ml.
7 tbsp.	butter, softened	105 ml.
2	egg yolks	2
1	egg	1
2 tsp.	grated lemon peel	10 ml.
¾ cup	raisins, soaked in hot water for 15 minutes and drained	175 ml.
1	egg white, lightly beaten	1
	blanched, slivered almonds or coarse sugar (optional)	

Mix the yeast and 1 tablespoon [15 ml.] of the sugar with ¼ cup [50 ml.] of the tepid milk; let the mixture stand for about 10 minutes in a warm place until it foams. To make the dough, combine the flour, the yeast mixture, the remaining sugar and milk, the salt, butter, egg yolks, whole egg and lemon peel. Knead well on a floured board for about 10 minutes to make a firm dough, then incorporate the raisins and knead for a further five minutes. Cover the dough and let it rise in a warm place for about one and a half hours, or until doubled in bulk.

Divide the dough into nine pieces and roll out the pieces into cylinders of equal length, but of three different widths: three pieces the thickness of two fingers, three pieces the thickness of one finger and three pieces half the thickness of a finger. Braid each of the three sets of dough. Brush the top of the medium-thick braid with egg white, and lay the thinnest braid on top of it, making sure the two braids stick firmly together. Then brush the top of the thickest braid with egg white and lay the assembled thin and medium braids on top of the thick one.

Place the resulting loaf on a buttered-and-floured baking sheet and let it rise for one and a half hours in a warm place, or until doubled in bulk. Glaze the whole loaf with egg white and, if you like, sprinkle with slivered almonds or coarse sugar. Bake the braid in a preheated 400° F. [200° C.] oven for one hour, or until a skewer inserted into the center of the bottom braid comes out clean.

OLGA HESS AND ADOLF FR. HESS
WIENER KÜCHE

Butter Cake

Butterkuchen

*To make one 20-by-16-inch
[50-by-40-cm.] cake*

4 cups	flour	1 liter
¼ oz.	package active dry yeast or ⅗ oz. [18 g.] cake fresh yeast	7½ g.
⅔ cup	tepid milk	150 ml.
6	egg yolks	6
14 tbsp.	butter, softened	210 ml.
¼ cup	sugar	50 ml.
	Chopped almond topping	
1	egg, beaten	1
1 cup	almonds, blanched and finely chopped	¼ liter
2 tbsp.	coarse sugar	30 ml.
4 tbsp.	butter	60 ml.

Mix the yeast with the milk and 2½ cups [625 ml.] of the flour; let this sponge rise for two hours in a warm place until doubled in bulk. Add the remaining flour, the egg yolks, butter and sugar. Knead well for about 10 minutes, then let rise for 30 minutes. Roll out the dough to fit a 20-by-16-inch [50-by-40-cm.] jelly-roll pan. Lay it in the well-buttered pan, brush it with the beaten egg, sprinkle it with the almonds and coarse sugar and dot it with the butter. Bake in a preheated 350° F. [180° C.] oven for 45 minutes, or until golden.

DOROTHEE V. HELLERMANN
DAS KOCHBUCH AUS HAMBURG

Crispies

To make 24 rolls

3 cups	flour	¾ liter
¼ oz.	package active dry yeast or ⅗ oz. [18 g.] cake fresh yeast	7½ g.
¼ cup	tepid water	50 ml.
7 tbsp.	butter, softened	105 ml.
¼ cup	milk	50 ml.
¾ cup	sugar	175 ml.
½ tsp.	salt	2 ml.
1	egg, beaten	1
½ cup	finely chopped nuts	125 ml.

In a bowl, mix the yeast with the water. Meanwhile, in a heavy saucepan, warm 4 tablespoons [60 ml.] of the butter in the milk until the butter melts; cool to lukewarm. To the yeast and water, add ¼ cup [50 ml.] of the flour, the butter-and-milk mixture, ¼ cup of the sugar and the salt. Beat the egg and ¼ cup of flour into this batter, then add the rest of the flour to make a stiff dough. Turn the dough out onto a floured surface and knead it until it is smooth—about 10 minutes. Return the dough to the bowl. Melt the remaining butter and use half of it to brush the top of the dough. Let the dough rise until doubled in bulk—about one hour.

Punch the dough down, and let it rise for 45 minutes. Punch it down, turn it out onto a lightly floured board and roll it into a 9-by-18-inch [23-by-45-cm.] rectangle about ½ inch [1 cm.] thick. Brush the top with the rest of the butter.

Combine the nuts and the remaining sugar, then sprinkle half of this mixture over the dough. Roll the dough up from one long side, as for a jelly roll, and seal the edge after moistening it with a little water. Cut the cylinder into slices 1 inch [2½ cm.] thick, sprinkle the rest of the sugar-nut mixture onto the kneading surface, place each slice of dough on it and flatten it lightly with a rolling pin to make a 3-inch [7-cm.] round. Turn the flattened roll over and press it into the sugar and nuts, so the top and bottom are well coated.

Butter two baking sheets and place the rolls on them carefully. Cover the rolls and let them rise in a warm place for about 30 minutes. Bake in a preheated 375° F. [190° C.] oven for about 10 minutes, or until the rolls are brown.

GRACE FIRTH
STILLROOM COOKERY

Nut Roll

Strucla Drożdżowa z Masą Orzechową

To make one 8-inch [20-cm.] rolled loaf

2¼ cups	flour	550 ml.
¼ oz.	package active dry yeast or one ⅗ oz. [18 g.] cake fresh yeast	7½ g.
6 tbsp.	granulated sugar	90 ml.
8 tbsp.	butter, softened and cut into pieces	120 ml.
2 tbsp.	tepid milk	30 ml.
	beaten egg yolk or milk (optional)	
	confectioners' sugar	
	Nut filling	
1 cup	granulated sugar	¼ liter
⅔ cup	water	150 ml.
14 oz.	walnuts or hazelnuts, finely ground in a nut grinder or a food processor operated in short spurts	400 g.
1 tbsp.	butter	15 ml.

Mix the flour and granulated sugar on a pastry board; work in the butter with your finger tips. Mix the yeast with the tepid milk and let it stand for 10 minutes. Using your hands, work the yeast into the butter-and-flour mixture. Knead the dough for 10 minutes, until smooth and elastic, then let it rise, covered, in a warm place for about one hour.

To make the filling, bring the sugar and water to a boil and simmer them over very low heat for eight to 10 minutes. Stir the nuts into this syrup and remove it from the heat. Stir in the butter; when it dissolves, let the mixture cool.

Roll out the dough into a rectangle about 10 by 8 inches [25 by 20 cm.] and about ½ inch [1 cm.] thick. Spread the filling over it, leaving a margin of about 1 inch [2½ cm.] at the edges. Roll up the dough like a jelly roll and, if desired, brush it with beaten egg yolk or milk. Butter and flour a baking sheet and put the roll on it. Cover the roll with a cloth and let it rise for up to one hour, or until doubled in bulk.

Bake the roll in a preheated 425° F. [220° C.] oven for 10 minutes, then reduce the heat to 400° F. [200° C.] and bake for 20 minutes, or until a pale golden color. Let the roll cool and sprinkle with confectioners' sugar.

LILI KOWALSKA
COOKING THE POLISH WAY

——————◆——————

Corsican Raisin and Walnut Buns

U Pan di i Morti o "Uga Siccati"

To make about 70 buns

13 cups	flour	3¼ liters
three ¼ oz.	packages active dry yeast or three ⅗ oz. [18 g.] cakes fresh yeast	three 7½ g.
4 cups	raisins, soaked in hot water for 15 minutes and drained	1 liter
4 cups	chopped walnuts	1 liter
¼ cup	tepid water	50 ml.
16 tbsp.	butter (½ lb. [¼ kg.]), softened	240 ml.
4	eggs	4
1 to 1½ tsp.	salt	5 to 7 ml.
2 cups	sugar	½ liter
2 tsp.	grated lemon peel	10 ml.
1 tbsp.	oil	15 ml.

Mix the yeast with the tepid water. Make a sponge by adding about ¾ cup [175 ml.] of the flour to the yeast. Cover the sponge and let it rise in a warm place for about two hours.

Pour the rest of the flour onto a work surface. Make a well in the center and add the butter, eggs, salt, sugar and grated lemon peel. Knead the mixture into a dough, and then add the yeast sponge. Knead the dough for 10 minutes, or until smooth and elastic. Add the raisins and walnuts and knead

until they are well incorporated. Put the dough in an earthenware bowl, cover, and let it rest for about one hour.

Shape the dough into small balls, each about 1½ inches [3 cm.] across. Place the balls on lightly oiled baking sheets. Bake in a preheated 425° F. [220° C.] oven for 35 to 40 minutes, or until the buns are golden brown. Cool before serving.

CHRISTIANE SCHAPIRA
LA CUISINE CORSE

——————◆——————

Russian Easter Bread

Koulich

To make confectioners'-sugar icing, sift 1 cup [¼ liter] of confectioners' sugar and stir into it 2 tablespoons [30 ml.] of milk or light cream and ½ teaspoon [2 ml.] of vanilla extract.

To make two 7-inch [18-cm.] cylindrical loaves

8 to 9 cups	sifted flour	2 to 2¼ liters
two ¼ oz.	packages active dry yeast or two ⅗ oz. [18 g.] cakes fresh yeast	two 7½ g.
1½ cups	tepid milk	375 ml.
8 tbsp.	butter, melted	120 ml.
½ cup	sugar	125 ml.
½ tsp.	salt	2 ml.
2 tbsp.	brandy	30 ml.
1 tsp.	vanilla extract	5 ml.
½ cup	tepid water	125 ml.
2	eggs, beaten	2
½ cup	almonds, blanched and slivered	125 ml.
1 cup	mixed candied pineapple and cherries, dusted with flour	¼ liter
½ cup	white raisins, soaked in hot water for 15 minutes and drained	125 ml.

To the milk, add the butter, sugar, salt, brandy and vanilla extract. Mix the yeast with the tepid water; add to the milk mixture. Stir in the eggs and 4 cups [1 liter] of the flour. Cover and let this sponge rise in a warm place until doubled in bulk (about one hour). On a pastry board, place the rest of the flour in a ring about the size of a dinner plate. Pour the sponge into the center of the ring; knead the flour into the sponge. Knead in the almonds and fruits. Butter two empty 3-pound shortening cans or two 2-pound coffee cans. Place half of the dough in each can. Cover; let the dough rise in a warm place until it reaches the tops of the cans. Bake in a preheated 375° F. [190° C.] oven for 40 minutes, or until a skewer inserted in the center of the bread comes out clean. The bread may be topped with confectioners'-sugar icing.

THE JUNIOR LEAGUE OF TAMPA
THE GASPARILLA COOKBOOK

Marston Buns

The book from which this recipe is taken was published in 1694. Marston is a small town in northern England.

To make 35 to 40 buns

10 cups	flour	2½ liters
two ¼ oz.	packages active dry yeast or two ⅗ oz. [18 g.] cakes fresh yeast	two 7½ g.
16 tbsp.	butter (½ lb. [¼ kg.])	240 ml.
2½ cups	tepid milk	625 ml.
5	eggs, beaten	5
1 cup	sugar	¼ liter
2 cups	dried currants, soaked in hot water for 15 minutes and drained, or 2 tbsp. [30 ml.] caraway seeds	½ liter
	freshly grated nutmeg	

Rub the butter into the flour. Mix the yeast with the tepid milk, add the eggs and set aside for 10 minutes, or until the yeast has begun to work. Add the mixture to the flour, and let the dough rise in a warm place for 30 minutes. Work in the sugar, currants or caraway seeds, and grated nutmeg to taste, and knead well. Then put pieces of dough into buttered muffin-pan cups, or shape the pieces into balls and place them on buttered-and-floured baking sheets. Let rise for 30 minutes and bake in a preheated 350° F. [180° C.] oven for 20 minutes, or until golden brown on top.

THE RECEIPT BOOK OF ANN BLENCOWE

Ground Raisin Nut Bread

This recipe was written by Anne Glass, who compiled the first edition of "An American Cook in Turkey."

To make one 8½-by-4½-inch [21-by-11-cm.] loaf

2 cups	flour, sifted	½ liter
¼ oz.	package active dry yeast or ⅗ oz. [18 g.] cake fresh yeast	7½ g.
¾ cup	raisins, ground or finely chopped	175 ml.
½ cup	chopped walnuts	125 ml.
1½ cups	tepid water	375 ml.
⅓ cup	sugar	75 ml.
6 tbsp.	butter or lard, cut into pieces	90 ml.
2 tsp.	salt	10 ml.

Mix the yeast with the water and 1 teaspoon [5 ml.] of the sugar. Cover and let the mixture stand in a warm place until foaming—about 10 minutes. In a large bowl, combine 1½ cups [375 ml.] of the flour with the yeast mixture and mix

well. Cover the dough with a cloth and leave it in a warm place until the mixture is spongy—about one hour. Then work in the butter or lard, the salt, the rest of the sugar, the raisins and the walnuts. Add the rest of the flour and knead well to make a stiff, smooth dough. Let the dough rise in a warm place until doubled in bulk. Punch it down, then let it rise again until doubled in bulk.

Put the dough into a buttered 8½-by-4½-inch [21-by-11-cm.] loaf pan. Let it rise for about an hour. Bake the loaf in a preheated 400° F. [200° C.] oven for 15 minutes. Then reduce the heat to 375° F. [190° C.]. The original recipe said to bake the bread for 50 minutes to one hour, but it often takes only 30 minutes, so be careful. The loaf is ready when it is golden brown and sounds hollow when rapped on the bottom.

ANNA G. EDMONDS (EDITOR)
AN AMERICAN COOK IN TURKEY

A Rich Scotch Bun

Scotch bun, also called black bun, is said to have been introduced to Scotland from Italy in the 16th Century. Once traditionally served on Twelfth Night (January 6), the bun is now baked for Hogmanay (New Year's Eve). This version is adapted from the 1841 edition of Mrs. Rundell's book, first published in 1806.

To make one 10-inch [25-cm.] bun

8 cups	flour	2 liters
two ¼ oz.	packages active dry yeast or two ⅗ oz. [18 g.] cakes fresh yeast	two 7½ g.
2 cups	tepid water	½ liter
24 tbsp.	butter (¾ lb. [⅓ kg.]), cut into pieces	360 ml.
2 tsp.	salt	10 ml.
1 tsp.	whole allspice	5 ml.
1 tsp.	peeled and chopped fresh ginger root	5 ml.
3 or 4	whole cloves	3 or 4
¾ cup	chopped candied orange peel	175 ml.
¾ cup	chopped candied lemon peel	175 ml.
¾ cup	chopped blanched almonds	175 ml.
4 cups	raisins, soaked in hot water for 15 minutes and drained	1 liter
4 cups	dried currants, soaked in hot water for 15 minutes and drained	1 liter
½ tsp.	grated nutmeg	2 ml.

Mix the yeast with the water. Mix it with the flour and salt, using your hands to work it in, until all of the ingredients are moist. Turn the dough out onto a floured board, mix in the butter and knead for about 15 minutes, until the dough is smooth and elastic. Put it into a warmed bowl, cover it and leave it in a warm place until doubled in bulk—about two hours. To make the flavoring, pound the allspice, ginger and cloves together in a mortar. Mix the spices with the chopped peels and add the almonds, raisins, currants and nutmeg.

Punch down the dough and knead it briefly until the air has been expelled. Slice off one third of the dough and reserve it. Flatten the larger piece of dough into a round about 1 inch [2½ cm.] thick. Sprinkle the flavoring mixture onto the dough. Then fold the dough over the flavoring, and knead well until the flavoring is evenly distributed.

Lightly flour a work surface and roll out the remaining dough into a sheet ¼ inch [6 mm.] thick and large enough to encase the fruit dough. Turn the sheet of dough over and place the fruit dough in the center. Pull the plain dough around the fruit dough, folding any excess plain dough into pleats on top of the bun. Press the pleats together firmly and turn the bun over. Gently flatten the bun until it is about 3 inches [8 cm.] thick. With a long needle, pierce the bun through to the bottom all over, to allow steam to escape during cooking. Lay the bun on a buttered-and-floured baking sheet. To ensure that the bun keeps its shape, encircle it with the hoop of a spring-form cake pan or with a ring of stiff cardboard covered with foil. The hoop or ring should be larger than the bun to allow for expansion during cooking.

Bake the bun in a preheated 375° F. [190° C.] oven for one hour, then remove the hoop or ring to let the sides of the bun brown. Bake for 30 minutes, until the bun is golden brown.

MRS. MARIA ELIZA RUNDELL
A NEW SYSTEM OF DOMESTIC COOKERY

Yeast Coffeecake
Babka Drożdżowa

The following is a traditional Polish recipe. The name babka, or grandmother, may have been given to it because the brioche mold the dough is baked in resembles a woman's wide skirts.

To make one 10-inch [25-cm.] coffeecake

4 cups	flour	1 liter
¼ oz.	package active dry yeast or ⅗ oz. [18 g.] cake fresh yeast	7½ g.
10 tbsp.	butter	150 ml.
6 tbsp.	sugar	90 ml.
3	egg yolks	3
¾ cup	seedless white raisins, soaked in hot water for 15 minutes and drained	175 ml.
	salt	
⅔ cup	tepid milk	150 ml.
¼ cup	slivered almonds	50 ml.
	confectioners' sugar	

Cream the butter until it is soft and then work in the sugar. Continue stirring and add the egg yolks, one by one. Add the

drained raisins. Mix the yeast with half of the tepid milk and stir the mixture until it is smooth. Allow it to stand in a warm place for 10 minutes. Add a pinch of salt to the butter-and-egg mixture and stir in the yeast, flour and milk. Beat very well with a wooden spoon until the dough develops bubbles and looks smooth and glossy, about 15 minutes. Butter and flour a 10-inch [25-cm.] brioche mold and stick slivered almonds against the fluted sides for decoration. Put in the dough and let it rise in a warm place until it has doubled in bulk, 30 to 40 minutes. Bake in a preheated 425° F. [220° C.] oven for 10 minutes. Reduce the heat to 375° F. [190° C.] and bake for 40 to 50 minutes longer. Let the cake cool and sprinkle it with confectioners' sugar.

LILI KOWALSKA
COOKING THE POLISH WAY

Fruit Bread
Birewecke

This recipe comes from the Sitter bakery in Colmar. Fruit bread is traditionally eaten at Christmas and is best made a week in advance. Serve in thin slices.

To make 3 small cylindrical loaves

1½ cups	flour	375 ml.
6 oz.	basic bread dough (recipe, page 164)	175 g.
2 cups	dried pear halves	½ liter
1 cup	dried apples	¼ liter
¾ cup	pitted dried prunes	175 ml.
¾ cup	chopped dried figs	175 ml.
2 cups	chopped mixed candied fruit peel	½ liter
1 cup	raisins	¼ liter
7 tbsp.	kirsch	105 ml.
1¾ cups	shelled walnuts	425 ml.
1 cup	almonds, blanched	¼ liter
4 tbsp.	ground cinnamon	60 ml.
1 cup	sugar	¼ liter

Boil the dried pears, apples and prunes for about 20 minutes to soften them; drain and cut them into large pieces. Mix them with the figs and mixed peel, add the raisins and let the fruits steep overnight in the kirsch. The next day, add most of the walnuts and almonds, reserving a few for decorating the loaves, and mix in the cinnamon. Then stir in the sugar. Work this mixture into the bread dough, then work in the flour. Shape into three cylindrical loaves, place them on buttered baking sheets and decorate with the reserved nuts. Bake in a preheated 375° F. [190° C.] oven for 30 to 40 minutes, or until a skewer inserted in the center comes out clean.

FOOD AND WINES FROM ALSACE, FRANCE

Walnut Loaf

Pain aux Noix

This bread should be eaten when a few days old, thinly sliced and spread with butter, honey or jam. It is perfect with tea.

To make one 7 ½-by-3 ½-inch [19-by-9-cm.] loaf

2 cups	flour	½ liter
¼ oz.	package active dry yeast or ⅗ oz. [18 g.] cake fresh yeast	7 ½ g.
1 cup	tepid milk	¼ liter
1	egg, beaten	1
1 cup	sugar	¼ liter
1 cup	chopped walnuts	¼ liter
	salt	

In a bowl, mix the yeast with the tepid milk. Stir in the beaten egg. Add the sugar, flour, walnuts and a pinch of salt, and stir the dough vigorously with a spoon for 10 minutes or so. Transfer the mixture to a buttered 7½-by-3½-inch [19-by-9-cm.] loaf pan and let rise in a warm place for 30 minutes. Bake in a preheated 375° F. [190° C.] oven for about 40 minutes, or until golden brown.

ZETTE GUINAUDEAU-FRANC
LES SECRETS DES FERMES EN PÉRIGORD NOIR

Hunting Bread

This recipe is from an anonymously written cookbook published in about 1827. Although the book is an excellent and comprehensive work, it was never republished, and the author's identity has never been discovered. Rose water is a flavoring produced in the Balkans, the Middle East and India by distilling the oil of rose petals; it is obtainable from pharmacies and specialty food stores.

To make about 40 cakes

6 cups	flour, sifted	1 ½ liters
¼ oz.	package active dry yeast or ⅗ oz. [18 g.] cake fresh yeast	7 ½ g.
2 cups	sugar	½ liter
1 or 2 tsp.	caraway seeds	5 or 10 ml.
1 or 2 tsp.	coriander seeds	5 or 10 ml.
¾ cup	tepid rose water	175 ml.
6	egg yolks, lightly beaten	6
4	egg whites	4

Mix the flour, sugar, and caraway and coriander seeds, as many as may be thought proper. Mix the yeast with ½ cup [125 ml.] of the tepid rose water. Beat the egg yolks and egg

whites with the rest of the rose water. Strain the egg-and-rose-water mixture through a sieve into the flour. Add the dissolved yeast and knead the mixture into a firm dough. Turn out the dough onto a lightly floured board and roll it out thin, about ½ inch [1 cm.] thick. Cut it into about 40 diamond-shaped pieces, and place them on buttered baking sheets. Bake the cakes in a preheated 400° F. [200° C.] oven for 15 to 20 minutes, or until they are golden brown. Remove them from the baking sheets to cool.

THE NEW LONDON COOKERY AND COMPLETE DOMESTIC GUIDE

Philadelphia Cinnamon Buns

To make 14 buns

3 to 3½ cups	flour	750 to 875 ml.
¼ oz.	package active dry yeast	7 ½ g.
¼ cup	tepid water	50 ml.
about ½ cup	sugar	about 125 ml.
½ tsp.	salt	2 ml.
2	egg yolks	2
1 cup	tepid milk	¼ liter
6 tbsp.	butter, melted	90 ml.
1 ½ cups	light brown sugar	375 ml.
½ cup	light corn syrup	125 ml.
½ cup	seedless raisins	125 ml.
2 tsp.	ground cinnamon	10 ml.

Pour the tepid water into a bowl and sprinkle the yeast and 1 teaspoon [5 ml.] of the sugar over it. Let it stand for two or three minutes, then stir well. Set in a warm place for five minutes, or until the yeast bubbles up.

Combine 3 cups [¾ liter] of the flour, ½ cup [125 ml.] of sugar and the salt in a bowl, and make a well in the center. Add the yeast mixture, egg yolks and tepid milk. With a large spoon, slowly mix the ingredients, and continue to stir until the dough is smooth and can be gathered into a ball.

Place the ball on a lightly floured surface and knead it. As you knead, sprinkle flour over the ball by the spoonful, adding up to ½ cup more flour, if necessary, to make a firm dough. Continue to knead for 10 minutes, or until the dough is smooth, shiny and elastic. Place the ball in a buttered bowl and turn the ball around to butter its entire surface. Drape the bowl with a kitchen towel and put it in the warm place for about one hour, or until doubled in volume.

In a small bowl, mix ¾ cup [175 ml.] of light brown sugar, 2 tablespoons [30 ml.] of the melted butter and the corn syrup to a smooth paste. Pour the mixture into two 9-inch [23-cm.] cake pans, tipping the pans back and forth to spread it evenly. In another bowl, stir the remaining ¾ cup of light brown sugar, the raisins and cinnamon together until they are well blended. Set aside.

Punch the dough down and, on a lightly floured surface, roll it out into an 18-by-10-inch [45-by-25-cm.] rectangle about ¼ inch [6 mm.] thick. Brush the dough with 2 tablespoons of the melted butter and sprinkle it evenly with the sugar-and-raisin mixture.

Starting at one long side, roll the dough tightly into a cylinder about 18 inches [45 cm.] long and 2½ inches [6 cm.] in diameter. Then, with a sharp knife, slice the cylinder crosswise into 14 rounds about 1¼ inches [3 cm.] thick. Place one slice cut side up in the center of each sugar-lined cake pan, and arrange the remaining slices in circles of six around each center slice. Set the buns aside in the draft-free place for about 45 minutes, or until they double in volume.

Preheat the oven to 350° F. [180° C.]. (If you have used the oven to let the buns rise, gently transfer them to a warm place to rest while the oven heats.) Brush the tops of the buns with the remaining 2 tablespoons of melted butter and bake in the middle of the oven for about 25 minutes, or until they are golden brown. Place a wire cake rack over each pan and, grasping rack and pan together firmly, quickly invert them. Let the cinnamon buns cool to lukewarm before serving.

FOODS OF THE WORLD/AMERICAN COOKING: THE EASTERN HEARTLAND

Irish Spice Bread

Bairn Brack

This is an 1829 version of a spice bread better known as barm brack or barmbrack (barm meaning homemade yeast). Once popular throughout the British Isles, the bread is now eaten chiefly on the Isle of Man and in Ireland. The author of this recipe recommends toasting the bread if it is not eaten immediately after baking.

To make one 16-by-10-inch
[40-by-25-cm.] bread

12 cups	flour, sifted	3 liters
three ¼ oz.	packages active dry yeast or three ⅗ oz. [18 g.] cakes fresh yeast	three 7½ g.
2½ cups	tepid milk	625 ml.
2¾ cups	brown sugar	675 ml.
32 tbsp.	butter (1 lb. [½ kg.])	480 ml.
8	eggs, well beaten	8
6 tbsp.	caraway seeds	90 ml.
	grated nutmeg	

Mix the yeast with ⅔ cup [150 ml.] of the tepid milk and 1 teaspoon [5 ml.] of the brown sugar, and leave the mixture in a warm place until foaming, about 10 minutes. Over very low heat, dissolve the butter in the remaining milk, cool to tepid, then mix with the flour. Add the eggs, the rest of the

sugar, the caraway seeds and a good pinch of nutmeg, and beat to form a fairly moist dough. Beat the dough for about 10 minutes, cover it with a cloth and set it in a warm place to rise for one hour, or until doubled in bulk.

When the dough is well risen, transfer it to a deep, well-buttered baking pan or dish about 16 by 10 inches [40 by 25 cm.] and bake it in a preheated 400° F. [200° C.] oven for 45 to 50 minutes, or until a skewer inserted into the center of the bread comes out clean.

MRS. DALGAIRNS
THE PRACTISE OF COOKERY

Chocolate Rolls

Petit Pains au Chocolat

To make 8 rolls

2 cups	bread flour	½ liter
¼ oz.	package active dry yeast or ⅗ oz. [18 g.] cake fresh yeast	7½ g.
1 tsp.	salt	5 ml.
about ⅓ cup	tepid milk	about 75 ml.
⅓ cup	tepid water	75 ml.
4 oz.	semisweet baking chocolate, broken into 8 equal pieces	125 g.
Milk-and-sugar glaze		
2 tsp.	milk	10 ml.
2 tbsp.	sugar	30 ml.

Sift the salt into the flour. Dissolve the yeast in the tepid milk and water, and leave it for 10 minutes. Pour the yeast mixture into the flour and mix lightly. If the dough is too stiff, add a little milk. Let the dough rise in a warm place.

When the dough has doubled in volume, punch it down, knead it very little, divide it in half, then in quarters, then in eighths. Roll or pat out each piece on a floured board into a rectangle large enough to fit around a piece of chocolate. Center a piece of chocolate on each rectangle. Fold over the ends, then the sides, to make neat parcels. Press the seams carefully together and brush the rolls with milk. Leave them on a floured baking sheet to recover their shape and volume; about 15 to 20 minutes should be sufficient.

Bake the rolls in a preheated 400° to 425° F. [200° to 220° C.] oven for 15 to 20 minutes, or until golden brown. Dissolve the sugar for the glaze in the milk, and brush the tops as soon as the rolls are removed from the oven to make them shiny.

Chocolate rolls should be eaten warm, either immediately after they are cooked or after they are reheated for a few minutes on the bottom shelf of a cool oven. The chocolate inside the roll must be just melting.

ELIZABETH DAVID
ENGLISH BREAD AND YEAST COOKERY

Yeast Puff Breads

*The recipe for a basic yeast puff dough appears
in Standard Preparations, page 166.*

Salted Crescent Rolls

Sörkifli

These savory rolls are traditionally eaten with beer.

To make 32 small rolls

4 cups	flour	1 liter
¼ oz.	package active dry yeast or ⅗ oz. [18 g.] cake fresh yeast	7½ g.
1¼ to 1¾ cups	tepid milk	300 to 425 ml.
1 tsp.	sugar	5 ml.
1 tsp.	salt	5 ml.
4 tbsp.	butter, softened	60 ml.
1	egg yolk, beaten	1

Salted caraway topping

1 tsp.	coarse salt, crushed	5 ml.
2 tbsp.	caraway seeds	30 ml.

Start the yeast working with 3 or 4 tablespoons [45 or 60 ml.] of the milk, mixed with the sugar. Leave in a warm place until the yeast foams on the surface of the milk, about 10 minutes. Pour the liquid into the flour, add the salt, and use a wooden spoon to stir in enough of the remaining milk to make a rather soft dough.

Work the dough thoroughly with the spoon, then knead it with your hands—dusting them with flour, if necessary, to make the dough easier to handle. Divide the dough into four portions. Roll each portion into a thin round about 10 inches [25 cm.] in diameter, and spread each round with the softened butter. Divide each round into eight wedges, and roll up each of these triangular wedges, starting from the base of the triangle. Bend the rolls slightly to form crescents, and lay them on three buttered baking sheets, leaving plenty of room between the crescents.

Let the crescents rise in a warm place for about two hours, or until doubled in size. Then brush them with the beaten egg yolk. Mix the caraway seeds with the coarse salt, and sprinkle the crescents with the mixture. Bake the crescents in a preheated 400° F. [200° C.] oven for 10 to 15 minutes, or until they are golden brown.

FRED MACNICOL
HUNGARIAN COOKERY

Bulgarian Cheese Bread

Tootmanik s Gotovo Testo

This typical Bulgarian bread is often made with lard instead of butter. The original version of the recipe calls for sirene cheese, the Bulgarian equivalent of Greek feta cheese. Because sirene cheese is unavailable in the United States, feta has been substituted.

To make one 10-by-8-inch [25-by-20-cm.] bread

1 lb.	basic bread dough (recipe, page 164)	½ kg.
10 tbsp.	butter, melted and cooled to tepid	150 ml.
3	eggs, lightly beaten	3
½ lb.	feta cheese, finely crumbled	¼ kg.

Make the bread dough in the usual way and let it rise once. When it has risen, punch it down and divide it into nine pieces. Roll out each piece into a round about 8 inches [20 cm.] across. Brush six of the dough rounds with half of the butter. Stack the buttered rounds in pairs, buttered sides uppermost, then top each pair with an unbuttered round. Roll out each dough "sandwich" to fit a 10-by-8-inch [25-by-20-cm.] baking pan or dish.

Reserve half of the beaten eggs for brushing the top of the bread, and mix the remainder with the crumbled cheese. Butter a baking pan with 2 tablespoons [30 ml.] of the reserved butter. Place a sheet of dough in the pan, brush the surface with butter and sprinkle it with half of the cheese-and-egg mixture. Cover with another sheet of dough, brush it with some more of the butter and sprinkle it with the remaining cheese-and-egg mixture to within ½ inch [1 cm.] of the edges. Put the third sheet of dough on top and brush it with the rest of the butter. Gently press down the edges into the pan. Let the bread rise in a warm place for one to one and a half hours, or until it has more than doubled in bulk.

Bake the bread in the upper part of a preheated 350° F. [180° C.] oven for about 30 minutes. Remove the bread from the oven, brush the surface with the reserved beaten egg and bake for another 10 to 15 minutes, or until the crust is a deep golden color and shiny. Serve the bread warm or cold, with tea or yogurt.

PENKA I. CHOLCHEVA
KNIGA ZA VSEKI DEN I VSEKI DOM

Danish Pastry

Wienerbrod

In Denmark, this pastry is called Wienerbrod, or "Vienna bread," reflecting its true origin. About 100 years ago, when the bakers of Copenhagen went on strike, their employers retaliated by importing German and Austrian bakers. Viennese pastry became so popular among the Danes that Danish bakers adopted the Viennese method of folding cold butter into yeast dough, and they went on to modify the pastry by filling it with jam and other sweet mixtures. This new "Danish pastry" was praised even in Austria.

If desired, the filling for the cockscombs may be flavored with 3 tablespoons [45 ml.] of thick applesauce or lemon custard instead of with crushed almond macaroons.

	To make 12 pastries	
2 cups	flour	½ liter
¼ oz.	package active dry yeast and ½ tsp. [2 ml.] sugar, or ⅗ oz. [18 g.] cake fresh yeast	7½ g.
⅓ cup	tepid water	75 ml.
1	egg, beaten	1
1 tsp.	sugar	5 ml.
	salt	
2 tbsp.	lard	30 ml.
10 tbsp.	butter	150 ml.
Raisin filling		
1	egg, beaten	1
2 tbsp.	butter, softened	30 ml.
2 tbsp.	superfine sugar	30 ml.
1 tsp.	ground cinnamon	5 ml.
¼ cup	seedless white raisins, soaked in hot water for 15 minutes and drained	50 ml.
Almond filling		
2 tbsp.	butter, softened	30 ml.
2 tbsp.	superfine sugar	30 ml.
¼ cup	crushed almond macaroons	50 ml.
1	egg, beaten	1
2 tbsp.	almonds, blanched and chopped	30 ml.
Sugar icing		
⅓ cup	confectioners' sugar	75 ml.
1 tsp.	water	5 ml.

Blend the fresh yeast into the tepid water. If using dry yeast, dissolve ½ teaspoon [2 ml.] of sugar in the water and then sprinkle the yeast over the top; stir the yeast into the water after a minute or so. Set aside the yeast mixture until frothy, about 15 minutes.

Add the beaten egg to the yeast liquid. In a large bowl, mix the flour, the teaspoon [5 ml.] of sugar and the salt. Rub the lard into the flour mixture, add the yeast-and-egg mixture and mix to a soft dough. Put the dough on a floured board and knead it until it is smooth and elastic, about 10 minutes. Place the dough in a lightly oiled plastic bag or encase it in plastic wrap, and refrigerate it for 10 minutes.

With a narrow metal spatula, work the butter until it is softened and shape it into a rectangle about ½ inch [1 cm.] thick. On a floured work surface, roll out the dough approximately 10 inches [25 cm.] square. Spread the butter down the center of the square to within 1 inch [2½ cm.] of the edges. Fold the sides over the butter to overlap in the middle by about ½ inch; seal the bottom and top. Roll out the dough into a rectangle about 6 by 18 inches [15 by 45 cm.]. Fold it evenly in three. Return the dough to the plastic bag or wrap, and let it rest in the refrigerator for 10 minutes.

Then return the dough to the floured work surface and roll it out in the opposite direction. Repeat the rolling, folding and resting processes twice more, ensuring that the dough is rolled in a different direction each time. Return the dough to the plastic bag or wrap, and refrigerate it overnight or for at least four hours. It will then be ready for use.

To make snails with raisin filling, roll out half of the dough into a 6-by-15-inch [15-by-38-cm.] rectangle. Brush the two short ends with some of the beaten egg to make a 1-inch border at both ends. Cream the butter with the superfine sugar and cinnamon. Spread this mixture on the dough and sprinkle it with the raisins. Roll up the dough from one short end to make a fat jelly-roll shape. Slice this roll into six pieces and place them on a buttered baking sheet. Flatten them slightly with your palm and brush them with beaten egg. Let them rise in a warm place for 30 minutes, or until well risen, before baking.

To make cockscombs with almond filling, roll out the rest of the dough into an 8-by-12-inch [20-by-30-cm.] rectangle. Slice the dough into six 4-inch [10-cm.] squares. Cream the butter with the superfine sugar and fold in the macaroons. Place a little of this filling in the center of each square. Brush the rest of the surface of the dough square with a little of the beaten egg, fold the square in half and make six to eight incisions along the fold. Bend each "comb" so that the "teeth" fan out. Brush the combs with the rest of the egg and scatter chopped almonds on them. Transfer the cockscombs to a buttered baking sheet and let them rise for 20 to 30 minutes, or until well risen.

Bake the snails and cockscombs in a preheated 400° F. [200° C.] oven for 10 minutes. Then reduce the heat to 350° F. [180° C.] and bake for a further 10 to 15 minutes, or until the pastries are golden brown. Cool the pastries on a wire rack. To ice the snails while they are cooling, sift the confectioners' sugar, blend in the water and beat the mixture until it is smooth. Trickle the icing over the pastries.

PAULINE VIOLA AND KNUD RAVNKILDE
COOKING WITH A DANISH FLAVOUR

Filled Croissants, Viennese-Style

Croissants Viennois Fourrés

Another method of making and shaping croissants is shown on pages 44-46. The croissants can also be filled with jam, in which case they are not iced, but glazed with egg yolk before baking and dusted with confectioners' sugar afterward.

To make 12 croissants

4 cups	flour	1 liter
¼ oz.	package active dry yeast or ⅗ oz. [18 g.] cake fresh yeast	7½ g.
about 1 cup	tepid milk	about ¼ liter
14 tbsp.	butter, softened	210 ml.
1 tsp.	salt	5 ml.
1 tbsp.	sugar	15 ml.
	Almond cream filling	
1	egg	1
2	egg yolks	2
⅓ cup	sugar	75 ml.
¼ cup	flour	50 ml.
½ cup	ground blanched almonds	125 ml.
2 cups	milk, simmered with a piece of vanilla bean for 3 minutes	½ liter
2 tbsp.	butter	30 ml.
	Almond topping	
1	egg white, lightly beaten	1
1 cup	confectioners' sugar	¼ liter
¾ cup	almonds, blanched and slivered	175 ml.

Prepare a yeast sponge by mixing the yeast with half of the tepid milk. Let stand for 10 minutes, then blend in one third of the flour to make a soft dough. Cover the mixture and let it rise in a warm place for 30 minutes. Mix the rest of the flour with half of the butter, the salt, sugar and remaining milk, adding more milk if necessary. Knead until a smooth, elastic dough is obtained. Mix this with the well-risen yeast sponge. Roll the dough into a ball, and let it rise in a cool place for at least two hours, or (preferably) overnight in the refrigerator.

Roll out the dough into a rectangle about ½ inch [1 cm.] thick. Divide the rest of the butter into small pieces and dot them over half of the dough. Fold the rectangle in half crosswise, enclosing the butter as if it were in a purse. Roll out the dough again and fold it in three crosswise, then give the dough a quarter turn and roll it out again. Fold it in three, cover, and let it rest for 20 minutes in the refrigerator.

Repeat these rolling, folding and resting processes twice more. Then roll out the dough a final time into a rectangle

about ⅛ inch [3 mm.] thick. Cut the rectangle into 12 equilateral triangles with 6-inch [15-cm.] sides. Roll up each triangle, starting from the base and rolling toward the apex; bend the ends slightly to make a crescent shape. Place the croissants on lightly buttered baking sheets and let them rise. The time needed will depend on the temperature of the room—20 minutes will suffice in a warm place, several hours in a cool one—or they may be refrigerated overnight.

Bake the croissants in a preheated 375° F. [190° C.] oven for 20 minutes, or until well risen and browned on the bottom. Cool the croissants on wire racks. While they cool, make the filling. Mix the egg and egg yolks with the sugar, flour and ground almonds. Gradually add the milk, stirring constantly. Put the mixture in a pan and set it over low heat, stirring constantly until the mixture begins to bubble. Remove the pan from the heat and stir in the butter. When the butter has melted, let the filling cool. Split the croissants lengthwise, fill them and sandwich them together again.

Beat the egg white and confectioners' sugar to form a stiff icing. Toast the almonds in an ungreased skillet over low heat until they are lightly browned. Ice the croissants, stick the almonds into the icing, then let the topping set.

B. DESCHAMPS AND J.-CL. DESCHAINTRE
LE LIVRE DE L'APPRENTI PÂTISSIER

———————◆———————

Breton Butter Loaf

Kouing-Aman

To make one 10-inch [25-cm.] round loaf

10 oz.	basic bread dough (recipe, page 164)	300 g.
10 tbsp.	butter, softened	150 ml.
¾ cup	superfine sugar	175 ml.

Make the bread dough in the usual way. Then, after the first rising, punch it down and roll it out on a floured board into a rectangle about ½ inch [1 cm.] thick. Spread it with the butter, leaving an unbuttered 1-inch [2½-cm.] margin around the edges of the rectangle. Sprinkle the butter with all but 1 tablespoon [15 ml.] of the sugar. Fold the dough in three lengthwise, then in three crosswise, to form it into a little parcel. Roll out the dough again, trying not to let the butter and sugar escape. Fold the dough lengthwise and crosswise again, but this time in two instead of in three. Then roll it out again, and shape it into a round about 10 inches [25 cm.] across and ½ inch thick.

Place the dough in a generously buttered 10-inch [25-cm.] spring-form pan set on top of two baking sheets. Let the dough rise for 20 minutes, then put it—still on the baking sheets—in a preheated 425° F. [220° C.] oven. Bake for about 20 minutes, or until the bread is golden and the surface caramelized. Remove the bread from the pan while it is still hot and sprinkle it with the reserved tablespoon of sugar. Serve it warm. If necessary, the bread can be reheated in a preheated 300° F. [150° C.] oven for about 10 minutes.

LES DESSERTS DE NOS PROVINCES

Chelsea Buns

To make 10 to 12 buns

5 cups	flour	1¼ liters
⅗ oz.	cake fresh yeast	18 g.
⅔ cup	tepid milk	150 ml.
1 tsp.	salt	5 ml.
2 tbsp.	sugar	30 ml.
16 tbsp.	butter (½ lb. [¼ kg.]), softened	240 ml.
2	eggs, beaten	2
2 tsp.	grated lemon peel	10 ml.
1 tsp.	ground cinnamon or allspice	5 ml.
4 tbsp.	superfine sugar, 2 tbsp. [30 ml.] mixed with 2 tbsp. milk	60 ml.

Chelsea-bun filling

6 tbsp.	butter, cut into pieces	90 ml.
¾ cup	dried currants, soaked in warm water for 15 minutes and drained	175 ml.
½ cup	brown sugar	125 ml.

Pour half of the milk over the yeast, and let the mixture foam. Mix the flour with the salt and sugar, then rub in the softened butter. Add the yeast and the eggs, lemon peel and cinnamon or allspice, then mix to a fairly stiff dough with the rest of the milk. Cover the bowl and leave it in a warm place for about two hours, until the dough has risen very high and is extremely light and puffy.

Break down the dough, knead it well, and divide it into two equal portions. Roll each into a rectangle. Spread each rectangle of dough with an equal quantity of butter, warmed currants and brown sugar. Fold each rectangle in three by folding one third over a second third and folding the remaining third on top of the other two. Turn the rectangles through a quarter circle, then roll them out again into rectangles approximately 8 by 10 inches [20 by 25 cm.]. Now roll up each piece of dough firmly, like a jelly roll. Seal the edges with water. Cut these rolls into slices from 1 to 2 inches [2½ to 5 cm.] thick, according to the size you want the buns to be, remembering that by the time they have risen and been baked, they will have doubled in volume.

Arrange the slices in even rows on a greased baking sheet—seven to a row used to be the rule of professional bakers—with a space of about 1 inch [2½ cm.] between each bun. The spacing is important, for during the rising period and as the buns grow in volume so that they almost merge, they begin to assume the characteristically square shape. (If they are too far apart they remain round.) When they are all but touching, sprinkle them with the 2 tablespoons [30 ml.] of superfine sugar. They are now ready for the oven. Bake them in a preheated 425° F. [220° C.] oven for 15 minutes. During baking, the merging process is completed. As soon as you take the buns from the oven, brush them with the sugar-and-milk glaze. Separate them only after they have cooled for a few minutes.

ELIZABETH DAVID
ENGLISH BREAD AND YEAST COOKERY

Aberdeen Butter Rolls

Buttery Rowies

To make about 20 rolls

4 cups	flour	1 liter
⅗ oz.	cake fresh yeast	18 g.
1 tbsp.	superfine sugar	15 ml.
1 tsp.	salt	5 ml.
1¾ cups	tepid water	425 ml.
12 tbsp.	butter, softened	180 ml.
12 tbsp.	lard, softened	180 ml.

Sift the flour into a warm bowl. Mix the yeast with the sugar and salt, and add it to the flour along with the water. Mix well, cover the dough with a warm, damp towel and set the bowl in a warm place until the dough rises to twice its bulk, about one and one half hours.

Beat the butter and lard together until they are thoroughly blended; then divide the mixture into three equal portions. On a floured board, roll out the dough (which is the better for being chilled after it has risen) into a strip three times as long as it is wide. Place small pats of the butter mixture all over the strip until the first portion is used up. Fold the dough in three and roll it out. Repeat this process twice, at intervals of 30 minutes, keeping the dough refrigerated or in a cool place during the intervening periods.

Divide the dough into about 20 pieces and shape each of these into an oval. Place the ovals a little apart on two greased-and-floured baking sheets, and let them rise in a warm place for 30 minutes. Bake in a preheated 400° F. [200° C.] oven for 20 to 25 minutes, or until golden brown.

F. MARIAN MC NEILL
THE SCOTS KITCHEN

Breads without Yeast

Soda Bread (White)

To make one 8-inch [20-cm.] round loaf

4 cups	flour	1 liter
½ tsp.	baking soda	2 ml.
½ tsp.	salt	2 ml.
1¼ cups	buttermilk or sour milk	300 ml.

Heat the oven to 400° F. [200° C.]. Butter an 8-inch [20-cm.] cast-iron pot or deep skillet and place it in the oven to warm.

Sift the flour, baking soda and salt into a bowl. Mix them into a soft dough with the buttermilk or sour milk. Turn out the dough onto a floured board and knead it with a pushing-and-pulling motion until smooth. Shape the dough into a round about 8 inches [20 cm.] across. Remove the pot or skillet from the oven and lay the round in it, floured side up. With a sharp knife, cut a cross in the top of the dough. Cover the pot or skillet with a tight-fitting lid and return it to the preheated oven for about 40 minutes, or until the bread is golden brown.

IRISH RECIPES TRADITIONAL AND MODERN

Baking Powder Biscuits

To make about 15 biscuits

2 cups	sifted bread flour	½ liter
1 tbsp.	baking powder	15 ml.
½ tsp.	salt	2 ml.
4 tbsp.	vegetable shortening	60 ml.
about ¾ cup	milk	about 175 ml.

To the flour, add the baking powder and salt, and sift together. Cut in the shortening with two knives or a pastry blender until the mixture is the consistency of coarse cornmeal. Stir in the milk to make a soft dough; then turn the dough out onto a lightly floured board and knead for half a minute. Roll out the dough about ½ inch [1 cm.] thick. Cut into 2-inch [5-cm.] rounds with a floured biscuit cutter, and bake on an ungreased baking sheet in a preheated 450° F. [230° C.] oven for 12 to 15 minutes, or until the biscuits are browned.

LOUIS P. DE GOUY
THE BREAD TRAY

Salt-Rising Bread

To make two 9-by-5-inch [23-by-13-cm.] loaves

8½ to 9½ cups	flour	2¼ to 2½ liters
½ cup	cornmeal, preferably stone-ground	125 ml.
4 cups	milk	1 liter
5 tbsp.	vegetable shortening, cut into bits	75 ml.
1 tbsp.	sugar	15 ml.
1 tbsp.	salt	15 ml.
1	egg, beaten with 1 tbsp. [15 ml.] milk	1

Starting a day ahead, measure the cornmeal into a heatproof bowl. Then heat 1 cup [¼ liter] of the milk in a small pan until bubbles form around the sides. Pour the milk over the cornmeal and stir until it is a smooth paste. Set the bowl in a warm, draft-free place overnight, or until the cornmeal mixture ferments and develops a strong cheeselike odor.

Place the shortening, sugar and salt in a mixing bowl 12 inches [30 cm.] across the top. Pour water to a depth of 2 inches [5 cm.] into a pot 12 inches in diameter. (The rim of the bowl should fit snugly over the pot; the pot must be deep so that the bottom of the bowl will be suspended above the water.) Bring the water to a boil, then remove the pot from the stove and cover tightly to keep the water hot.

In a heavy saucepan, heat the remaining milk until bubbles form around the sides of the pan. Pour the milk over the shortening mixture and stir until the sugar and salt dissolve. When the mixture is tepid, add 3½ cups [875 ml.] of flour and, after it is incorporated, add the cornmeal mixture.

Set the bowl over the pot of water and drape the bowl with a kitchen towel. Let the dough rise for about two hours, or until surface bubbles indicate that it has fermented. The water under the bowl must be kept tepid; check the pot occasionally and replenish with boiling water if necessary.

When the dough has fermented, remove the bowl from the pot. Stir into the dough 5 to 6 cups [1¼ to 1½ liters] more flour, 1 cup [¼ liter] at a time, to make a firm ball. If the dough becomes difficult to stir, work in the flour with your hands. Place the dough on a lightly floured surface and knead it for 20 minutes, or until it is smooth and elastic. Divide the dough in half and shape each piece into a cylindrical loaf about 8 inches [20 cm.] long and 4 inches [10 cm.] wide. Place the loaves in buttered 9-by-5-inch [23-by-13-cm.] loaf pans and set them aside in the draft-free place for two hours, or until the loaves double in bulk.

Brush the tops of the loaves with the egg-and-milk mixture and bake on the middle shelf of a preheated 400° F. [200° C.] oven for 10 minutes. Reduce the temperature to 350° F. [180° C.] and bake for 25 to 30 minutes longer, or until the bread is golden brown. To test for doneness, turn the loaves out and rap the bottoms with your knuckles. The loaves should sound hollow. Cool the loaves on racks before serving.

FOODS OF THE WORLD/AMERICAN COOKING: THE EASTERN HEARTLAND

Beaten Biscuits

To make about 36 biscuits

3 cups	flour	¾ liter
½ tsp.	sugar	2 ml.
½ tsp.	salt	2 ml.
3 tbsp.	butter, cut into pieces and chilled	45 ml.
3 tbsp.	lard, cut into pieces and chilled	45 ml.
½ cup	milk, chilled	125 ml.
about ½ cup	water, chilled	about 125 ml.

Sift the flour, sugar and salt into a mixing bowl. Add the butter and lard and, with two knives or a pastry blender, cut them into the flour until the mixture resembles coarse meal. Add the milk and enough water to make a stiff dough. Toss the mixture with a fork. Knead the dough for 15 minutes; then beat it with a mallet for 20 minutes, or until well blistered. Or put the dough through the coarse disk of a food grinder, folding the dough over frequently. When ready, the dough should be smooth and glossy.

Roll out the dough ½ inch [1 cm.] thick and cut it into rounds with a small, floured biscuit cutter. Prick the rounds with the tines of a fork and bake on baking sheets in a preheated 325° F. [160° C.] oven for 30 minutes.

JEAN HEWITT
THE NEW YORK TIMES SOUTHERN HERITAGE COOKBOOK

Bran Muffins

Buttermilk or plain yogurt can be used instead of sour milk.

To make 12 muffins

1 cup	sifted flour	¼ liter
1 tsp.	baking soda	5 ml.
1 cup	bran breakfast cereal	¼ liter
4 tbsp.	butter	60 ml.
¼ cup	sugar	50 ml.
1	egg, beaten	1
½ tsp.	salt	2 ml.
1 cup	sour milk	¼ liter
½ cup	seedless raisins or chopped dates (optional)	125 ml.

Cream the butter with the sugar. Add the egg and beat well. Mix the dry ingredients—bran, flour, baking soda and

salt—and add them to the butter-and-egg mixture alternately with the sour milk. Stir in the raisins or dates, if desired. Fill the buttered cups of a muffin pan two thirds full. Bake the muffins in a preheated 400° F. [200° C.] oven for 20 to 25 minutes, or until golden brown.

CHEZZETCOOK HISTORICAL SOCIETY COOKBOOK

Sister Olive Wheeler's Soda Biscuits

To make 12 to 16 biscuits

2 cups	flour	½ liter
½ tsp.	baking soda	2 ml.
1 tsp.	cream of tartar	5 ml.
½ tsp.	salt	2 ml.
½ cup	milk	125 ml.

Sift together the flour, cream of tartar and salt. Dissolve the baking soda in the milk and stir the mixture into the sifted ingredients. Pat the dough thin, cut it into 12 to 16 squares, and bake the squares on a greased baking sheet in a preheated 400° F. [200° C.] oven for 10 minutes, or until browned.

AMY B. W. MILLER AND PERSIS W. FULLER (EDITORS)
THE BEST OF SHAKER COOKING

Triticale Muffins

To make 8 large muffins

1¾ cups	triticale flour	425 ml.
2 tsp.	baking powder	10 ml.
½ tsp.	salt	2 ml.
⅓ cup	hominy grits, boiled, drained and cooled	75 ml.
¾ cup	milk	175 ml.
1	egg, lightly beaten	1
2 tbsp.	unsalted butter, melted and cooled	30 ml.
2 tbsp.	blackstrap molasses	30 ml.
¼ cup	freshly brewed strong black coffee, cooled	50 ml.

Sift the flour, baking powder and salt into a bowl. In a separate bowl, combine the cooled grits, milk, egg, butter, molasses and coffee. Pour the grits mixture into the flour mixture and stir well. Spoon the batter into the oiled cups of a muffin pan. Bake in a preheated 400° F. [200° C.] oven for 20 minutes, or until the muffins are crusty on top. Serve hot.

JULIA OLDER AND STEVE SHERMAN
SOUP AND BREAD

Graham Bread

Graham flour is another name for whole-wheat flour. The name comes from Sylvester Graham, an early 19th Century American dietician who pioneered the use of flour made from the whole grain.

To make two 8 ½-by-4 ½-inch [21-by-11-cm.] loaves

4 cups	graham flour	1 liter
⅔ cup	all-purpose flour	150 ml.
2 tsp.	baking soda	10 ml.
¼ cup	sugar	50 ml.
2 tsp.	salt	10 ml.
½ cup	molasses	125 ml.
2 tbsp.	butter or lard, melted and cooled	30 ml.
2 ½ cups	milk	625 ml.

Sift the flours, baking soda, sugar and salt together. Add the molasses, melted butter or lard, and the milk. Beat well—air and the baking soda are the only rising agents. Put the dough into two greased 8½-by-4½-inch [21-by-11-cm.] loaf pans and bake in a preheated 375° F. [190° C.] oven for one hour, or until a skewer inserted in the center of the loaf comes out clean.

AMY B. W. MILLER AND PERSIS W. FULLER (EDITORS)
THE BEST OF SHAKER COOKING

Rye Drop Cakes

To make about twelve 4-inch [10-cm.] cakes

about 2 cups	rye meal	about ½ liter
1 tsp.	baking soda	5 ml.
2 cups	buttermilk	½ liter
2	eggs	2
½ tsp.	salt	2 ml.

To the buttermilk add the eggs, baking soda, salt and enough rye meal to make a batter that will spread a little, but not run. With a spoon, drop the batter into muffin rings placed on a lightly greased hot griddle. For baking, the cakes will require six to seven minutes—about twice the time of griddlecakes.

MRS. M. E. PORTER
MRS. PORTER'S NEW SOUTHERN COOKERY BOOK

Buttermilk Oaten Bread

To make four 8 ½-by-5-by-5-inch [21-by-13-by-13-cm.] wedges

1 ¼ cups	flour	300 ml.
2 ⅓ cups	rolled oats, pulverized in a blender or food processor, and steeped overnight in 1 ¼ cups [300 ml.] buttermilk or sour milk	575 ml.
½ tsp.	baking soda	2 ml.
½ tsp.	salt	2 ml.

Mix the flour, soda and salt together in a bowl. Stir in the oat mixture. If necessary, add a little more buttermilk or sour milk to make the mixture into a soft dough. Knead the dough until it is smooth—about 10 minutes.

Roll out the dough into a round about 2 inches [5 cm.] thick, and lay it on a well-buttered baking sheet. With a sharp knife, cut it into quarters. Bake the bread in a preheated 375° F. [190° C.] oven for about 25 minutes, until the bread is golden.

IRISH RECIPES TRADITIONAL AND MODERN

Rice Bread

Pain de Riz

To make one 8-inch [20-cm.] round or square bread

¼ cup	raw unprocessed rice, boiled, cooled and pressed through a sieve	50 ml.
2 cups	white cornmeal, sifted	½ liter
2 ½ tsp.	baking powder	12 ml.
2 ½ cups	milk	625 ml.
3	eggs, beaten	3
1 tsp.	salt	5 ml.
1 tbsp.	butter, melted	15 ml.

Gradually pour the milk into the eggs while mixing. Mix the salt and baking powder with the cornmeal and add it to the milk and eggs. Beat well. Then add the melted butter and the rice. Mix all thoroughly and beat until very light. Then grease the bottom of a shallow, round or square 8-inch [20-cm.] baking pan and turn the mixture into it. Bake in a preheated 400° F. [200° C.] oven for 30 minutes, or until a skewer inserted in the center comes out clean. Serve hot, buttering the slices freely.

THE PICAYUNE CREOLE COOK BOOK

Granny's Oatcakes

For the beef drippings called for, use the fat melted from a beef roast; lard may be substituted. Steel-cut oatmeal is obtainable from most health-food stores and some European-food specialty stores.

These oatcakes are always best made in small batches. If a large number is to be made, repeat the small batches.

To make about ten 3-inch [8-cm.] oatcakes		
1½ cups	steel-cut oatmeal	375 ml.
½ tsp.	baking soda	2 ml.
4 tsp.	beef drippings	20 ml.
5 or 6 tbsp.	boiling water	75 or 90 ml.
	salt	

Melt the beef drippings in the water, then add this to the oatmeal along with the baking soda and a pinch of salt. Work the mixture into a stiff dough. Roll out the dough very thin on a board sprinkled with oatmeal. Cut the dough into rounds with a 3-inch [8-cm.] biscuit cutter or a coffee cup, and place the rounds a few at a time on a hot, lightly greased griddle or skillet. Cook them until the edges curl, about three minutes. Do not turn the oatcakes over, but transfer them to a baking sheet and put them under a broiler for two or three minutes to brown the tops lightly.

PETITS PROPOS CULINAIRES I

Brown Oatmeal Bread

To sour 1¼ cups [300 ml.] of milk, add 1 tablespoon [15 ml.] of vinegar or lemon juice to the milk and let the mixture stand for five minutes.

To make two 8-inch [20-cm.] round flatbreads		
4 cups	whole-wheat flour	1 liter
⅓ cup	steel-cut oatmeal	75 ml.
1 tsp.	baking soda	5 ml.
1 tsp.	salt	5 ml.
4 tbsp.	lard	60 ml.
about 1¼ cups	sour milk	about 300 ml.

Sift together the salt, baking soda and flour and mix very thoroughly. Rub in the fat until the mixture has the consistency of fine bread crumbs, then mix in the oatmeal. Make a

well in the center of the mixture, and add enough sour milk to produce a dry but spongy dough—a sticky dough will make the bread heavy. Turn the dough out onto a floured board, divide it in half and, with your palms, quickly pat and roll the dough into two flat cakes. Place these on two floured baking sheets. Score each bread lightly into four quarters with a sharp knife and bake the breads in a preheated 425° F. [220° C.] oven for 20 to 30 minutes, or until the tops of the breads are brown and crisp.

ANNE PASCOE
CORNISH RECIPES OLD AND NEW

Whole-wheat Griddle Breads

Chappati

Chappati dough can be made and cooked within a few minutes. Personally, I like to leave the dough overnight in the refrigerator, covered with a damp muslin cloth.

To make about eight 5-inch [13-cm.] round flatbreads		
2 cups	whole-wheat flour	½ liter
1 tsp.	salt	5 ml.
about 1 cup	water	about ¼ liter

Mix the flour and salt and place them on a pastry board. Sprinkle some of the water in the middle and gradually work it in until the flour has absorbed it. Stop adding water as soon as the dough is supple and elastic. Knead the dough well—the longer the better. Ten minutes gives a specially light finish, but five minutes is adequate. Cover with a wet muslin cloth and leave for 30 minutes at least. If the dough is left for a longer period of time, it should be kept in a cool place. Knead lightly again before shaping the dough.

Form the dough into small, round balls and flatten them with the palm of your hand. Dust the rounds with a little flour on each side, place them on a board and roll each of them out as thin as a sheet of parchment paper. They should be the same diameter as your griddle or skillet. Have the griddle or skillet at medium heat (a little hotter if it is very thick) and turn a flatbread onto it. Wait until the first bubbles rise in the bread, about three minutes. Turn it over, using a spatula or your hand. After a minute or so, press on the edges a little and gently rotate the bread. Now pick up the bread with the spatula and, if you are using a gas range, hold the bread steady over a high flame. Otherwise, set the bread under the broiler for a few seconds. In both cases, the bread should puff up and then be ready to eat.

To serve, heat a deep dish, line it with hot napkins and stack the bread. Keep the bread covered with the napkins and take it to the table.

DHARAMJIT SINGH
INDIAN COOKERY

Whole-wheat Buttered Griddle Bread

Paratha

Lovage seeds can be purchased from Indian or Middle Eastern food stores.

To make six 7-inch [18-cm.] flatbreads

1¾ cups	whole-wheat flour	425 ml.
¾ tsp.	salt	4 ml.
12 to 16	lovage seeds, roughly bruised	12 to 16
½ cup	milk	125 ml.
½ cup	water	125 ml.
2 to 4 tbsp.	butter, melted	30 to 60 ml.

Sift the flour and salt onto a board and make a well in the center. Drop the lovage seeds into the well and pour in the milk and water. Combine the ingredients to form a very soft dough, almost a batter. Knead or beat it until it is smooth. Cover with a damp cloth and let the dough rest at room temperature for at least one and a half hours, but preferably for eight hours or overnight.

Divide the dough into six portions and roll each of them into a circle, about 7 inches [18 cm.] across. Brush the circles with a little of the melted butter. Fold the circles in half and then fold again to make triangles. Roll out the triangles again to form circles about 7 inches across. Brush the circles with melted butter and repeat the folding and rolling process. Do this at least three times more. The more times you repeat the process, the crisper your bread will be.

Cook one *paratha* at a time on a lightly buttered griddle or in a heavy skillet over medium heat until it is a pale brown, mottled with a dark brown. Turn the *paratha* over and cook on the other side. Serve hot.

DHARAMJIT SINGH
INDIAN COOKERY

Navajo Fry Bread

To make three 8-inch [20-cm.] round flatbreads

2 cups	flour	½ liter
2 tsp.	baking powder	10 ml.
½ cup	nonfat dry milk	125 ml.
½ tsp.	salt	2 ml.
2 tbsp.	lard, cut into small pieces	30 ml.
½ cup	ice water	125 ml.
1 lb.	lard for deep frying	½ kg.

Combine the flour, dry milk, baking powder and salt, and sift them into a deep bowl. Add the small pieces of lard and, with your finger tips, rub the flour and fat together until the

mixture resembles coarse meal. Pour in the water and toss the ingredients together until the dough can be gathered into a ball. Drape the bowl with a kitchen towel and let the dough rest at room temperature for about two hours.

Cut the dough into three equal pieces. Then, on a lightly floured surface, roll each piece into a round about 8 inches [20 cm.] in diameter and ¼ inch [6 mm.] thick. Cut two 4- to 5-inch [10- to 13-cm.] parallel slits completely through the center of each round, spacing the slits 1 inch [2½ cm.] apart.

In a heavy skillet, melt the remaining lard over medium heat until it is very hot but not smoking. The melted fat should be about 1 inch deep; add more lard if necessary. Fry the breads one at a time for about two minutes on each side, turning them once with tongs or a slotted spatula. The bread will puff slightly and become crisp and brown. Drain the Navajo fry bread on paper towels and serve warm.

FOODS OF THE WORLD/AMERICAN COOKING: THE GREAT WEST

Norman Flatbread

La Foncée

This traditional flatbread from Normandy is nearly identical to that eaten in Scandinavia, and can thus almost certainly be traced back to the Normans' Viking ancestors.

To make one 10-inch [25-cm.] flatbread

2 cups	flour	½ liter
2	eggs, beaten	2
	salt	
16 tbsp.	butter (½ lb. [¼ kg.]), softened and cut into pieces	240 ml.
1 cup	heavy cream	¼ liter
1	egg yolk, beaten	1

Put the flour into a bowl. Make a well in the center and pour in the eggs. Add a pinch of salt, the butter and the cream. Knead well with your finger tips to form a smooth dough. Cover and let the dough stand for 30 minutes.

Roll out the dough and fold it into quarters. Roll out the dough again and repeat the folding. Then shape the dough into a ball, cover, and let it rest for 15 minutes before rolling it into a round about 10 inches [25 cm.] in diameter and the thickness of a finger. Lay this round on a buttered baking sheet. Score a cross lightly with the point of a sharp knife to divide the round into quarters. Brush the round with the egg yolk. Bake in a preheated 425° F. [220° C.] oven for about 30 minutes, or until brown.

MARIE BISSON
LA CUISINE NORMANDE

Telemark Flatbread

This crisp flatbread will keep indefinitely if stored in an air-tight container.

To make two 12- to 14-inch [30- to 35-cm.] round flatbreads

2 cups	all-purpose flour	½ liter
2 cups	oat flour	½ liter
2 cups	barley flour	½ liter
2 cups	light rye flour	½ liter
2 cups	water	½ liter
½ tsp.	salt	2 ml.

Mix all of the ingredients together and work them into a pliable dough. Divide the dough in half, roll out each half into a thin round, and cook over low heat on a hot, buttered cast-iron griddle or skillet until crisp, about 10 minutes on each side. Cool the flatbreads on wire racks.

ELISE SVERDRUP
NORWAY'S DELIGHT: DISHES AND SPECIALITIES

Tortillas

A comal is a small, round iron or earthenware griddle. The author suggests you may use any other heavy griddle. The tortillas may be flattened—between sheets of plastic wrap or wax paper—with a rolling pin instead of a tortilla press.

To make about twelve 5-inch [13-cm.] tortillas

2 cups	corn flour	½ liter
1⅓ cups	tepid water	325 ml.
1 tsp.	salt	5 ml.

Mix the ingredients to form a soft dough. Divide the dough into balls the size of small eggs and flatten them in a tortilla press, lined with two plastic bags or two sheets of plastic wrap or wax paper, to form thin, round cakes about 5 inches [13 cm.] across. If the tortillas stick to the plastic wrap or wax paper, the dough is too moist: Scrape it off, add a little more corn flour to the dough and begin again. It does not hurt the dough to handle it.

Place an ungreased *comal* over medium heat and cook the tortillas one at a time for about two minutes on each side, or until the edges brown lightly and begin to lift.

Tortillas can be kept warm for several hours in a preheated 150° F. [65° C.] oven. Have ready a cloth napkin wrung out in hot water. As you make the tortillas, wrap them first in paper towels and then in the napkin, and put them in the oven. When all of the tortillas are stacked up, dampen the napkin again, wrap the lot in aluminum foil and keep in the oven until needed.

ELISABETH LAMBERT ORTIZ
THE COMPLETE BOOK OF MEXICAN COOKING

Barley Flatbread

Ohrarieska

Pearl barley is whole barley with the husks removed. It is obtainable at health-food stores.

This is a thick, chewy bread with a subtly sour taste.

To make one 8-inch [20-cm.] square flatbread

¼ cup	barley flour	50 ml.
2 cups	pearl barley	½ liter
2½ cups	buttermilk	625 ml.
1	egg, lightly beaten	1
1½ tsp.	sea salt	7 ml.
1 tbsp.	oil or melted butter	15 ml.

Soak the barley flour and pearl barley in the buttermilk at room temperature for seven to eight hours or overnight.

Butter an 8-inch [20-cm.] square glass baking dish. Add the egg and salt to the barley-and-buttermilk mixture and blend well. Pour the batter into the baking dish and bake it in a preheated 350° F. [180° C.] oven for 30 minutes, then brush the top of the flatbread with oil or butter. Continue baking the bread for 30 minutes to one hour, or until the top and sides are brown and crisp. Serve warm or cold.

ULLA KÄKÖNEN
NATURAL COOKING THE FINNISH WAY

Philpy

This is a traditional rice bread from Charleston, South Carolina. Rice was introduced into North America when Captain John Thurber brought a bag of rice from Madagascar to Charleston in 1680.

To make one 10-inch [25-cm.] flatbread

1 cup	cornmeal	¼ liter
1 cup	raw unprocessed rice, boiled in 2 cups [½ liter] water and cooled	¼ liter
1 cup	milk	¼ liter
2	eggs, beaten	2
1 tbsp.	butter, melted	15 ml.
½ tsp.	salt	2 ml.

Mix the rice with the milk, cornmeal, eggs, butter and salt. Beat well and pour into a well-buttered 10-inch [25-cm.] pie-pan. The mixture should be thin. Bake in a preheated 375° F. [190° C.] oven until nicely browned—about 30 minutes. Break in pieces and serve with butter.

HELEN BROWN
HELEN BROWN'S WEST COAST COOK BOOK

Popovers

There are two methods of baking popovers, both satisfactory, although the hot-oven method turns out a popover with a firmer inside.

To make 8 medium-sized popovers

1 cup	sifted flour	¼ liter
1 cup	milk	¼ liter
1 tbsp.	butter, melted	15 ml.
½ tsp.	salt	2 ml.
2	eggs	2

To make popovers using the hot-oven method, preheat the oven to 425° F. [220° C.]. Grease the cups of a popover pan generously and set the pan aside. (If using glass or earthenware cups, preheat them in the hot oven before greasing them. Remove and grease the cups just before filling them.) With a rotary beater, wire whip or fork, beat together just until smooth the milk, butter, flour and salt. Beat in the eggs, one at a time, but do not overbeat. Ladle the batter into the cups. Bake in the preheated oven, without peeking, for 30 minutes. Then reduce the heat to 350° F. [180° C.] and continue baking for 5 to 10 minutes, or until the popovers are firm, puffy and well browned. Serve them immediately.

To make the popovers by the cold-oven method, mix the batter as directed above. Fill the greased baking cups less than two thirds full. Place them in a cold oven and set the heat at 425° F. Bake, without peeking, for about 30 to 35 minutes, or until the popovers are firm, puffy and well browned. If the popovers brown too quickly, reduce the heat to 375° F. [190° C.] for the last 10 or 15 minutes.

NIKA HAZELTON
AMERICAN HOME COOKING

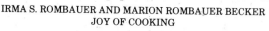

Dierdre's Favorite Walnut Popovers

To make about 12 popovers

2 cups	sifted flour	½ liter
3	eggs	3
2 cups	milk	½ liter
1 tsp.	grated lemon peel	5 ml.
½ tsp.	salt	2 ml.
⅓ cup	chopped walnuts	75 ml.
	cold butter pieces, jam or warmed maple syrup	

Beat the eggs with a rotary beater or wire whisk until thick and lemon-colored. Add the milk. To the flour add the lemon peel, salt and nuts. Add all at once to the egg-milk mixture, beating briskly until the batter is smooth. Have buttered, sizzling-hot popover molds or muffin pans or ovenproof-glass

custard cups ready. Fill the cups half-full. Bake in a preheated 425° F. [220° C.] oven for 20 minutes until the popovers have "popped"; reduce the heat to 350° F. [180° C.] and bake until the tops are firm and golden brown. Turn off the heat. Prick the side of each popover with the tines of a fork, or make a slit with a knife tip, to let steam escape. Return the popovers to the oven for five to 10 minutes. Insert into the slits pieces of cold butter or a little jam or warm maple syrup.

TED AND JEAN KAUFMAN
THE COMPLETE BREAD COOKBOOK

Cheese Popovers

To make about 9 popovers

1 cup	flour	¼ liter
1 cup	milk	¼ liter
1 tbsp.	butter, melted	15 ml.
¼ tsp.	salt	1 ml.
2	eggs, beaten	2
⅛ tsp.	paprika	½ ml.
	cayenne pepper	
½ cup	grated sharp Cheddar or Parmesan cheese	125 ml.

Beat the milk, butter, flour and salt together, just until smooth. Add the eggs, one at a time, but do not overbeat; the batter should be no heavier than whipping cream. Add the paprika and a few grains of cayenne pepper to the grated cheese. Butter the cups of deep muffin or popover pans; dust them with grated cheese. Pour a scant tablespoon of batter into each cup and cover it with a few teaspoons of cheese, then add another tablespoon of batter. Bake at once in a preheated 450° F. [230° C.] oven for 15 minutes, then reduce the heat—without peeping—to 350° F. [180° C.] and bake for about 20 minutes longer.

To test for doneness, remove a popover to be sure the side walls are firm. If not cooked long enough, the popover will collapse. After baking, you may want to insert a sharp paring knife gently into the popovers to let the steam escape.

IRMA S. ROMBAUER AND MARION ROMBAUER BECKER
JOY OF COOKING

Mrs. Macnab's Scones

Mrs. Macnab was the wife of a farmer who lived near Ballater in the Grampian highlands. Such was her reputation as a baker that King Frederick of Prussia and other distinguished guests at Balmoral used frequently to go over and have tea with her. It is not possible to impart Mrs. Macnab's lightness of touch, but here, at least, is the recipe for her celebrated scones. The secret of success lies in not overworking the dough.

To make 15 to 20 scones

4 cups	flour	1 liter
1 tsp.	baking soda	5 ml.
2 tsp.	cream of tartar	10 ml.
1 tsp.	salt	5 ml.
4 tbsp.	butter, softened and cut into pieces	60 ml.
1	egg, beaten	1
1¼ cups	buttermilk	300 ml.

In a bowl, mix thoroughly the flour, baking soda, cream of tartar and salt. Rub in the butter. Gradually stir in the egg and buttermilk. Turn out the dough onto a floured board, flour the top, and knead very briefly with your hand. Cut off pieces of dough about the size of eggs and flatten them with your knuckles (to a thickness of about ½ inch [1 cm.]), but do not roll them out at all. Prick each scone with a fork and mark it into quarters. Butter and flour a baking sheet and place the scones on it. Bake in a preheated 400° F. [200° C.] oven for 10 to 15 minutes, or until lightly browned.

F. MARIAN MC NEILL
THE SCOTS KITCHEN

———————◆———————

Vanilla-Cream Bread

A delicately flavored bread good to serve with your favorite homemade jam.

To make one 9-by-5-inch [23-by-13-cm.] loaf

2½ cups	flour, sifted with 2½ tsp. [12 ml.] baking powder	625 ml.
2	large eggs, the yolks separated from the whites	2
⅔ cup	heavy cream	150 ml.
2 tbsp.	sugar	30 ml.
½ tsp.	vanilla extract	2 ml.
⅔ cup	milk	150 ml.
¼ tsp.	salt	1 ml.

In a large bowl, beat the egg yolks with the cream, sugar, vanilla extract and milk. Beat the egg whites until very stiff. Sift the flour and salt into the egg-yolk mixture, add the beaten egg whites and carefully fold all of the ingredients together until evenly mixed. Spoon the mixture into a buttered 9-by-5-inch [23-by-13-cm.] loaf pan. Bake on the upper shelf of a preheated 375° F. [190° C.] oven for 40 minutes, or until the loaf is well risen and firm to the touch. Serve hot.

LORNA WALKER AND JOYCE HUGHES
THE COMPLETE BREAD BOOK

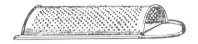

Cheesy Bread

To make 10 rolls

2 cups	flour	½ liter
1 tbsp.	baking powder	15 ml.
1 tsp.	salt	5 ml.
1 cup	finely shredded Cheddar cheese	¼ liter
1	medium-sized potato, boiled, peeled, mashed and pressed through a sieve (about ½ cup [125 ml.])	1
about ½ cup	milk	about 125 ml.

Sift together the flour, baking powder and salt, making sure there are no lumps remaining, particularly of baking powder. Gradually add the cheese and potato, blending the mixture quickly with your finger tips. Gradually add enough milk to make a soft, dry dough; shape it into 10 small balls, handling the dough as little as possible. Place the balls on a floured baking sheet and bake them in a preheated 450° F. [220° C.] oven for 10 to 15 minutes, or until they are golden brown. Eat them while they are still warm.

ANN PASCOE
CORNISH RECIPES OLD AND NEW

———————◆———————

Sage Biscuits Chicoutimi

These biscuits are named for the steamship *Chicoutimi*, famed for her trips up the Saguenay River in Canada.

To make about 16 biscuits

2 cups	flour	½ liter
1 tsp.	baking powder	5 ml.
½ cup	oil	125 ml.
⅔ cup	milk	150 ml.
¼ cup	chopped fresh sage leaves	50 ml.
1 tsp.	salt	5 ml.

Sift the flour into a bowl and add the baking powder, oil, milk and sage. Stir with a wooden spoon and add the salt. Blend until smooth. Drop the batter by spoonfuls onto a greased baking sheet. Bake in a preheated 475° F. [250° C.] oven for 10 to 12 minutes.

FRANCES D. & PETER J. ROBOTTI
FRENCH COOKING IN THE NEW WORLD

Sweet Potato Biscuits

To make about 12 biscuits

2 cups	sifted flour	½ liter
4 tsp.	baking powder	20 ml.
1 tsp.	salt	5 ml.
10 tbsp.	shortening	150 ml.
1	medium-sized sweet potato, boiled, peeled and mashed (about 1 cup [¼ liter])	1
about 3 tbsp.	milk	about 45 ml.

Sift the flour, baking powder and salt, cut in the shortening and blend in the sweet potatoes. Add enough milk to make a soft dough. Knead lightly. On a lightly floured board, roll out the dough to about ¾ inch [2 cm.] thick. Cut the dough into squares, or into rounds with a biscuit cutter. Bake the biscuits on an ungreased baking sheet in a preheated 400° F. [200° C.] oven for 15 to 20 minutes.

JUNIOR LEAGUE OF JACKSON, MISSISSIPPI
SOUTHERN SIDEBOARDS

Stuffed Parathas

To make about 10 parathas

2½ cups	whole-wheat flour	625 ml.
½ tsp.	salt	2 ml.
¾ cup	water	175 ml.
6 tbsp.	*ghee*	90 ml.
	Potato stuffing	
2	large potatoes	2
1 tbsp.	*ghee*	15 ml.
1	small onion, finely chopped	1
2 tbsp.	chopped fresh coriander	30 ml.
½-inch	slice fresh ginger root, peeled and finely chopped	1-cm.
1½ tsp.	salt	7 ml.
1 tsp.	*garam masala*	5 ml.
½ tsp.	cayenne pepper (optional)	2 ml.
1 tbsp.	puréed mango pulp or 2 tsp. [10 ml.] fresh lemon juice	15 ml.

Put 2 cups [½ liter] of the flour into a bowl with the salt and gradually add the water to make a soft dough. Pound and knead by hand for several minutes: The more the dough is kneaded, the lighter the bread will be. Let the dough rest for at least one hour, then knead it once again and, if necessary, sprinkle a little more water on it.

Warm the *ghee* and have it by you. Divide the dough into 10 pieces, shape each into a ball and, with a little of the reserved flour sprinkled on the work surface, roll out the dough into a round about ¼ inch [6 mm.] thick. Using a spoon, spread some of the warm *ghee* on the round, then fold it over and spread a little more *ghee* on the top. Repeat the rolling, spreading and folding processes two or three times, and then roll out the *paratha* to make a fairly thin round. Repeat with the rest of the dough.

To make the potato stuffing, boil the potatoes in their jackets; when cool, peel and mash them. Heat the *ghee* in a frying pan and fry the onion, coriander and ginger gently for a few minutes. Add the salt, *garam masala*, cayenne pepper if using, and the mango pulp or lemon juice. Mix in the mashed potatoes and let the mixture sizzle for two to three minutes. Remove it from the heat and let it cool.

Spread warm *ghee* on each *paratha* and place a tablespoon [15 ml.] or more of the stuffing in the center. Fold the *paratha* over the stuffing to enclose it. Using some of the remaining flour, roll out the *paratha* as thin and as round as you can.

Grease a griddle or heavy frying pan well with butter or extra *ghee,* heat to medium hot and put a *paratha* on it. When one side is partially cooked—about five minutes— turn the *paratha* over and spread *ghee* liberally on it; do the same to the other side. When ready, the *parathas* should be golden brown and well soaked with *ghee*. They should be served piping hot.

SAVITRI CHOWDHARY
INDIAN COOKING

Apple Breakfast Rolls

To make about 18 rolls

2 cups	flour	½ liter
½ tsp.	baking soda	2 ml.
1 tsp.	cream of tartar	5 ml.
1 cup	milk	¼ liter
½ cup	sugar	125 ml.
1½ cups	finely diced apples	375 ml.
	lard	

Make a batter of the flour mixed with the cream of tartar, the baking soda, milk and sugar. Put in the diced apples last. Grease the cups of muffin pans with lard, place a dab of lard in the bottom of each well, and get the pans sizzling hot on top of the stove. Fill the cups two thirds full with batter, and let them stand for a good minute; then put the pans into a preheated 400° to 425° F. [200° to 220° C.] oven and bake quickly, about 10 minutes.

HELEN LYON ADAMSON
GRANDMOTHER IN THE KITCHEN

Spiced Apple Bread

Guernsey Gâche Melée

This traditional bread from Guernsey in the Channel Islands is partially leavened by the malic acid in the apples.

To make one 12-by-8-inch [30-by-20-cm.] bread

4 cups	whole-wheat flour	1 liter
3	medium-sized cooking apples, peeled, cored and chopped into small pieces	3
16 tbsp.	butter (½ lb. [¼ kg.]), softened	240 ml.
2⅔ cups	dark brown sugar	650 ml.
1 tsp.	ground cinnamon	5 ml.
2 tsp.	grated nutmeg	10 ml.
3	eggs, beaten	3

Mix the flour and apples thoroughly, and let them stand in a warm place for three hours. Cream the butter with the sugar and add the cinnamon and grated nutmeg. Mix all of the ingredients together, add the eggs and mix again thoroughly. Transfer the mixture to a greased 12-by-8-inch [30-by-20-cm.] baking pan and bake in a preheated 325° F. [160° C.] oven for one and one half hours, or until a knife dipped into the bread comes out clean.

J. STEVENS COX (EDITOR)
GUERNSEY DISHES OF BYGONE DAYS

Apricot Bread

To make one 8½-by-4½-inch [21-by-11-cm.] loaf

2 cups	sifted flour	½ liter
2 tsp.	baking powder	10 ml.
¼ tsp.	baking soda	1 ml.
2 cups	dried apricots	½ liter
1 cup	sugar	¼ liter
2 tbsp.	butter, softened	30 ml.
1	egg	1
¼ cup	water	50 ml.
½ cup	fresh orange juice	125 ml.
1 tsp.	salt	5 ml.
⅓ to ⅔ cup	raisins, soaked in hot water for 15 minutes and drained	75 to 150 ml.

Soak the apricots in warm water to cover for 30 minutes. Drain, and cut the apricots into strips. Cream the sugar and butter. Add the egg, water and orange juice to the creamed mixture. Sift together the flour, baking powder, soda and salt; add them gradually. Stir in the apricots and raisins. Pour the batter into a well-greased 8½-by-4½-inch [21-by-11-cm.] loaf pan. Bake the bread in a preheated 350° F. [180° C.] oven for one and one quarter hours, or until a skewer inserted into the loaf comes out clean.

THE JUNIOR LEAGUE OF GREENVILLE, INC.
300 YEARS OF CAROLINA COOKING

Carrot-Apricot Steamed Bread

To make two 5-inch [13-cm.] cylindrical loaves

2 cups	all-purpose flour	½ liter
1 cup	whole-wheat flour, preferably stone-ground	¼ liter
2 tsp.	baking powder	10 ml.
1 tsp.	salt	5 ml.
2	eggs	2
⅔ cup	honey	150 ml.
1⅓ cups	milk	325 ml.
4 tbsp.	unsalted butter, melted	60 ml.
1 tsp.	grated orange peel	5 ml.
1 cup	grated raw carrots	¼ liter
1 cup	chopped dried apricots	¼ liter

Sift together the all-purpose flour, baking powder and salt. Add the whole-wheat flour and mix well with a fork.

In a large bowl beat the eggs until they are light and thick. Add the honey, milk, butter and grated orange peel, beating to mix. Stir in the grated carrots and chopped apricots. Add the flour mixture, and blend thoroughly but gently with a rubber spatula or wooden spoon.

Divide the batter between two buttered 1-pound coffee cans. Cover the tops with foil, and secure it tightly around the cans with string or tape. Place the cans on a trivet or cake rack in a large pot of boiling water, which should reach halfway up the cans. Cover the pot tightly and let the water simmer (not boil) for three hours. Remove the cans from the water and carefully remove their covers. Place the cans in a preheated 300° F. [150° C.] oven for about 10 minutes to dry out the bread slightly. Then let the cans sit on a rack for five minutes or so before sliding the loaves out. Let them finish cooling on the rack if you are not serving immediately.

ELLEN FOSCUE JOHNSON
THE GARDEN WAY BREAD BOOK

Pineapple Muffins

To make about 20 muffins

1⅓ cups	flour	325 ml.
2 tsp.	baking soda	10 ml.
½ cup	sugar	125 ml.
⅓ cup	vegetable shortening	75 ml.
⅓ cup	honey	75 ml.
2	eggs	2
1⅓ cups	bran cereal	325 ml.
½ tsp.	salt	2 ml.
1 cup	half-and-half cream	¼ liter
1 cup	canned crushed pineapple, well drained	¼ liter

Cream the sugar, shortening and honey together, then add the other ingredients and mix lightly. Fill greased muffin-pan cups two thirds full. Bake for 25 minutes in a preheated 350° F. [180° C.] oven. (Or cover the pans with wax paper and refrigerate them overnight to bake up fresh in the morning.)

WILF AND LOIS COPPING
THE COUNTRY INNKEEPERS' COOKBOOK

Griddlecake

Cacen Gri

To make one 8-inch [20-cm.] cake

2 cups	flour	½ liter
½ tsp.	baking soda	2 ml.
¼ tsp.	salt	1 ml.
8 tbsp.	butter	120 ml.
¼ cup	sugar	50 ml.
⅓ cup	dried currants, soaked in hot water for 15 minutes and drained	75 ml.
1	egg, well beaten	1
½ cup	buttermilk or milk	125 ml.

Put the flour into a bowl with the salt. Rub in the butter. Add the sugar and currants, and mix thoroughly. Make a well in the center of the mixture. Dissolve the baking soda in the milk and pour it into the well. Then add the egg. Blend and knead the mixture to a soft dough. Turn the dough out onto a floured board, shape it into a ball, and flatten it to form a round cake about ½ inch [1 cm.] thick. Bake the cake on a lightly greased griddle or heavy skillet over medium heat until browned, about 10 minutes on each side. Halve the cake horizontally while still warm and spread it with butter.

S. MINWEL TIBBOTT
WELSH FARE

Raspberry Buns

To make 8 to 10 buns

1 cup	all-purpose flour	¼ liter
¾ cup	rice flour	175 ml.
½ tsp.	baking powder	2 ml.
	salt	
4 tbsp.	butter	60 ml.
¼ cup	sugar	50 ml.
¼ cup	tepid milk	50 ml.
1	large egg, beaten	1
8 to 10 tsp.	raspberry jam	40 to 50 ml.

Mix the flours, salt and baking powder together. Rub in the butter, and then work in the sugar. Add the milk to the egg and incorporate them into the dry ingredients.

Form the mixture into eight to 10 balls and place them on a buttered baking sheet. Make a well in each ball with your finger and put 1 teaspoon [5 ml.] of raspberry jam into he well. Fold the dough over the well to seal it, and bake the buns in a preheated 400° F. [200° C.] oven for 15 to 20 minutes, or until golden brown. Let cool on a wire rack.

ABERDEEN SCHOOL OF DOMESTIC SCIENCE
PLAIN COOKERY RECIPES

Boston Brown Bread

You may freeze this bread, tightly wrapped, and reheat it in foil for about 20 minutes in a preheated 350° F. [180° C.] oven, or slice it and toast it. Delicious with cream and jam.

To make two 6-inch [15-cm.] cylindrical loaves

1½ cups	rye flour	375 ml.
1½ cups	water-ground cornmeal	375 ml.
1 tsp.	baking soda	5 ml.
½ tsp.	salt	2 ml.
2 cups	milk	½ liter
1	egg, well beaten	1
½ cup	dark molasses, warmed	125 ml.
1 cup	raisins, soaked in hot water for 15 minutes and drained (optional)	¼ liter

Sift the cornmeal, rye flour, baking soda and salt together. Stir the milk and egg into the molasses. Combine all of the ingredients and mix them well. Add the raisins, if using.

Butter two 1½-quart [1½-liter] molds, or use 1-pound coffee cans. Make tight lids for them out of foil, which you can tie on securely so that no steam escapes. Pour the batter into the molds, filling them not more than three quarters full to allow for rising. Cover them tightly.

Pour water into a Dutch oven or large kettle to a depth of 1 inch [2½ cm.]. Cover the Dutch oven or kettle tightly and bring the water to a boil. Place the molds in the water and re-cover the pan tightly. Steam the bread for three hours; check occasionally to be sure that the water does not boil away, and add enough water to maintain the 1-inch level in the pan.

To serve the bread, let the covered molds stand on a rack for about five minutes to let the steam subside. Then remove the covers and upend the molds onto a plate. Cut the bread into ¾-inch [2-cm.] slices while it is still hot. Slice only as much as you will need for a meal and serve with butter.

JANE MOSS SNOW
A FAMILY HARVEST

French Spice Bread

Pain d'Épice

To make one 14-by-11-inch [35-by-28-cm.] rectangular flatbread or two 7-inch [18-cm.] round breads

4 cups	rye flour, or substitute bread flour	1 liter
2 tsp.	baking powder	10 ml.
1 tsp.	baking soda	5 ml.
1¼ cups	honey	300 ml.
7 tbsp.	superfine sugar	105 ml.
½ cup	almonds, blanched and chopped	125 ml.
½ cup	chopped mixed candied fruit peel	125 ml.
1 tsp.	anise seeds	5 ml.
⅛ tsp.	ground cinnamon	½ ml.
⅛ tsp.	ground cloves	½ ml.
1½ tsp.	grated lemon or orange peel (optional)	7 ml.
¼ cup	milk	50 ml.
2 tbsp.	sugar	30 ml.

Heat the honey to the boiling point; skim the froth from the surface, remove the honey from the heat and cool to tepid. Sift the flour into a bowl, make a well in the center and pour in the honey. Mix with a wooden spoon until a firm paste is obtained. It may be necessary to add additional flour, as some flours are more absorbent than others. Shape the paste into a ball, wrap it in a cloth and let it rest for one hour. Then knead in the superfine sugar, baking powder, baking soda, chopped almonds and candied peel. Knead in the anise seeds, cinnamon, ground cloves and grated peel, if using. Knead the dough vigorously for about 10 minutes to give it body.

Roll out the dough into a 14-by-11-inch [35-by-28-cm.] rectangle and place it on a buttered jelly-roll pan or divide it between two buttered 7-inch [18-cm.] cake pans. Bake the spice bread in a preheated 350° F. [180° C.] oven for one hour. As soon as the bread is cooked, brush the surface quickly with the milk sweetened with the sugar and heated to a syrup-like consistency, and return the bread to the oven for a few seconds to set the glaze. Cool the bread before serving.

PROSPER MONTAGNÉ
THE NEW LAROUSSE GASTRONOMIQUE

Cinnamon Muffins

To make 12 muffins

1½ cups	sifted flour	375 ml.
2¼ tsp.	baking powder	11 ml.
⅓ cup	sugar	75 ml.
½ tsp.	grated nutmeg	2 ml.
¼ tsp.	salt	1 ml.
1	extra-large egg	1
½ cup	milk	125 ml.
4 tbsp.	butter, melted and cooled to tepid	60 ml.
Cinnamon topping		
5 tbsp.	butter, melted	75 ml.
1 tsp.	ground cinnamon, mixed with ⅓ cup [75 ml.] sugar	5 ml.

Sift together onto a piece of wax paper the flour, baking powder, sugar, nutmeg and salt; carefully pick up the paper and return the dry ingredients to the sifter. Sift them into a mixing bowl. The second sifting is to ensure complete mixing of the dry ingredients. Break the egg into a small bowl and beat it with a wire whisk or fork until the white and yolk are thoroughly combined. Stir the milk and then the butter into the beaten egg.

Make a small well in the center of the dry ingredients and pour the liquid ingredients into the well. With the mixing spoon, stir only enough to dampen all of the dry ingredients. The batter should be lumpy. Carefully spoon the batter into the well-buttered cups of a muffin pan, filling each cup two thirds full of batter. Fill empty cups in the muffin pan with water to maintain even heating throughout the pan. Bake the muffins in a preheated 425° F. [220° C.] oven for about 12 minutes, or until golden brown.

When the muffins have cooled for three or four minutes, remove them from the pan to a rack. Dip the top of each muffin first in the melted butter and then in the cinnamon-sugar mixture. These muffins are best served warm.

KATHLEEN THORNE-THOMSEN AND LINDA BROWNRIDGE
WHY THE CAKE WON'T RISE AND THE JELLY WON'T SET

Spanish Nut Bread

Pan de Nueces

To make one 7 ½-by-3 ½-inch [19-by-9-cm.] loaf

2¼ cups	flour	550 ml.
1 tsp.	baking powder	5 ml.
1½ tbsp.	butter, softened	22 ml.
1	egg, beaten	1
¾ cup	sugar	175 ml.
1 cup	milk	¼ liter
⅔ cup	raisins, soaked in hot water for 15 minutes and drained	150 ml.
1 cup	coarsely chopped walnuts	¼ liter

In a bowl, beat together the butter, egg and sugar until creamy. Add half the flour alternately with the milk, then the raisins and nuts, and finally the remaining flour and the baking powder. Turn out the dough onto a floured work surface and knead lightly with your fingers for 10 minutes. Butter and flour a 7½-by-3½-inch [19-by-9-cm.] pan. Put in the dough and let it rise in a warm place for 30 minutes.

Bake the loaf in a preheated 325° F. [170° C.] oven for one hour, or until a skewer inserted into the loaf comes out clean. If the bread browns too quickly, cover the top with wax paper to prevent burning. The flavor will be improved if the loaf is wrapped, after cooling, in a clean cloth or aluminum foil and left in a cool, dry place for 24 hours.

SIMONE ORTEGA
MIL OCHENTA RECETAS DE COCINA

Grandmother's Corn Pone

In parts of the South these fried pones were referred to as hoecakes because they were fried over open fires on hoes. Settlers who came from the North might have called them "johnnycakes," probably derived from journey cakes.

To make about five 3-inch [8-cm.] cakes

1 cup	cornmeal	¼ liter
1 tsp.	salt	5 ml.
1 cup	boiling water	¼ liter
4 tbsp.	rendered bacon fat	60 ml.

Mix together the salt and the cornmeal. Pour the water over them and stir well. Immediately wet your hands in cool water and form the mixture into rounds about 3 inches [8 cm.] across. Melt the bacon fat in a frying pan over medium heat, and fry the rounds until they are golden brown on each side.

LINDA KENNEDY ROSSER (EDITOR)
PIONEER COOKERY AROUND OKLAHOMA

Scalded-Meal Jonny Cakes

The author of this recipe and the one below uses the 18th Century spelling for johnnycake.

To make about 18 small cakes

1½ cups	white water-ground cornmeal	375 ml.
about 10 tbsp.	butter, 1 tbsp. [15 ml.] softened, the rest cut into thick slices	about 150 ml.
1 tsp.	salt	5 ml.
1 tsp.	molasses	5 ml.
about 1½ cups	boiling water	about 375 ml.
	milk	

Place the cornmeal, softened butter, salt and molasses in a bowl and pour over these enough boiling water to make a stiff dough. Beat thoroughly and let stand for a few minutes while the mixture thickens. Thin down the dough with milk to a consistency that will readily drop off the end of a spoon.

Drop the dough by the tablespoonful onto a well-greased hot griddle. Cook over low heat for 10 to 15 minutes, turning once to brown both sides lightly.

Split the hot jonny cake in half and place a slice of butter between the halves. When the butter has melted, serve.

CEIL DYER
THE NEWPORT COOKBOOK

Milk Jonny Cakes

To make 12 to 14 small cakes

1 cup	white water-ground cornmeal	¼ liter
1 tsp.	sugar	5 ml.
½ tsp.	salt	2 ml.
about 1¾ cups	milk	about 425 ml.
	rendered bacon fat	

Put the cornmeal, sugar and salt in a bowl. Add the milk and mix thoroughly.

Bake on a hot griddle greased with bacon fat, as you would bake griddlecakes. Since the meal continues swelling for some time, add more milk to the batter as necessary to keep the mixture at the proper thin consistency.

CEIL DYER
THE NEWPORT COOKBOOK

Dodgers, Dabs or Cornmeal Puffs

To make about 12 puffs

2 cups	cornmeal	½ liter
⅓ cup	boiling water	75 ml.
1 tsp.	butter, softened	5 ml.
1 tsp.	sugar	5 ml.
½ tsp.	salt	2 ml.
2 or 3 tbsp.	milk	30 or 45 ml.
2	eggs, the yolks separated from the whites, the yolks beaten, and the whites stiffly whipped	2

Scald the cornmeal with the boiling water so that the meal is all wet but not soft. Add the butter, sugar, salt and milk. When the mixture is cold, add the beaten egg yolks and fold in the whites. The batter should drop easily from the spoon—not thin enough to be poured, nor stiff enough to be scraped out.

Have your muffin pans well buttered and hissing hot. Drop heaping spoonfuls of the batter into each compartment of the pans, dividing the batter evenly among the compartments, and bake in a preheated 400° F. [200° C.] oven for about 20 minutes, or until brown and puffy.

MRS. MARY J. LINCOLN
MRS. LINCOLN'S BOSTON COOKBOOK

Spider Corncake

A spider is an 18th Century cast-iron frying pan with long legs that hold the pan above the coals in a hearth.

To make one 9-inch [23-cm.] bread

1½ cups	yellow cornmeal	375 ml.
½ cup	flour	125 ml.
1 tsp.	baking soda	5 ml.
1 cup	buttermilk	¼ liter
2 cups	milk	½ liter
2 tsp.	sugar	10 ml.
½ tsp.	salt	2 ml.
2 tbsp.	rendered bacon fat or butter	30 ml.

Combine the cornmeal, flour and baking soda in a mixing bowl. Add the buttermilk, half of the milk, the sugar and the

salt. Stir well. Meanwhile, put the bacon fat or butter in a 9-inch [23-cm.] cast-iron skillet or heavy baking dish, and place the vessel in an oven preheated to 350° F. [180° C.]. When the skillet or baking dish is thoroughly hot, remove it from the oven and pour in the cornmeal batter. Carefully pour the remaining milk over the top of the batter. Bake for 50 minutes, or until the cake is firm and the top is golden.

JEAN HEWITT
THE NEW YORK TIMES NEW ENGLAND HERITAGE COOKBOOK

Skillet Corn Bread and Corn Sticks

The technique of preparing corn sticks appears on page 88.

To make one 9-inch [23-cm.] round loaf or fourteen 5½-inch [14-cm.] sticks

1½ cups	cornmeal, preferably white water-ground	375 ml.
½ cup	flour	125 ml.
1 tbsp.	baking powder	15 ml.
1 tsp.	salt	5 ml.
2	eggs	2
1½ cups	buttermilk	375 ml.

Combine the cornmeal, flour, baking powder and salt, and sift them into a deep bowl. In a separate bowl, beat the eggs lightly with a wire whisk or fork, then add the buttermilk and mix well. Pour the liquid ingredients over the dry ones and, with a wooden spoon, stir them together until the batter is smooth; do not overbeat.

To make corn bread, place a heavy 9-inch [23-cm.] skillet with an ovenproof handle over high heat for about two minutes, or until the skillet is very hot. Remove the skillet from the heat and, with a pastry brush, quickly coat the bottom and sides with melted butter. Immediately pour in the batter, spreading it even and smoothing the top with a rubber spatula. Bake in a preheated 350° F. [180° C.] oven for 30 to 35 minutes, or until the corn bread begins to draw away from the edges of the skillet and the top is a rich golden brown.

To serve, run a knife around the edges of the skillet to loosen the sides of the bread. Place a warmed platter upside down over the skillet and, grasping platter and skillet together, invert them. Rap the platter sharply on a table and the bread should slide easily out of the skillet. Cut the bread into wedge-shaped pieces and serve at once.

To make corn sticks, brush the inside surfaces of the molds in a corn-stick pan with melted butter. Spoon the batter into the molds, dividing it evenly among them. Bake in a preheated 350° F. [180° C.] oven for 25 to 30 minutes, or until the corn sticks are golden brown. Turn the corn sticks out of the pan, arrange on a warmed platter and serve at once.

FOODS OF THE WORLD/AMERICAN COOKING: SOUTHERN STYLE

Josephine's Batter Bread

To make one 6- to 7-inch [15- to 18-cm.]
round bread

1 cup	cornmeal, sifted	¼ liter
1 tsp.	baking powder	5 ml.
1 tsp.	sugar	5 ml.
2 cups	milk	½ liter
3	eggs	3
4 tbsp.	butter	60 ml.

Mix the dry ingredients; beat the milk and eggs together and add them. In a deep 1-quart [1-liter] baking dish, melt the butter and swish it around in the dish so that the sides will be evenly coated. Pour the batter into the baking dish. Bake for about 30 minutes in a preheated 350° F. [180° C.] oven, or until a knife comes out clean from the center of the bread. Do not let it become too dry. Serve the bread with butter.

MARION BROWN
THE SOUTHERN COOK BOOK

Carrot Corn Bread

To make one 9- to 10-inch
[23- to 25-cm.] round loaf

1 cup	cornmeal, preferably stone-ground	¼ liter
1 cup	all-purpose flour	¼ liter
2 tsp.	baking powder	10 ml.
½ tsp.	salt	2 ml.
2	eggs	2
2 tbsp.	honey	30 ml.
2 tbsp.	unsalted butter, melted	30 ml.
1 cup	half-and-half cream or light cream	¼ liter
1½ cups	shredded or grated carrots	375 ml.

Sift together the flour, baking powder and salt; mix in the cornmeal with a fork. Beat the eggs until they are light and slightly thickened. Add the honey and beat; beat in the melted butter and the cream. Stir in the carrots. Add the flour-cornmeal mixture and blend lightly but thoroughly. Butter a 9- to 10-inch [23- to 25-cm.] heavy skillet and heat it briefly in a preheated 375° F. [190° C.] oven. Pour the batter into the skillet and bake the bread for about 30 minutes, or until the center is firm.

ELLEN FOSCUE JOHNSON
THE GARDEN WAY BREAD BOOK

Cornmeal Apple Pone

To make one 8-inch [20-cm.]
square bread

1 cup	cornmeal	¼ liter
2 tsp.	baking powder	10 ml.
1 cup	boiling water	¼ liter
1	egg, beaten	1
1 tsp.	sugar	5 ml.
1	medium-sized apple, peeled, cored and chopped	1
1 tbsp.	butter, melted	15 ml.
½ tsp.	salt	2 ml.
	heavy cream, warmed maple syrup, or confectioners' sugar	

Place the cornmeal in a bowl and scald it with the boiling water. Stir until smooth, then let cool. When cold, add the beaten egg and beat vigorously for five minutes. Stir in the sugar, chopped apple, butter, salt and baking powder. Mix well. Bake in a well-buttered, shallow, 8-inch [20-cm.] square baking pan in a preheated 350° F. [180° C.] oven for 25 to 30 minutes, or until the top is golden brown. Serve the pone warm. Pass a pitcher of heavy cream or warm syrup, or sift a soft cloud of confectioners' sugar over the pone.

TED AND JEAN KAUFMAN
THE COMPLETE BREAD COOKBOOK

Maple Corn Bread

To make one 9-inch [23-cm.] square bread

⅔ cup	cornmeal	150 ml.
1⅓ cups	flour	325 ml.
1 tbsp.	baking powder	15 ml.
½ tsp.	salt	2 ml.
⅓ cup	maple syrup	75 ml.
8 tbsp.	shortening, melted and cooled	120 ml.
2	eggs, beaten	2

Sift together the cornmeal, flour, baking powder and salt. Add the syrup, shortening and eggs. Stir until well mixed, but do not beat. Turn the batter into a greased 9-inch [23-cm.] square cake pan and bake in a preheated 425° F. [220° C.] oven for 25 minutes.

SARA B. B. STAMM
YANKEE MAGAZINE'S FAVORITE NEW ENGLAND RECIPES

Italian Sweet Corn Bread

Pizza di Polenta

If citron is not available, use chopped candied fruit peel.

To make one 10-by-8-inch
[25-by-20-cm.] bread

3½ cups	cornmeal	875 ml.
½ cup	flour	125 ml.
4 tbsp.	butter, softened	60 ml.
⅓ cup	oil	75 ml.
2 tbsp.	sugar	30 ml.
	salt	
2 cups	hot water	½ liter
1¼ cups	seedless white raisins	300 ml.
½ cup	pine nuts	125 ml.
½ cup	chopped candied citron	125 ml.

Put the cornmeal and flour in a large mixing bowl, make a well in the center, and add the butter, oil, sugar and a pinch of salt. Mix all of the ingredients together and bind them with the water to form a batter the consistency of thick cream. Add the raisins, pine nuts and candied citron, and incorporate them well and evenly into the batter.

Butter and flour a 10-by-8-inch [25-by-20-cm.] baking pan. Gently pour the mixture into the pan and bake in a preheated 375° F. [190° C.] oven for about 30 minutes, until the edges are golden brown.

LUIGI VOLPICELLI AND SECONDINO FREDA (EDITORS)
L'ANTIARTUSI: 1000 RICETTE

Steamed Togus Loaf

To make one 6- or 7-inch
[15- or 18-cm.] round loaf

½ cup	flour, sifted	125 ml.
1½ cups	yellow cornmeal	375 ml.
½ tsp.	baking soda	2 ml.
1 tsp.	salt	5 ml.
¼ cup	molasses	50 ml.
1½ cups	milk	375 ml.
½ cup	sour milk	125 ml.

Combine the sifted flour with the baking soda and salt, and sift into a large bowl. Blend in the cornmeal. Mix the molas-

ses with the sweet milk and sour milk; stir into the cornmeal mixture. The batter will be thin. Grease a 1½-quart [1½-liter] mold. Pour the batter into the mold; if the mold does not have a lid, cover it with wax paper or aluminum foil and tie it down with string. Set the mold in a deep kettle, pour in boiling water to within 3 inches [8 cm.] of the rim of the mold, and boil gently for three hours. Add boiling water to the kettle from time to time to maintain the water level.

The top of the bread must be firm but not sticky before it is unmolded. Carefully unmold the loaf and serve it steaming hot with butter.

YVONNE YOUNG TARR
THE NEW YORK TIMES BREAD AND SOUP COOKBOOK

Green Chili and Cheese Corn Bread

To roast fresh chilies, place them under a broiler, or spear each chili with a fork and hold it over the flame of a gas burner. Turn the chilies so that the skin blisters and chars slightly but evenly. Wrap the chilies in a damp towel and leave them for 15 to 20 minutes before peeling them. The number of chilies used in the bread may be varied to taste, and canned or bottled jalapeño peppers may be used instead of fresh chilies.

To make one 10-inch [25-cm.] round bread

2 cups	whole-grain cornmeal	½ liter
1 tsp.	baking soda	5 ml.
3	eggs	3
2 cups	buttermilk, plain yogurt or sour cream	½ liter
⅓ cup	oil	75 ml.
1 tsp.	salt	5 ml.
4	long, green fresh chilies, roasted, peeled, halved, seeded and chopped	4
1 to 2 cups	grated sharp Cheddar cheese	¼ to ½ liter

Mix together the eggs, the buttermilk, yogurt or sour cream and the oil. Stir together the cornmeal, baking soda and salt, pressing out lumps; add to the egg mixture. Stir in the chopped chilies and all but ¼ cup [50 ml.] of the cheese.

Preheat the oven to 450° F. [230° C.]. Heat an oiled 10-inch [25-cm.] cast-iron skillet in the oven. Pour the batter into the hot skillet; top with the reserved grated cheese. Bake for 25 to 30 minutes, or until the bread is set and slightly brown on top. Cool the bread slightly before cutting it into wedges and serving it.

MARLENE ANNE BUMGARNER
THE BOOK OF WHOLE GRAINS

Doughnuts

The techniques for making doughnuts are demonstrated on pages 38-39.

Funnel Cakes

To make about twelve 6-inch [15-cm.] cakes

2 cups	flour	½ liter
1 tsp.	baking powder	5 ml.
	vegetable oil	
1 tbsp.	sugar	15 ml.
¼ tsp.	salt	1 ml.
2	eggs, lightly beaten	2
1 to 1¼ cups	milk	250 to 300 ml.
	molasses or maple syrup	

Preheat the oven to its lowest setting. Line two large baking sheets with paper towels and place them in the oven. Pour vegetable oil into a large, heavy skillet to a depth of about 1½ to 2 inches [4 to 5 cm.] and heat the oil until it is very hot but not smoking.

Meanwhile, combine the flour, baking powder, sugar and salt, and sift them together into a deep bowl. Make a well in the center, and pour in the eggs and 1 cup [¼ liter] of the milk. With a large spoon, gradually mix the dry ingredients into the liquid ones and stir until the batter is smooth.

To make the cakes, ladle ½ cup [125 ml.] of batter into a funnel with a tube ½ inch [1 cm.] in diameter, keeping the tip of the tube closed with your forefinger. Dribble the batter directly into the hot oil, using your finger to control the flow; move the funnel in a circle to build a snail-like coil of three or four rings about 6 inches [15 cm.] in diameter. Form two or three cakes and deep fry them for about two minutes on each side, turning them once with a slotted spatula. When the cakes are brown, arrange them side by side on the paper-lined sheets and keep them warm in the oven. Repeat the procedure four or five times, using ½ cup of batter for each batch. If the batter becomes stiff, add up to ¼ cup [50 ml.] more milk, a tablespoon [15 ml.] at a time.

Serve the cakes warm, with molasses or maple syrup.

FOODS OF THE WORLD/AMERICAN COOKING: THE EASTERN HEARTLAND

Golden Puffs

To make about 30 puffs

2½ cups	sifted flour	625 ml.
1 tbsp.	baking powder	15 ml.
¼ cup	sugar	50 ml.
1 tsp.	salt	5 ml.
1 tsp.	ground mace	5 ml.
¼ cup	corn oil	50 ml.
¾ cup	milk	175 ml.
1	egg, beaten	1
	oil or fat for deep frying	

Sift the flour, baking powder, sugar, salt and mace together; then add the oil, milk and beaten egg. Stir with a fork until thoroughly mixed. Drop by the teaspoonful [5 ml.] into deep hot oil or fat heated to 375° F. [190° C.]. Fry the puffs until golden brown—about three minutes. Drain on absorbent paper. Roll the warm puffs in sugar.

WILF AND LOIS COPPING
THE COUNTRY INNKEEPERS' COOKBOOK

French Doughnuts

To make ten to twelve 3-inch [8-cm.] doughnuts

1 cup	sifted flour	¼ liter
3 tbsp.	lard	45 ml.
¼ tsp.	salt	1 ml.
1 cup	hot water	¼ liter
3	eggs	3
	lard for deep-fat frying	

To the hot water, add the 3 tablespoons [45 ml.] of lard and the salt and bring to a boil. Add the flour all at once and stir vigorously until the mixture forms a ball. Cool until tepid. Add the eggs, one at a time, beating thoroughly after each addition. Chill the dough for one hour or longer. Pipe the dough through a pastry bag fitted with a No. 8 or 9 star or plain tube onto the edges of 3-inch [8-cm.] rounds of greased brown paper or parchment paper. Heat lard to 365° F. [185° C.] and lower the doughnuts, two or three at a time, into the lard with the paper sides up. Fry until brown on one side. Remove the paper rounds, turn and brown on the second side. Cool the doughnuts on a cake rack and sprinkle them with confectioners' sugar.

JEANNE M. HALL
500 MORE RECIPES BY REQUEST

Maple-frosted Doughnuts

To make 36 doughnuts

3 cups	sifted flour	¾ liter
¼ oz.	package active dry yeast	7½ g.
1 cup	milk	¼ liter
2 tbsp.	shortening	30 ml.
2 tbsp.	sugar	30 ml.
1 tsp.	salt	5 ml.
¼ cup	tepid water	50 ml.
1	egg	1
	oil	

Maple frosting

2 cups	sifted confectioners' sugar	½ liter
8 tbsp.	butter, softened	120 ml.
½ tsp.	maple flavoring	2 ml.
	hot water	

Scald the milk. Stir in the shortening, sugar and salt. Cool to tepid. Sprinkle the yeast onto the tepid water; stir to mix. Add the yeast, egg and 1 cup [¼ liter] of the flour to the milk mixture. Beat with an electric mixer at medium speed until smooth, about two minutes, scraping the bowl occasionally. Or beat with a spoon until the batter is smooth.

Gradually add the remaining flour, blending thoroughly. Cover the dough and let it rise in a warm place until doubled, about one hour.

Roll out the dough ¼ inch [6 mm.] thick on a floured surface. With a floured knife, cut the dough into 3-by-1½-inch [8-by-4-cm.] bars. Place the bars on floured wax paper. Cover and let the bars rise until doubled, about 45 minutes.

In oil heated to 375° F. [190° C.], fry a few doughnuts at a time until golden brown, turning once. Drain the doughnuts on paper towels.

To make the frosting, combine the confectioners' sugar with the butter. Beat in the maple flavoring and enough hot water to make a creamy maple frosting. Beat until smooth.

When the doughnuts cool, spread them with the frosting.

ELISE W. MANNING (EDITOR)
COUNTRY FAIR COOKBOOK

Yeast Potato Doughnuts

Fasnachts

To make thirty-six 2-by-3-inch [5-by-8-cm.] rectangles

6 cups	sifted flour	1½ liters
¼ oz.	package dry yeast	7½ g.
1	medium-sized potato, peeled and sliced	1
2¾ cups	water	675 ml.
4 tbsp.	butter	60 ml.
½ cup	granulated sugar	125 ml.
2	eggs, beaten	2
1 tsp.	salt	5 ml.
	fat for deep frying	
	superfine sugar	

Cook the potato slices in 2½ cups [625 ml.] of boiling salted water until tender. Drain, saving 1½ cups [375 ml.] of the potato cooking water. Melt the butter in this hot water. Mash the potato and measure out ¼ cup [50 ml.]. Using an electric mixer, if you like, beat the ¼ cup of mashed potato with the sugar in a large mixing bowl until well blended. Add the eggs and salt; mix well. Gradually add the reserved potato water. Mix the yeast with ¼ cup of tepid water and add to the potato mixture. Beat in half of the flour and then mix in the last 3 cups [¾ liter] of flour by hand. The dough will be soft.

Knead on a well-floured surface until smooth and elastic. Place the dough in a greased bowl, then turn the dough upside down so the top surface is greased. Cover and let rise in a warm place, free from drafts, until doubled in bulk, two to three hours.

Turn out onto a floured surface and knead for one minute. Divide the dough in half. Roll each half into a rectangle ⅓ inch [1 cm.] thick. With a pastry wheel or knife, cut the dough into 2-by-3-inch [5-by-8-cm.] rectangles, making a slit 1 inch [2½ cm.] long in the center of each. Place the rectangles on a cloth, away from any drafts, and cover with another cloth. Let the rectangles rise again until they have doubled in size, about one hour.

Fry a few of the rectangles at a time in deep fat preheated to 375° F. [190° C.]. Drain on paper towels. Roll the doughnuts in superfine sugar.

EDNA EBY HELLER
THE ART OF PENNSYLVANIA DUTCH COOKING

Sour-Cream Doughnuts

To make about eighteen 2-by-3-inch [5-by-8-cm.] rectangles

about 4 cups	flour	about 1 liter
1 tsp.	baking powder	5 ml.
1½ cups	sour cream	375 ml.
1	egg, beaten	1
¼ cup	granulated sugar	50 ml.
	fat for deep frying	
	confectioners' sugar	

Mix together the sour cream and beaten egg. Sift together the flour, sugar and baking powder. Stir into the sour cream mixture. If necessary to make the dough easy to roll out, add more flour. Turn out the dough onto a floured board and roll it out ½ inch [1 cm.] thick. Cut the dough into 2-by-3-inch [5-by-8-cm.] rectangles and cut a slit in the center of each. Fry in deep fat heated to 360° F. [185° C.] until the doughnuts are brown on both sides. Drain on brown paper. When cool, sprinkle the doughnuts with confectioners' sugar.

EDNA EBY HELLER
THE ART OF PENNSYLVANIA DUTCH COOKING

Maine Buttermilk Doughnuts

To make 48 doughnuts

4 cups	flour	1 liter
1 tsp.	baking powder	5 ml.
1 tsp.	baking soda	5 ml.
2	eggs	2
1 cup	sugar	¼ liter
4 tbsp.	shortening, melted	60 ml.
1 cup	buttermilk	¼ liter
½ tsp.	grated nutmeg	2 ml.
1 tsp.	salt	5 ml.
	fat for deep frying	

Beat the eggs. Add the sugar and beat well. Add the melted shortening and the buttermilk.

Sift together the flour, baking powder, baking soda, nutmeg and salt. Add this to the egg mixture, and again be sure to mix all together very thoroughly. On a floured board, roll out the dough and cut it into doughnuts with a doughnut cutter. Let the doughnuts stand for a short while—10 to 15 minutes. Then fry in deep fat heated to 375° F. [190° C.] for about four minutes, or until golden brown, turning the doughnuts once while they are frying. Let the doughnuts cool for two and a half minutes before sampling them.

HAYDN S. PEARSON
COUNTRY FLAVOR COOKBOOK

Yogurt Doughnuts

These doughnuts are not sweet. You may dust them with powdered sugar, glaze them with an icing of confectioners' sugar and a little water, or roll them in cinnamon sugar.

To make about 18 medium-sized doughnuts

3 cups	flour	¾ liter
1 tsp.	baking powder	5 ml.
1 tsp.	baking soda	5 ml.
2	eggs	2
¼ cup	honey	50 ml.
1 cup	plain yogurt	¼ liter
2 tbsp.	unsalted butter, melted	30 ml.
½ tsp.	salt	2 ml.
¼ tsp.	grated nutmeg	1 ml.

In a large bowl, beat the eggs until they are light in color and somewhat thickened. Beat in the honey, yogurt and melted butter. Sift together the flour, baking powder, soda, salt and nutmeg. Combine this with the egg-yogurt mixture, blend gently, and turn out the dough onto a lightly floured board. Pat the dough together with your hands and knead it gently a few times until it holds together. A pastry scraper is helpful in folding the dough over on itself. If the dough seems quite sticky, add a little more flour. Wrap the dough in plastic wrap or wax paper and chill for at least 30 minutes.

On a lightly floured board, roll the dough out with a floured rolling pin to a thickness of about ½ inch [1 cm.]. Cut with a doughnut cutter or two biscuit cutters (one large, one small). Dip the cutters in flour each time. Let the doughnuts and their cut-out centers rest on the board for 10 to 15 minutes, uncovered.

Heat deep fat or oil in a pot to 375° F. [190° C.]. If you have one, use a deep-frying thermometer and leave it in the pot so you can constantly check the temperature. Place the doughnuts and their centers on a spatula and slide them, one at a time, into the hot fat. Cook only a few at once; do not crowd the pot. Fry until golden brown on both sides, about three minutes in all. Remove with a slotted spoon and drain on paper towels. Break open one of the first ones to test for proper doneness. Repeat frying with the remaining doughnuts and their cut-out centers.

ELLEN FOSCUE JOHNSON
THE GARDEN WAY BREAD BOOK

Spicy Doughnuts

To make 14 doughnuts

3½ cups	sifted flour	875 ml.
2 tsp.	baking powder	10 ml.
1 tsp.	baking soda	5 ml.
2 tsp.	ground cinnamon	10 ml.
¼ tsp.	ground cloves	1 ml.
¼ tsp.	grated nutmeg	1 ml.
¼ tsp.	ground mace	1 ml.
½ tsp.	salt	2 ml.
4	egg yolks	4
1 cup	sugar	¼ liter
2 tbsp.	butter, softened	30 ml.
¾ cup	buttermilk	175 ml.
1 tsp.	rum extract	5 ml.
	oil for deep frying	

Cinnamon-sugar coating

½ tsp.	ground cinnamon	2 ml.
1 cup	sugar	¼ liter

Sift together the flour, baking powder, baking soda, cinnamon, cloves, nutmeg, mace and salt.

Beat together the egg yolks and sugar until light. Add the butter, buttermilk and rum extract. Add the sifted dry ingredients all at once, stirring just until smooth. (The dough is very soft.) Knead the dough lightly on a floured surface. Cover, and refrigerate for at least one hour.

Roll out the dough ⅜ inch [9 mm.] thick on a floured surface. Cut out doughnuts with a floured doughnut cutter.

In oil heated to 375° F. [190° C.], fry a few doughnuts at a time until golden brown, turning once. Drain the doughnuts on paper towels. Roll them in the cinnamon-sugar coating.

ELISE W. MANNING (EDITOR)
COUNTRY FAIR COOKBOOK

Spiced Sour-Cream Doughnuts

Smultringer

To make 30 doughnuts

about 4 cups	flour	about 1 liter
1 tsp.	baking soda	5 ml.
2 tsp.	baking powder	10 ml.
2	eggs	2
1 cup	sugar	¼ liter
1 cup	sour cream	¼ liter
½ tsp.	ground cardamom or grated nutmeg	2 ml.
½ tsp.	salt	2 ml.
	lard or oil for deep frying	

Beat the eggs well; add the sugar, sour cream, baking soda, cardamom or nutmeg, salt and just enough flour to make a dough that can be rolled. Chill the dough, roll it out, and cut out doughnuts with a doughnut cutter. Cook the doughnuts in hot lard or oil, turning them over as soon as they rise to the surface. Drain the doughnuts on paper towels.

ALICE B. JOHNSON
THE COMPLETE SCANDINAVIAN COOKBOOK

Cinnamon and Nutmeg Crullers

To make about 50 crullers

12 cups	flour	3 liters
2 tbsp.	baking soda	30 ml.
24 tbsp.	butter (¾ lb. [⅓ kg.])	360 ml.
about 2¼ cups	sugar	about 550 ml.
1 tsp.	ground cinnamon	5 ml.
1 tsp.	grated nutmeg	5 ml.
1 cup	rose water	¼ liter
10	eggs, beaten	10
	lard for deep frying	

Rub the butter, 2¼ cups [550 ml.] of sugar and the flour well together, and add the spices, rose water and baking soda, and the eggs. Knead the dough thoroughly and roll it out to about ½ inch [1 cm.] thick. Cut the dough into 5-inch [13-cm.] strips about 1 inch [2½ cm.] wide. Twist these into various forms and fry them in hot lard until they are light brown. Sift sugar over them.

MRS. M. E. PORTER
MRS. PORTER'S SOUTHERN COOKERY BOOK

Jelly Doughnuts

An alternative technique for filling jelly doughnuts is demonstrated on page 36.

To make 36 doughnuts

3 to 4 cups	flour	¾ to 1 liter
two ¼ oz.	packages active dry yeast and ¼ cup [50 ml.] tepid water, or two ⅗ oz. [18 g.] cakes fresh yeast	two 7½ g.
2 tbsp.	sugar	30 ml.
1 cup	tepid milk	¼ liter
1	egg	1
2	egg yolks	2
1 tsp.	grated lemon peel	5 ml.
1 tsp.	salt	5 ml.
4 tbsp.	butter, softened	60 ml.
1½ cups	jam	375 ml.
	fat for deep frying	
	vanilla sugar	

If dry yeast is used, mix it with the tepid water and the sugar, and let it stand for 10 minutes. If fresh yeast is used, cream it with the sugar to make a syrup. Add to the yeast the milk, egg, egg yolks and lemon peel. Mix well. Add the salt and enough flour to make a medium-firm dough, working in the softened butter at the same time. Knead well until the dough is smooth and elastic. Place the dough in a bowl. Dust the dough lightly with flour. Cover the bowl. Place it in a draft-free place until the dough doubles in bulk.

After the dough has risen, punch it down. Cover the bowl. Let the dough rise a second time.

Shape doughnuts by pinching off egg-sized pieces of dough and forming each into a smooth, slightly flattened ball. Place the balls on a floured towel. Let the balls rise until all are doubled in size.

While the doughnuts are rising, heat the fat to 375° F. [190° C.]. Drop the doughnuts into the fat, two or three at a time. Fry until the undersides are a deep golden brown; then turn and fry until the second sides are also well browned, about five minutes in all.

Remove the doughnuts from the fat with a skimmer. Drain them on paper towels or brown paper.

When the doughnuts are thoroughly cool, fill them by squirting jam into their centers with a pastry bag fitted with a long, narrow tube. Dust the doughnuts with vanilla sugar.

PAULA PECK
THE ART OF FINE BAKING

Carnival Jelly Doughnuts

Faschingskrapfen

An alternative technique for filling doughnuts is demonstrated on page 36.

To make about 30 doughnuts

about 3½ cups	flour	about 875 ml.
two ⅗ oz.	cakes fresh yeast, finely crumbled	two 18 g.
⅓ cup	sugar	75 ml.
1 cup	tepid milk	¼ liter
4 tbsp.	unsalted butter, melted and cooled until tepid	60 ml.
6	egg yolks	6
2 tsp.	grated lemon peel	10 ml.
¾ tsp.	salt	4 ml.
2 tbsp.	rum	30 ml.
1 cup	apricot jam	¼ liter
	vegetable shortening and corn oil for deep frying	
	confectioners' sugar	

Add 2 tablespoons [30 ml.] of the sugar and ⅔ to ¾ cup [150 to 175 ml.] of the flour to the tepid milk. Stir. Add the yeast. Cover the mixture with a kitchen towel. Let the mixture rise in a draft-free place until bubbles appear on the surface.

While the sponge is rising, stir the cooled butter and sugar until creamy. Add the egg yolks, lemon peel and salt. Add several spoons of flour and the yeast sponge. Beat well with a wooden spoon. Add the rum and gradually beat in the remaining flour. If necessary, add more flour, but keep the dough soft. Beat the dough for about 10 minutes until it is satiny and shiny, and blisters form on its surface. Cover. Let the dough rise in a draft-free place until it is more than double its original bulk. Punch down the dough. Beat it with a few strokes. Let it rise again for about 15 minutes.

Turn the dough over onto a well-floured pastry board. With a lightly floured rolling pin, roll it out to less than ¼ inch [6 mm.] thick. With a biscuit cutter 2½ inches [6 cm.] in diameter (or the rim of a glass), mark (but do not cut) rounds close together in the dough.

Place about ½ teaspoon [2 ml.] of apricot jam on the centers of half of the rounds. Cut out the other rounds and set them on top of the ones dotted with jam. Press the edges together. Then cut out the whole filled doughnut with a slightly smaller biscuit cutter (or glass). Cover the doughnuts and let them rise for about 15 minutes.

While the doughnuts are rising, heat shortening in a large kettle or a deep 10-inch [25-cm.] frying pan to 375° F. [190° C.]. (The shortening will be less likely to burn if it is combined with corn oil. Use two parts of shortening to one part of corn oil.)

Place four or five doughnuts in the hot fat, leaving enough room for them to expand. They have to "swim" in deep, hot fat to get a light band around their middle, the distinctive mark of the *faschingskrapfen*. Cover the kettle or frying pan for about one minute. Remove the cover and let the doughnuts fry until golden brown on one side, then turn them over to fry the other side. Remove the doughnuts with a slotted spoon. Transfer them to absorbent paper.

Doughnuts are at their best when eaten fresh, still lukewarm. Before serving, sprinkle them generously with confectioners' sugar.

LILLY JOSS REICH
THE VIENNESE PASTRY COOKBOOK

Pancakes and Waffles

The techniques for making pancakes and waffles are demonstrated on pages 86-87. The recipe for basic pancakes and waffles appears in Standard Preparations, page 166.

Cotton Cakes

To make twelve 4-inch [10-cm.] pancakes

1 cup	sifted flour	¼ liter
1 tsp.	baking soda	5 ml.
4	eggs, 3 with the yolks separated from the whites, and the whites stiffly beaten	4
2 tbsp.	sugar	30 ml.
½ tsp.	salt	2 ml.
1 cup	light cream	¼ liter
1 tbsp.	fresh lemon juice	15 ml.

With an electric mixer on high speed, beat one whole egg and three egg yolks with the sugar and salt until they form a heavy ribbon when the beater is lifted from the bowl—after about 10 minutes. Keep the mixer on high speed and add the cream, mixed with the lemon juice. Blend in the flour, mixed with the baking soda. Whip the egg whites and fold them into the batter. Cook promptly.

MADELEINE KAMMAN
THE MAKING OF A COOK

Pumpkin Griddlecakes

To make about ten 6-inch [15-cm.] pancakes

1 cup	flour	¼ liter
½ cup	yellow cornmeal	125 ml.
2 tsp.	baking powder	10 ml.
1 cup	boiling water	¼ liter
¼ cup	cooked, well-drained and mashed pumpkin flesh	50 ml.
⅞ cup	milk, scalded and cooled until tepid	200 ml.
¾ tsp.	salt	4 ml.
1½ tsp.	sugar	7 ml.
1 tsp.	ground allspice	5 ml.
1	egg, beaten	1

Combine the cornmeal and water, and let stand for five minutes. Add the pumpkin and tepid milk, and stir until smooth. Sift the flour, baking powder, salt, sugar and allspice together, and add to the cornmeal mixture. Stir the beaten egg in. Mix all well together. Drop the batter by ladlefuls onto a well-greased hot griddle. Bake each cake until bubbles form all over, then turn and bake the other side until golden and crisp. Serve the cakes with maple syrup.

AMY B. W. MILLER AND PERSIS W. FULLER (EDITORS)
THE BEST OF SHAKER COOKING

Oatmeal Pancakes

To make about twelve 4-inch [10-cm.] pancakes

1 cup	quick-cooking rolled oats	¼ liter
½ cup	flour	125 ml.
2 tsp.	baking powder	10 ml.
1 cup	hot water or milk	¼ liter
2	eggs, the yolks separated from the whites, and the whites stiffly beaten	2
½ cup	milk	125 ml.
2 tbsp.	corn oil	30 ml.
1 tsp.	salt	5 ml.

Soak the oats in the hot water or milk for about five minutes. Beat the egg yolks with the ½ cup [125 ml.] of cold milk and the oil. Add to the oatmeal mixture. Combine the baking powder, salt and flour, and stir into the oatmeal mixture. Fold in the stiffly beaten egg whites.

GLADYS MANYAN
THE COUNTRY SEASONS COOKBOOK

Whole-wheat Pancakes

To make about twenty 4-inch [10-cm.] pancakes

2 cups	whole-wheat flour	½ liter
3 tsp.	baking powder	15 ml.
1 tsp.	salt	5 ml.
1 tbsp.	brown sugar or honey	15 ml.
3	eggs, the yolks separated from the whites, the yolks beaten and the whites stiffly beaten	3
2 cups	milk	½ liter
½ cup	oil	125 ml.

Sift the flour with the baking powder, salt and sugar. If you are using honey, add it to the milk and oil. Beat the milk and oil into the egg yolks. Combine the yolks, milk and oil with the dry ingredients until just blended, then fold in the stiffly beaten egg whites. Cook on a greased griddle or in a frying pan.

EDWARD ESPE BROWN
THE TASSAJARA BREAD BOOK

Grandma's Hot Cakes

To make about twenty 3-inch [8-cm.] pancakes

1 cup plus 2 tbsp.	flour	280 ml.
¼ cup	whole-grain cornmeal	50 ml.
½ cup	rolled oats	125 ml.
¾ tsp.	baking powder	4 ml.
2 tsp.	baking soda	10 ml.
2 cups	buttermilk	½ liter
¾ tsp.	salt	4 ml.
½ cup	sour cream	125 ml.
2	eggs	2
⅔ cup	sugar	150 ml.

Pour the buttermilk into a 1½-quart [1½-liter] mixing bowl. Add the baking soda and salt. Add sour cream and stir until the mixture foams. Add the eggs and beat with a spoon until they are mixed in. Add the rolled oats. Combine the flour, sugar, baking powder and cornmeal, and sift them into the buttermilk mixture; beat until the flour lumps disappear. Heat and oil a griddle or large, heavy frying pan. Pour on batter by large tablespoonfuls. Keep the pancakes 1 inch [2½ cm.] apart. When deep brown on one side, turn to brown the other side. (Watch, they scorch easily!) Accompany with syrup, honey, jam, jelly or preserves.

IDA BAILEY ALLEN
BEST LOVED RECIPES OF THE AMERICAN PEOPLE

Cornmeal Pancakes

To make about 40 small pancakes

1 cup	yellow cornmeal	¼ liter
¼ cup	flour	50 ml.
¼ tsp.	baking soda	1 ml.
1 tsp.	salt	5 ml.
1 cup	boiling water	¼ liter
2 tbsp.	butter, melted	30 ml.
1 cup	buttermilk	¼ liter
1	egg, lightly beaten	1

Combine the cornmeal and salt. Slowly stir in the boiling water and melted butter. Cover and let stand for 10 minutes. Stir in the buttermilk and egg. Combine the flour and the baking soda, and stir quickly into the batter. The batter will be very thin.

Bake on a well-greased griddle over medium heat, using a tablespoon [15 ml.] of batter for each cake. Stir the batter often and keep the griddle well greased. When each pancake is golden brown underneath, turn it to brown the other side. Turn only once. Serve with warmed maple syrup.

WILF AND LOIS COPPING
THE COUNTRY INNKEEPERS' COOKBOOK

Apple-Cheese Pancakes

To make about twelve 4-inch [10-cm.] pancakes

¾ cup	all-purpose flour, or ½ cup [125 ml.] all-purpose flour and ¼ cup [50 ml.] whole-wheat flour	175 ml.
1½ cups	grated firm-textured cooking apples	375 ml.
1 cup	cottage or ricotta cheese, pressed through a sieve	¼ liter
1 tbsp.	honey	15 ml.
1 tsp.	fresh lemon juice	5 ml.
1 tbsp.	sunflower seeds or chopped almonds	15 ml.
½ tsp.	ground cinnamon	2 ml.
⅛ tsp.	grated nutmeg or ground allspice	½ ml.
½ tsp.	salt	2 ml.
4	eggs, the yolks separated from the whites	4

Mix all of the ingredients together except the egg whites. Beat the egg whites until stiff and fold them into the batter. Drop the batter ¼ cup [50 ml.] at a time onto a hot buttered griddle or skillet set over medium heat. Fry the pancakes on both sides until brown. Serve with maple syrup, preserves, sour cream, yogurt, fresh fruit or cinnamon sugar.

MOLLIE KATZEN
THE MOOSEWOOD COOKBOOK

Sour-Cream Blueberry Pancakes

To make about twelve 4-inch [10-cm.] pancakes

1 cup	sifted flour	¼ liter
1 tbsp.	baking powder	15 ml.
¼ tsp.	salt	1 ml.
2 tbsp.	sugar	30 ml.
1	egg	1
1 cup	milk	¼ liter
¼ cup	sour cream	50 ml.
2 tbsp.	butter, melted and cooled	30 ml.
½ cup	fresh blueberries	125 ml.

Sift the flour, baking powder, salt and sugar together. Beat together the egg, milk and sour cream, and pour over the dry mixture. Beat until the batter is smooth. Stir in the butter and fold in the blueberries. Cook the pancakes on a greased griddle until the edges bubble; turn once only.

AMY B. W. MILLER AND PERSIS W. FULLER (EDITORS)
THE BEST OF SHAKER COOKING

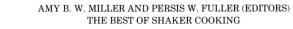

Yeasty Pancakes with Bacon

To make eight 10-inch [25-cm.] pancakes

4 cups	flour	1 liter
two ¼ oz.	packages active dry yeast or two ⅗ oz. [18 g.] cakes fresh yeast	two 7½ g.
1 lb.	sliced lean bacon	½ kg.
½ cup	tepid water	125 ml.
3½ cups	tepid milk	875 ml.
1 tsp.	salt	5 ml.
2	eggs, beaten	2
3 tbsp.	butter	45 ml.
	maple syrup	

Sauté the bacon slices until they are brown. Drain on paper towels. Mix the yeast with the tepid water and let stand for 10 minutes. Stir in the tepid milk. Combine the flour with the salt and sift together. Add the dry ingredients to the yeast mixture a little at a time, stirring well after each addition. Beat in the eggs for a smooth batter.

Heat the butter in a 10-inch [25-cm.] skillet. Arrange two or three strips of bacon in the butter, and pour in enough batter to cover the bottom of the skillet completely. Shake the skillet occasionally as the pancake browns to loosen its edges. Turn once to brown the other side. Repeat until all of the bacon and batter have been used. Serve hot with syrup.

YVONNE YOUNG TARR
THE NEW YORK TIMES BREAD AND SOUP COOKBOOK

Sour-Cream Pancakes

To make six 3-inch [8-cm.] pancakes

⅓ cup	flour	75 ml.
1 tsp.	baking powder	5 ml.
¼ tsp.	salt	1 ml.
2	eggs	2
1 cup	sour cream	¼ liter

Sift the flour, baking powder and salt into a bowl. Beat the eggs with the sour cream and stir (but do not beat) into the dry ingredients. Bake on an ungreased griddle. These are delicious with sautéed apple rings.

JANET E. C. WURTZBURGER (EDITOR)
PRIVATE COLLECTIONS: A CULINARY TREASURE

Sarah's Sourdough Pancakes

Pancakes made with yeast need longer cooking at lower temperatures than ordinary pancakes. These very flavorful pancakes are moist inside and somewhat chewy; if you like them drier, warm them in the oven for a few minutes.

To make twenty 4-inch [10-cm.] pancakes

3 cups	whole-wheat flour	¾ liter
¼ oz.	package active dry yeast or ⅗ oz. [18 g.] cake fresh yeast	7½ g.
½ tsp.	baking soda	2 ml.
about 3 cups	tepid water	about ¾ liter
1 tbsp.	plain yogurt	15 ml.
1 tsp.	salt	5 ml.

Mix the yeast with 2 cups [½ liter] of tepid water. Add the yogurt and 2 cups of flour, beating this batter until very smooth. Cover loosely and set aside overnight.

Next morning, stir together the remaining flour, the soda and salt, and add them with 1 cup [¼ liter] of tepid water to the batter; let the mixture rest for 15 minutes. Spoon onto a seasoned griddle preheated over medium heat, immediately spreading the batter about ¼ inch [6 mm.] thick. Turn each pancake when the top is no longer shiny.

LAUREL ROBERTSON, CAROL FLINDERS AND BRONWEN GODFREY
LAUREL'S KITCHEN: A HANDBOOK FOR
VEGETARIAN COOKERY & NUTRITION

Buttermilk Pancakes

To make about fourteen 4-inch [10-cm.] pancakes

1½ cups	flour	375 ml.
1½ tsp.	baking powder	7 ml.
½ tsp.	baking soda	2 ml.
2	eggs	2
1½ cups	buttermilk	375 ml.
3 tbsp.	butter, melted	45 ml.
1 tbsp.	sugar	15 ml.
½ tsp.	salt	2 ml.

Beat the eggs; add the remaining ingredients and beat with a rotary beater until smooth. Grease a heated griddle. To test, sprinkle the griddle with water; if the drops of water jump around, the griddle is ready. Pour batter from a large spoon. Turn the pancakes when puffed and full of bubbles. Bake the other side of each pancake until golden brown.

WILF AND LOIS COPPING
THE COUNTRY INNKEEPERS' COOKBOOK

Buttermilk Whole-wheat Waffles

The same amount of yogurt, thinned with a little water, can be used instead of buttermilk. For crisper waffles, reduce the flour to 2 cups [½ liter].

To make about four 9-inch [23-cm.] square waffles

2¼ cups	whole-wheat flour	550 ml.
1½ tsp.	baking powder	7 ml.
½ tsp.	baking soda	2 ml.
2	eggs, the yolks separated from the whites, and the whites stiffly beaten	2
2 tbsp.	corn oil	30 ml.
2 cups	buttermilk	½ liter
½ tsp.	salt	2 ml.

Beat the egg yolks with the oil and add the buttermilk. Combine the flour, baking powder, baking soda and salt, then add the buttermilk mixture. Fold in the beaten egg whites.

GLADYS MANYAN
THE COUNTRY SEASONS COOKBOOK

Buttermilk-Bran Waffles

To make about three 9-inch [23-cm.]
square waffles

¾ cup	flour	175 ml.
1 tsp.	baking powder	5 ml.
½ tsp.	baking soda	2 ml.
¼ cup	sugar	50 ml.
¼ tsp.	salt	1 ml.
1 cup	bran cereal or bran buds	¼ liter
2	eggs, the yolks separated from the whites, and the whites stiffly beaten	2
1 cup	buttermilk or sour milk	¼ liter
6 tbsp.	butter, melted and cooled	90 ml.

Preheat a waffle iron. Sift together the flour, baking powder, baking soda, sugar and salt. Add the bran cereal or buds. Add the egg yolks, buttermilk and butter. Stir until well blended. Fold the egg whites into the batter. Bake the batter—in batches—in the waffle iron until golden brown.

THE JUNIOR LEAGUE OF FAYETTEVILLE, INC.
THE CAROLINA COLLECTION

Cornmeal Waffles

To make about three 9-inch [23-cm.]
square waffles

2 cups	cornmeal, sifted	½ liter
1 tbsp.	flour	15 ml.
½ tsp.	baking soda	2 ml.
1 tsp.	salt	5 ml.
2	eggs, the yolks separated from the whites, the yolks beaten and the whites stiffly beaten	2
1 tbsp.	butter, melted and cooled	15 ml.
2 cups	milk	½ liter

Sift together the cornmeal, flour, baking soda and salt. Mix together the egg yolks, butter and milk. Add the sifted dry ingredients. Add last the stiffly beaten egg whites.

MRS. M. E. PORTER
MRS. PORTER'S NEW SOUTHERN COOKERY BOOK

Rice Waffles

To make about four 9-inch [23-cm.]
square waffles

2½ cups	flour	625 ml.
4 tsp.	baking powder	20 ml.
3	eggs, the yolks separated from the whites, and the whites stiffly beaten	3
1 tsp.	salt	5 ml.
2 cups	milk	½ liter
⅓ cup	raw unprocessed rice, boiled in 2 cups [½ liter] water for 15 minutes, drained and cooled	75 ml.
4 tbsp.	butter, melted and cooled	60 ml.

Beat the egg yolks until thick and lemon-colored. Sift together the flour, baking powder and salt. Add the flour mixture and milk alternately to the egg yolks and beat until smooth. Stir in the rice. Add the melted butter and fold in the stiffly beaten egg whites.

THE WOMAN'S AUXILIARY OF OLIVET EPISCOPAL CHURCH
VIRGINIA COOKERY—PAST AND PRESENT

Cheese Waffles

To make six 9-inch [23-cm.] square
waffles

2 cups	flour	½ liter
2 tsp.	baking powder	10 ml.
2 tbsp.	sugar	30 ml.
1 tsp.	salt	5 ml.
1 cup	finely shredded Cheddar cheese	¼ liter
2	eggs, the yolks separated from the whites, the yolks beaten and the whites stiffly beaten	2
1½ cups	milk	375 ml.
4 tbsp.	butter, melted	60 ml.

Sift together into a bowl the flour, baking powder, sugar and salt. Add the cheese. Stir in the beaten egg yolks, the milk and butter. Fold in the stiffly beaten egg whites. Bake in a hot waffle iron.

THE SETTLEMENT COOKBOOK

Standard Preparations

Basic Bread Dough

Wherever basic bread dough is called for in the recipe section of this book, this method can be followed, using any desired flour—in the proportions shown on page 9.

The techniques of making basic bread dough are demonstrated on pages 14-15. The dough may be shaped and baked in any of the ways shown on pages 16-31. This recipe will produce enough dough for two 8-inch [20-cm.] round loaves, two 8½-by-4½-inch [21-by-11-cm.] rectangular loaves, two 14-inch [35-cm.] cylindrical loaves or approximately thirty 3-inch [8-cm.] rolls.

To make about 2 ½ pounds [1 ¼ kg.] dough

about 6 cups	flour	about 1½ liters
¼ oz.	package active dry yeast or ⅗ oz. [18 g.] cake fresh yeast	7½ g.
1 to 2 tsp.	salt	5 to 10 ml.
about 2 cups	tepid water	about ½ liter

In a small bowl or a measuring cup, mix the yeast with the tepid water, and leave it to soften in a warm place for about 10 minutes. Sift the flour and salt into a large bowl. Pour the yeast mixture into the flour. Mix the flour and liquid together into a stiff, sticky dough, adding more flour or tepid water if necessary. Transfer the dough to a work surface and knead the dough for about 15 minutes, until it is elastic and glossy.

Shape the dough into a ball and return it to a clean bowl. Cover the bowl with plastic wrap and let the dough rise in a warm, draft-free place until doubled in volume—a process that may require from one to two and a half hours. The dough is ready when the insertion of a finger into it leaves a dent that does not immediately smooth out.

Punch the dough down with a blow of your fist. Put the dough on a work surface and cut it in half with a knife. Knead each half into a ball, cover the balls with a cloth and let them rise for 10 to 15 minutes. The dough is now ready for shaping and baking.

Milk-and-Butter Dough

This dough produces bread with a tender crumb and a soft crust. The dough is particularly suitable for making loaves that are braided *(pages 22-23)* or baked in covered bread pans *(pages 24-25)*, and for creating rolls *(pages 26-28)*. This recipe will produce enough dough for one 12-inch [30-cm.]

braided loaf, a covered-pan loaf and for about twenty-four 3-inch [8-cm.] rolls.

To make 2 pounds [1 kg.] dough

about 5 cups	flour	about 1¼ liters
¼ oz.	package active dry yeast or ⅗ oz. [18 g.] cake fresh yeast	7½ g.
about 1½ cups	tepid milk	about 375 ml.
1 tsp.	salt	5 ml.
3 tbsp.	butter, softened	45 ml.

Stir the yeast into ¼ cup [50 ml.] of the tepid milk and leave it in a warm place for about 10 minutes. Sift the flour and salt into a bowl. Pour the yeast mixture and the remaining tepid milk into the flour and salt, and work in the softened butter. The dough will be sticky. Turn the dough out onto a floured board, and knead it vigorously for 10 to 15 minutes, or until the dough is elastic, smooth and glossy. The dough should be fairly firm; add more flour if necessary. Put the dough into a clean, dry bowl, cover the bowl with plastic wrap or a damp cloth, and set it in a warm, draft-free place until the dough has doubled in volume—about one to two and a half hours. The dough is ready when the insertion of a finger leaves a dent that does not immediately fill out. Punch down the dough, knead it into a ball and let it rest for about 10 minutes. It is now ready for shaping and baking.

Simple Egg-Bread Dough

The techniques of making simple egg-bread dough are demonstrated on pages 34-35. This recipe will produce enough dough for two 10-inch [20-cm.] ring loaves or two 8½-by-4½-inch [21-by-11-cm.] rectangular loaves. To make two of the braided, egg-dough loaves known as challahs, reduce the quantity of milk to ¾ cup [175 ml.].

To make about 2 ½ pounds [1 ¼ kg.] dough

about 6 cups	flour	about 1½ liters
two ¼ oz.	packages active dry yeast or two ⅗ oz. [18 g.] cakes fresh yeast	two 7½ g.
1 cup	tepid milk	¼ liter
1 tbsp.	sugar	15 ml.
3	eggs	3
16 tbsp.	butter (½ lb. [¼ kg.]), softened	240 ml.
1½ tsp.	salt	7 ml.

Mix the yeast with the tepid milk, add the sugar, and leave the mixture in a warm place for about 10 minutes, or until slightly foaming. Then whisk in about 1 cup [¼ liter] of the flour, adding it gradually until the mixture has the consistency of a thick batter. Cover the bowl with plastic wrap and leave it in a warm place until this yeast sponge has doubled in volume—about one hour.

Break the eggs into the sponge and whisk them in. Add the softened butter in walnut-sized pieces. Gradually stir in the rest of the flour a handful at a time, adding only enough flour to give the dough a firm consistency. Lumps of butter will remain in the dough, but they will be incorporated during the kneading.

Turn out the dough onto a floured work surface, and knead thoroughly for about 10 to 15 minutes, until the dough is smooth, glossy and elastic. Gather the dough into a ball and place it in a clean, dry bowl. Cover with plastic wrap and set the bowl in a warm place for about one and one half to two and one half hours, until the dough has risen to three to four times its previous volume. The dough is now ready for shaping and baking.

Rich Egg-Bread Dough

The techniques of making rich egg-bread dough are demonstrated on pages 40-43. This recipe produces enough dough for about twelve 3-inch [8-cm.] brioches or two 8-inch [20-cm.] brioches. Instead of being baked in fluted brioche molds, the dough may be formed into a 10- to 12-inch [25- to 30-cm.] ring and the surface cut with scissors, following the technique demonstrated on page 20. In this case, the bread is known as a *brioche couronne* (crown brioche).

To make 2 pounds [1 kg.] dough

about 4 cups	flour	about 1 liter
¼ oz.	package active dry yeast or ⅗ oz. [18 g.] cake fresh yeast	7½ g.
¼ cup	tepid water	50 ml.
¼ cup	sugar	50 ml.
1 tsp.	salt	5 ml.
6	eggs	6
20 tbsp.	unsalted butter, softened	300 ml.

Mix the yeast with the tepid water, and leave it for 10 minutes. Put the flour, sugar and salt into a bowl. Add the yeast mixture and break in the eggs. Mix the eggs and yeast, gradually pulling flour from the sides of the well, until all of the flour has been moistened. The dough should be very soft and sticky.

Turn the dough out onto a cool, unfloured work surface. Using your hands and a pastry scraper, knead the dough

thoroughly for about 10 minutes, or until it loses its stickiness and becomes smooth and elastic.

Break off walnut-sized pieces of the butter and, using the pastry scraper or a spatula, fold them one at a time into the dough. Knead again until the dough is smooth. Put the dough into a large bowl, cover it with plastic wrap, and leave it in a warm place for three to four hours, or until the dough has tripled in volume.

Punch the dough down several times to expel the air, then knead it lightly in the bowl for two or three minutes. Cover the bowl with plastic wrap and let the dough rise again. For best results, let the dough rise in the refrigerator for six to eight hours or overnight. If that is not possible, let the dough rise at room temperature until doubled in bulk— three to four hours—and then chill it for at least half an hour before shaping it.

Yeast-Dough Fillings

Any of these fillings is suitable for Danish pastries, filled croissants or buns, or coffeecakes.

Almond paste. Blanch 2 cups [½ liter] of almonds in boiling water for a minute or so, then drain the almonds and— when cool enough to handle—slip off their skins. Grind the almonds in a nut grinder, or in a food processor operated in short spurts. In a bowl, mix the ground almonds with ½ cup [125 ml.] of superfine sugar, 1 cup [¼ liter] of confectioners' sugar and 2 teaspoons [10 ml.] of grated lemon peel. Add one lightly beaten egg white and stir to form a thick paste. Yield: about 2 cups [½ liter].

Apple and cinnamon. Simmer 2 cups [½ liter] of peeled, cored and diced apples with 1 cup [¼ liter] of sugar, ⅔ cup [150 ml.] of water, 2 tablespoons [30 ml.] of fresh lemon juice, 1 teaspoon [5 ml.] of grated lemon peel and ½ teaspoon [2 ml.] of ground cinnamon. When the apples are soft, in about 10 minutes, press the mixture through a strainer or mash it with a fork. Add 2 tablespoons of rum. If necessary, cook the mixture over high heat until it is thick enough to hold its shape in a spoon. Yield: about 2 cups [½ liter].

Cheese and egg. Sieve 1 cup [¼ liter] of ricotta or farmer cheese. Beat an egg into the cheese, then blend in 1⅓ cups [325 ml.] of freshly grated Parmesan and a pinch of cayenne pepper. Yield: about 2 cups [½ liter].

Poppy seed. Grind 2 cups [½ liter] of poppy seeds—½ cup [125 ml.] at a time—in a food processor operated in short spurts. In a saucepan, combine the poppy seeds with 1 cup [¼ liter] of milk and simmer for five minutes, stirring constantly. Stir in ½ cup of sugar, 2 tablespoons [30 ml.] of butter and ½ teaspoon [2 ml.] of vanilla extract. Simmer for five minutes, stirring constantly. Yield: about 2 cups [½ liter].

Recipe Index

All recipes in the index that follows are listed by their English titles except in cases where a bread of foreign origin, such as zwieback, is universally recognized by its source name. Entries also are organized by the major ingredients specified in the recipe titles and — in the case of specialty-grain breads — by the type of flour or meal used. Foreign recipes are listed by country or region of origin. Recipe credits appear on pages 173-175.

General Index/ Glossary

Included in this index to the cooking demonstrations are definitions, in italics, of special culinary terms not explained elsewhere in this volume. The Recipe Index begins on page 168.

All-purpose flour: characteristics, 6, 8; combining with other flours, 8; in Irish soda bread, 78-79; mixing and kneading a basic yeast dough, 14-15; in pancakes, 84-85; storing, 8; substitutions for, 8-9
Almond paste: filling Danish pastries with, 47-48; mixing, 47
Altitude: effect of, 7
Anchovies, salt: *whole cleaned headless fish, packed in salt. Sold in cans or by weight at markets that specialize in French, Greek or Italian foods.*
Bagels, 58-59; adding milk, 58; egg glaze, 59; enriching basic yeast dough with butter and egg white, 58; poaching, 58; shaping rings, 59
Baguette: rolling out and shaping a freestanding loaf, 22-23; slashing, 23.

See also French bread
Baking powder: in banana bread, 72, 82-83; biscuits, 80-81; composition, 7, 73, 80; in corn sticks, 88; history of, 7; as leavening agent, 73, 80; in pancakes, 84-85; ratio of, to flour, 80; in waffles, 86-87
Baking soda: history of, 6-7; as leavening agent, 73, 78; leavening Irish soda bread, 78-79; lightening crumpets with, 56; neutralizing with an acid, 73, 78
Banana bread, 72; blending ingredients in small batches, 82; leavened with baking powder, 82-83; preventing toughness, 82
Banneton: basket to encase dough while rising, 54-55
Barley flour: characteristics, 8-9; substituting, 8-9
Bashing: of cottage loaves, 18
Basic yeast bread: baguette (long loaf) of French bread, 22-23; baked in pan with a hinged lid, 24-25; baking, 16-17; baking bread on carbon-steel sheets, 16; baking on quarry tiles in the home oven, 16, 17; basic dough baked in a loaf pan, 24-25; braided loaf, 22-23; bread sticks, 30, 31; cooling, 7, 17, 24; effect of altitude and weather, 7; effect of materials used for baking, 24; English cottage

loaf, 18; freezing, 7; history of breadmaking, 5-7; humidifying oven, 16; kneading dough, 14-15; looped pretzels, 30-31; mixing dough, 14-15; notched cylindrical loaf, 19-20; *pita,* 29; rising and proofing, 13, 14; rolls, 12, 26-28; round loaves, 16-17; shaping dough, 16-17; size of pan to use, 24; storing, 7; substituting flours, 8-9; tapered cylindrical loaf, 21. *See also* Enriched yeast bread; Flavored yeast bread; Yeast dough
Batters. *See* Nonyeast batter; Yeast-leavened batter
Bel Paese or butter cheese: *a type of uncooked, semisoft, mild-flavored Italian cheese, obtainable at cheese specialty stores and some supermarkets.*
Biscuits: fat in, 80; leavened by baking powder, 80-81; working dough, 81
Blueberries: flouring, before adding to muffin batter, 80
Braided loaf: glazing, 23; made with three strands, 22-23
Bran: described, 7; separating, 5; in whole-wheat flour, 60
Bread flour: characteristics, 6, 8; storing, 8; substitutions for, 8-9
Bread sticks: coating with coarse salt, 31; cutting strips for, 30, 31

Breakfast bread: blueberry muffins, 80-81; brioche, 40-43; croissants, 44-46; Danish pastry, 47-49; filled coffeecakes, 50-51; pancakes, 84-85; waffles, 86-87; yeast doughnuts, 36-37
Brioche: baking in a mold with a topknot, 40-43; folding in butter, 40; glazing, 42; kneading on a marble slab, 41; preliminary dough, 40; punching down dough, 40, 41; ratio of flour to butter and eggs, 40; rising under refrigeration, 40, 41; shaping dough, 42-43; three risings, 40
Buckwheat flour: characteristics, 8-9; in pancakes, 84-85; in sourdough bread, 54-55; substituting, 8-9
Butter: in enriched bread dough, 33, 34; glazing rolls with, 28; and gluten, 24, 33; ratio of, in brioche, 40; softening, 35; in yeast puff dough, 33, 44
Buttermilk: in corn sticks, 88; in doughnuts, 36; in Irish soda bread, 78; neutralizing baking soda, 78
Caramel: syrup for sticky buns, 38, 39
Cast-iron cookware: for corn sticks, 88; for flatbreads, 74-75; and Irish soda bread, 78-79; for johnnycakes, 76-77; popover mold,

78-79; seasoning pans, 76; waffle iron, 86-87

Chappatis, 74-75; cooking in two stages, 75; puffing up by steam, 73, 74

Cheddar cheese: incorporating into bread dough, 66-67

Cheese: bread, 66-67; fat content of and effect on rising dough, 66; filling braided coffeecake with ricotta and Parmesan, 50; filling Danish pastry cockscombs, 49; flavoring breads with, 66; incorporating into dough, 66, 67; Muenster, in picnic loaf, 70-71

Cheese bread, 66-67; dividing with a string, 66

Chocolate: melting and adding to pumpernickel bread, 64-65

Cloverleaf rolls, 28

Coarse salt: on bread sticks and pretzels, 31; sprinkled on herb bread, 67

Coarse sugar: *a specially refined, large crystalline form of sugar designed for use in decorations. Obtainable from baking-supply stores and some gourmet-food specialty stores.*

Cockscombs (Danish pastry), 47, 49

Coffeecake, 32; braided and filled with cheese, 50-51; fillings, 50; fruit filling, 50; glazing, 51; twisted ring filled with fruit and spices, 50-51

Confectioners' sugar: in almond paste, 47; dusting Danish pastries with, 48; dusting yeast doughnuts with, 36, 37

Corn flour (masa harina), 8; characteristics, 8-9; substituting, 8-9

Corn sticks, 88; making a crisp crust, 88

Cornmeal: absorbing liquid, 76; in American flatbreads (johnnycakes), 76-77; in corn sticks, 88; dusting baking sheet with, 16, 20, 23, 29, 31, 65; mixing, 76; in pumpernickel bread, 64-65

Cornstarch, in baking powder, 7

Cracked wheat, garnishing whole-wheat bread, 60

Cream of tartar: in baking powder, 7, 73, 80

Croissants, 44-46; cutting and shaping dough, 44, 45-46; folding and rolling dough, 44-45; glazing, 46; mixing yeast puff dough, 44; working dough on marble, 44

Crullers, 36

Crumpets: adding baking soda, 56, 57; beating batter to develop gluten in, 56; mixing batter, 56-57; producing a honeycombed texture, 56

Crust: adding milk to bagel dough to retard crispness, 58; affected by pan material, 24; bread with a high proportion of (cottage loaf), 18; brushing loaf with egg yolk and water, 23; as determined by type of flour used, 8-9; dusting baking sheet with cornmeal or semolina to make a

crisp bottom, 16; dusting dough with flour, 26; forming during baking, 16; forming in yeast rolls, 26; making a crust crisp, 24, 60; seasoning crust with salted water, 27; slashing dough to obtain a secondary crust, 16, 19, 21

Cylindrical loaves, 19-21; decorating with seeds, 21; developing gluten in, 19; notching a loaf with scissors, 20; shaping a blunt-ended loaf, 19-20; slashing to reveal a secondary crust, 19, 21; tapering a cylinder, 21

Danish pastries, 47-49; almond paste filling, 47, 48; cheese filling, 49; chilling dough, 47; cockscombs, 47, 49; envelopes, 47; glaze, 47, 48, 49; handling dough, 47; jam filling, 48; mixing almond paste filling, 47; pinwheels, 47, 48; twists, 47, 48-49

Deep frying: yeast doughnuts, 36-37

Dough. See Egg-and-butter dough; Milk-and-butter dough; Nonyeast dough; Sourdough bread; Unleavened dough; Yeast dough; Yeast puff dough

Doughnuts: cutting, 36, 37; deep frying, 36-37; dusting with sugar, 37; flavorings, 36; frying jam-filled, 36-37; made of simple egg-bread dough, 36-37; using buttermilk or yogurt in place of milk, 36

Egg-and-butter dough: baking brioche in a mold with a topknot, 40-43; deep frying doughnuts in oil, 36-37; developing gluten in, 33, 34; fat in, 33, 34; filled slices of dough arranged as fans, 38; forming and baking a ring of, 34-35; glazing ring of, 35; kneading, 34, 35; mixing dough, 34-35; moisture in, 34; preparing sponge, 34; punching down dough to expel gas, 40, 41; ratio of butter, eggs and flour in brioche, 40; replacing milk with buttermilk or yogurt, 36; rising under refrigeration, 40; sticky buns, 38-39. See also Enriched yeast bread

Eggs: egg-and-water glaze, 26, 27, 35, 67; egg-white-and-water glaze, 26, 65; egg-yolk-and-water glaze, 23, 26, 38, 42, 46, 47, 48, 49, 51, 58, 59, 70; in enriched bread dough, 33, 34; lightening pancakes with whites, 84; ratio of, in brioche, 40; raw, in picnic loaf, 70-71; -white wash, to bind doughnuts filled with jam, 36

English cottage loaf, 18; bashing, 18; joining spheres of dough, 18

Enriched yeast bread, 33, 34-51; braided and filled coffeecake, 32, 50-51; brioche, 40-43; croissants, 44-46; preparing the dough, 33; ring of simple egg-and-butter dough, 34-35; slices of filled egg-bread dough arranged as fans, 38; small Danish pastries, 47-49; sticky buns, 38-39; storing, 7; twisted ring of coffeecake, 50-51; yeast doughnuts, 36-37. See

also Egg-and-butter dough; Yeast puff dough

Envelopes (Danish pastry), 47

Fats: incorporating in egg-and-butter dough, 34; inhibiting gluten development, 33; softening gluten in flour, 24

Filling: almond paste, for Danish pastry, 47, 48; cheese, for Danish pastry, 49; coffeecake, 50; jam, for Danish pastry twists, 48; ricotta and Parmesan cheeses, in braided coffeecake, 50; for sticky buns, 38

Flatbread: *chappatis, 74-75; from cornmeal, 76; flavored with sage, 66, 67; flours used to make, 74; johnnycake, 76-77; kneading, 74; parathas, 74; pita, 29; stuffing with puréed vegetables, 74*

Flavored yeast bread, 53, 54-71; adding baking soda to a yeast-leavened batter, 56; adding Cheddar cheese, 66, 67; adding fruit or vegetable purées, 62-63; adding ingredients to dough, 53; adding molasses, 53, 64; adding raw fruits and vegetables, 62-63; adding whole grains, 62; bagels, 58-59; cheese bread, 66-67; combining many and various ingredients, 64; crumpets, 56-57; with dried fruit and nuts, 68-69; firm and hard cheeses in, 66; flavoring a basic bread dough with rye and buckwheat flours and bran, 54-55; French bread baked in a frame, 61; fresh cheese in, 66; herb bread flavored with sage, 66, 67; kneading herbs into dough, 66, 67; leavening dough with baking soda, 56; mixing flours in pumpernickel bread, 64; mixing a soft, moist dough for French bread, 61; picnic loaf, 70-71; poaching a yeast-leavened dough, 58; pumpernickel bread, 64-65; pumpkin bread, 62-63; ring-shaped loaf of sourdough bread, 54-55; Scotch bun, 52, 68-69; using a sourdough starter, 54-55; whole-wheat bread, 60; working with whole-wheat flour, 60; zucchini bread, 62-63

Flour: adding to bread dough, 8; bleaching, 6; characteristics of specialty flours, 8-9; dusting dough with to obtain firm crust, 26; dusting top crust with, 19, 26; as ingredient, 8-9; milling in recent times, 6; milling in Roman times, 6; storing, 8; substituting in yeast breads, 8-9; temperature of, for mixing, 14; used in making flatbread, 74; warming before use, 8, 14. *See also* All-purpose flour; Barley flour; Bread flour; Buckwheat flour; Corn flour; Gluten flour; Millet flour; Oat flour; Rice flour; Rye flour; Soy flour; Triticale flour; Whole-wheat flour

Freezing bread, 7

French bread: baking in a frame, 61; kneading a moist dough, 61; rising, 61; shaping a freestanding baguette, 22-23; slashing dough, 61

Fruits: adding purée to bread dough, 62; adding purée to quick bread batter, 82; dried, in Scotch bun, 68-69; preparing coffeecake filling from fresh and dried, 50; purée, in waffle batter, 86; simmering fresh fruits to make a glaze, 50

Garam masala: *a mixture of ground spices, usually peppercorns, coriander, cumin, cloves, cinnamon and cardamom. Obtainable from Indian-food specialty stores.*

Ghee: *the Indian version of clarified butter. To make it, start with at least one third more butter than the amount of ghee desired. Melt the butter over low heat without browning it. Then bring the butter to a boil. When it foams, reduce the heat to very low. Simmer, uncovered, for 45 minutes. Strain the clear liquid ghee through a sieve lined with four layers of dampened cheesecloth. Discard the milk solids.*

Glaze: beaten egg-and-water, 26, 27, 35, 67; egg-white-and-water, 26, 65; egg-yolk-and-water, 23, 26, 28, 42, 46, 47, 48, 49, 51, 58, 59, 70; made with fresh fruit, 60; milk, cream or butter, 26, 28; salted water, 26, 27

Gluten: developed in enriched dough, 33; developing in whole-wheat flour, 8; developing in yeast dough, 5, 10, 13, 14-15, 16-17; developing in yeast-leavened batter, 56; inhibited by presence of fats, 33; in nonyeast breads, 73; in nonyeast dough, 74; preventing overdevelopment of, in pancakes, 84; preventing overdevelopment of, in yeast puff dough, 44; relaxing gluten mesh, 14, 15; relaxing, in flatbread, 74; softened by butter, 24, 33; in specialty flours, 8; in wheat flour, 6, 8; in whole-wheat flour, 60

Gluten flour: baking bread with, 8; characteristics, 8-9; in *pita* bread, 29; storing, 8; substituting, 8-9

Grains: adding to bread dough, 62

Herbs: baking a sage flatbread, 66, 67; flavoring bread with, 66-67

Hogmanay cake. See Scotch bun

Irish soda bread: kneading, 78; leavening process, 78; made with white and whole-wheat flours, 78-79; scoring loaf, 79

Jam: filling Danish pastry twists, 48; filling doughnuts for deep frying, 36-37

Johnnycake: made from a batter, 76-77; scalded-meal dough, 76-77

Julienne: *a French term for vegetables or other food cut into thin — usually matchstick-sized —strips.*

Kneading: basic yeast dough, 14-15; brioche dough, 41; croissants, 44; developing gluten mesh, 5, 14; flatbread, 74; French bread, 61; herbs into dough, 66; on a marble slab, 34, 41; pumpernickel bread, 64; simple egg dough, 34, 35; a sourdough ring,

characteristics of, 8-9, 60; garnishing loaf of whole-wheat bread, 60; gluten in, 8, 60; in Irish soda bread, 78-79; in *parathas*, 74; in pumpernickel bread, 64-65; rising time, 60; substituting, 8-9; using additional yeast, 60; using in combination with other flours, 60

Yeast: activating dry, 10; adding baker's yeast to sourdough culture, 11, 54; adding extra yeast to whole-wheat bread, 60; adding to sourdough starter, 53, 54; baker's, 10; cultivating wild yeasts in a sourdough starter, 11, 54; in Egypt, 5; fermentation process, 10; growth while bread is rising, 5, 10, 13, 14; history of, 5, 6; nourishing, 60; preparing a sourdough starter, 10-11;

preparing a sponge for simple egg-and-butter dough, 34; producing on a wide scale, 6; softening, 10; starch for, 10; storing commercial, 10; wild yeasts, 10, 11, 54; yeast production and temperature of dough, 14, 40

Yeast dough: baking bread from basic yeast dough, 13, 14-17; bashing, 18; basic dough baked in a covered pan, 24-25; basic dough baked in loaf pan, 24-25; braiding a loaf, 22-23; cutting and shaping pretzels and bread sticks, 30-31; developing gluten, 10, 13; enriching basic dough with butter and eggs, 33-51; flavoring basic dough, 53-71; handling dough for pretzels, 30; inflating during baking to form a pocket *(pita)*, 29; kneading, 14-15;

making a tiered loaf, 18; mixing by hand, 14-15; molding a ball into a cylinder, 19-20; notching a cylinder with scissors, 20; punching down, 14; resting, 15; rising and proofing, 13, 14; rising while refrigerated, 14; rolling out a baguette, 22-23; shaping and baking rolls from bread dough, 26-28; shaping into loaves and rising, 16-17; slashing tops of shaped dough, 16, 18, 19, 21, 23, 25, 26, 27, 61; substituting flours, 8-9; tapering a cylindrical loaf, 21; testing after dough has risen, 14; testing baked bread, 17; using a sourdough starter, 10-11. *See also* Basic yeast bread; Egg-and-butter dough; Milk-and-butter dough; Yeast puff dough

Yeast-leavened batter: beating,

56; crumpets, 56-57; developing gluten, 56; lightening with baking soda, 56

Yeast puff dough: in braided and filled coffeecake, 32, 50-51; butter in, 44; chilling dough, 47; in cockscombs, 47, 49; in envelopes, 47; fat in, 33; folding and rolling, 44-45; handling for Danish pastry, 47; kneading, 44; making croissants, 44-46; milk in, 44; mixing dough, 44; in pinwheels, 47, 48; relaxing dough, 44; shaping and filling Danish pastries, 47-49; twisted ring, 50-51; in twists, 47, 48-49; working on marble slab, 44. *See also* Enriched yeast bread

Zucchini: adding to bread dough, 62; bread, 62-63; getting rid of excess liquid, 62; salting, 62

Recipe Credits

The sources for the recipes in this volume are shown below. Page references in parentheses indicate where the recipes appear in the anthology.

Aberdeen School of Domestic Science, *Plain Cookery Recipes.* Published by Robert Gordon's Technical College, Aberdeen, 1913(148).

Acton, Eliza, *The English Bread-Book for Domestic Use.* Published by Longman, Brown, Green, Longmans, & Roberts, London, 1857(118).

Adam, Hans Karl, *Das Kochbuch aus Schwaben.* © Copyright 1976 by Verlagsteam Wolfgang Hölker. Published by Verlag Wolfgang Hölker, Münster. Translated by permission of the publisher(123).

Adamson, Helen Lyon, *Grandmother in the Kitchen.* © 1965 by Helen Lyon Adamson. Published by Crown Publishers, Inc. By permission of the publisher(144).

Akerström, Jenny, *Prinsessornas Kokbok.* © 1945 Albert Bonniers Boktryckeri, Stockholm. Published by Albert Bonniers Förlag, A. B., Stockholm. By permission of the publisher(115).

Allen, Ida Bailey, *Best Loved Recipes of the American People.* Copyright © 1973 by Ruth Allen Castelli. Published by Doubleday & Company, Inc. By permission of the publisher(160).

Androuet, Pierre, *La Cuisine au Fromage.* © 1978, Éditions Stock. Published by Éditions Stock, Paris. Translated by permission of the publisher(113).

Artocchini, Carmen, *400 Ricette della Cucina Piacentina.* Published by Gino Molinari, Piacenza. Translated by permission of the author(96).

Bar-David, Molly Lyons, *The Israeli Cookbook.* © 1964 by Crown Publishers, Inc. Published by Crown Publishers, Inc. By permission of the publisher(96).

Bates, Margaret, *The Scottish and Irish Baking Book.* Copyright © Pergamon Press Ltd. Published in 1965 by Pergamon Press Ltd., London. By permission of the publisher(147).

Bisson, Marie, *La Cuisine Normande.* © Solar, 1978. Published by Solar, Paris. Translated by permission of the publisher(140).

Bringer, Rodolphe, *Les Bons Vieux Plats du Tricastin.* Published by Les Amis du Tricastin. Reprinted by Éditions Daniel Morcrette, Luzarches. Translated by permission of the publisher(120).

Brown, Edward Espe, *The Tassajara Bread Book.* © by the Chief Priest, Zen Center, San Francisco. Published by Shambhala Publications, Inc., 1920 13th Street, Boulder, Colorado 80301. By permission of the publisher (160).

Brown, Helen, *Helen Brown's West Coast Cook Book.* Copyright 1952 by Helen Evans Brown. Published by Little, Brown and Company, Boston. By permission of the publisher(141).

Brown, Marion, *The Southern Cook Book.* © 1968 The University of North Carolina Press. Published by The University of North Carolina Press, Chapel Hill. By permission of the publisher(152).

Bumgarner, Marlene Anne, *The Book of Whole Grains.* Copyright © 1976 by Marlene Anne Bumgarner. Published by St. Martin's Press. By permission of the publisher(92, 108, 153).

Calvel, Raymond, *La Boulangerie Moderne.* © 1978 Eyrolles. Published by Éditions Eyrolles, Paris, 1978. Translated by permission of the publisher(98, 104).

Cavazzuti, Giorgio (Editor), *Il Mangiarfuori: Almanacco della Cucina Modenese.* Published by Camera di Commercio, Modena, 1965. Translated by permission of Camera di Commercio Industria Artigianato e Agricoltura(119).

Chamberlin-Hellman, Maria (Editor), *Food Notes.* © Copyright 1974, The Rudolf Wittkower Fellowship Fund. Published for the benefit of The Rudolf Wittkower Fellowship Fund, Department of Art, History and Archaeology, Columbia University, New York. By permission of Maria Chamberlin-Hellman(91).

Chezzetcook Historical Society Cookbook. Published by Women's Clubs Publishing Co. Inc., Chicago, c. 1973(137).

Cholcheva, Penka I., *Kniga za Vseki Den i Vseki Dom.* Published by the State Publishing House "Technika," 1979. Translated by permission of Jusautor Copyright Agency, Sofia, for the author(132).

Chowdhary, Savitri, *Indian Cooking.* Copyright © Savitri Chowdhary 1954, 1975. Published by André Deutsch, London, 1954 and Pan Books, London, 1975. By permission of André Deutsch(144).

Clayton, Bernard, Jr., *The Complete Book of Breads.* Copyright © 1973 by Bernard Clayton Jr. Published by Si-

mon & Schuster, a division of Gulf & Western Corporation. By permission of the publisher(90, 107, 112, 124).

Copping, Wilf and Lois, *The Country Innkeepers' Cookbook.* Copyright © 1978 by Yankee, Inc. Published by Yankee, Inc., Dublin, New Hampshire. By permission of the publisher(148, 154, 160, 162).

Corsi, Guglielma, *Un Secolo di Cucina Umbra.* Published by Tipografia Porziuncola, Assisi, 1968. Translated by permission of the publisher(114).

Cox, J. Stevens (Editor), *Guernsey Dishes of Bygone Days.* © James and Gregory Stevens Cox. Published by The Toucan Press, St. Peterport, Guernsey, 1974. By permission of Gregory Stevens Cox(145).

Dalgairns, Mrs., *The Practise of Cookery.* Printed for Cadell & Co., Edinburgh, 2nd edition, 1829(104, 131).

David, Elizabeth, *English Bread and Yeast Cookery.* Copyright © Elizabeth David, 1977. Published by Penguin Books Ltd., London, 1979. By permission of the publisher(131, 135).

de Bonnefons, Nicolas, *Les Délices de la Campagne.* 1655(117).

De Gouy, Louis P., *The Bread Tray.* Copyright © 1944 by Louis P. De Gouy. Copyright renewed 1972 by Jacqueline S. Dooner. Published by Dover Publications, Inc. By permission of the publisher(136).

de Groot, Roy Andries, *The Auberge of the Flowering Hearth.* Copyright © 1973 by Roy Andries de Groot. Published by The Bobbs-Merrill Company, Inc. By permission of Robert Cornfield, agent for the author(119).

de Zuliani, Mariù Salvatori, *La Cucina di Versilia e Garfagnana.* Copyright © by Franco Angeli Editore, Milano. Published by Franco Angeli Editore, Milan, 1969. Translated by permission of the publisher(92, 115).

Deschamps, B. and J.-Cl. Deschaintre, *Le Livre del'Apprenti Pâtissier.* © 1978 Éditions Jacques Lanore C.L.T. Published by Éditions Jacques Lanore C.L.T., Malakoff. Translated by permission of the publisher(134).

Les Desserts de nos Provinces. © Hachette, 1974. Published by Librairie Hachette, Paris. Translated by permission of the publisher(134).

Dolby, Richard, *The Cook's Dictionary and House-Keeper's Directory.* Published by Henry Colburn and Richard Bentley, London, 1830(105).

Dyer, Ceil, *The Newport Cookbook.* Copyright © 1972 by Ceil Dyer. Published by Weathervane Books. By permission of Hawthorn Books, a division of Elsevier/Dutton Publishing Co., Inc.(150, 150).

Edmonds, Anna G. (Editor), *An American Cook in Turkey.* Published by Redhouse Press, Istanbul, 1961, 1966, 1971, 1978. By permission of Anna Edmonds for Redhouse Press(128).

Ellis, Eleanor A. (Editor), *Northern Cookbook.* © Minister of Supply and Services Canada 1979. Published by Hurtig Publishers, Edmonton, Alberta. By permission of the publisher and the Minister of Supply and Services Canada(146).

Ellis, W., *The Country Housewife's Family Companion.* Published in London, 1750(95).

Firth, Grace, *Stillroom Cookery.* Copyright © 1977 Grace Firth. Published by EPM Publications, Inc., McLean, Virginia. By permission of the publisher (106, 126).

Food and Wines from Alsace, France. Published by Centre d'Information du Vin d'Alsace, Colmar, 1979. By permission of the publisher(129).

Foods of the World, *American Cooking: The Eastern Heartland; American Cooking: The Great West; American Cooking: Southern Style.* Copyright © 1971 Time-Life Books Inc.; Copyright © 1971 Time Inc.; Copyright © 1971 Time Inc. Published by Time-Life Books, Alexandria, Virginia(130, 136, 154; 140; 151).

Francesconi, Jeanne Caròla, *La Cucina Napoletana.* Copyright 1965 by Casa Editrice Fausto Fiorentino, Napoli. Published by Fausto Fiorentino Editore, Naples. Translated by permission of the author(114, 117).

Grant, Doris, *Your Daily Food: Recipe for Survival.* © Doris Grant 1973. Published by Faber & Faber Limited, 1973. By permission of the publisher(94).

The Great Cooks' Guide to Breads. Copyright © 1977 by Albert G. Lowenthal. Published by Random House, Inc. By permission of Carol Cutler (114 — Carol Cutler).

Grigson, Jane, *English Food.* Copyright © 1974 Jane Grigson. Published by Macmillan London Limited, 1974. By permission of Macmillan, London and Basingstoke(97, 105).

Groff, Betty and José Wilson, *Good Earth & Country Cooking.* Published by Stackpole Books, Harrisburg, Pennsylvania, 1974. By permission of the publisher (91).

Guinaudeau-Franc, Zette, *Les Secrets des Fermes en Périgord Noir.* © 1978, Éditions Serg, Paris. Published by Éditions Serg, Paris. Translated by permission of the author(130).

Haitsma Mulier-van Beusekom, C. A. H. (Editor), *Culinaire Encyclopedie.* Published by Elsevier © 1957. Revised edition 1974 by N.V. Uitgeversmaatschappij Elsevier Nederland and E.H.A. Nakken-Rovekamp. Translated by permission of B.V. Uitgeversmaatschappij Elsevier Focus, Amsterdam(93).

Hall, Jeanne M., *500 More Recipes By Request.* Copyright © 1960 by Jeanne Hall Senderhauf. Published by Bramhall House, a division of Clarkson N. Potter, Inc., by arrangement with Hearthside Press, Inc. By permission of Nedda Anders-Richard Anders(154).

Hazelton, Nika, *American Home Cooking.* Copyright © 1980 by Nika Hazelton. Published by The Viking Press. By permission of Viking Penguin, Inc.(142).

Heller, Edna Eby, *The Art of Pennsylvania Dutch Cooking.* Copyright © 1968 by Edna Eby Heller. Published by Doubleday & Company, Inc. By permission of the publisher(155, 156).

Hellermann, Dorothee V., *Das Kochbuch aus Hamburg.* © copyright 1975 by Verlagsteam Wolfgang Hölker. Published by Verlag Wolfgang Hölker, Münster. Translated by permission of the publisher(100, 126).

Hess, Olga and Adolf Fr., *Wiener Küche.* 37th edition 1977. Copyright © by Franz Deuticke, Vienna, 1963. Translated by permission of Franz Deuticke(125).

Hewitt, Jean, *The New York Times New England Heritage Cookbook.* Copyright © 1972 and 1977 by The New York Times Company. Introduction © 1977 by Jean Hewitt. Published by G. P. Putnam's Sons. By permission of Curtis Brown Ltd., New York, agents for the author(151). *The New York Times Southern Heritage Cookbook.* Copyright © 1972 and 1976 by The New York Times Company. Published by

G. P. Putnam's Sons. By permission of Curtis Brown Ltd.(137).

Hirschfeld, Florence Kerr, *Cooking With Love.* Copyright © 1965 by Florence Kerr Hirschfeld. Published by Houghton Mifflin Company, 1965. By permission of the publisher(100).

Irish Recipes Traditional and Modern. Published by Mount Salus Press Limited, Dublin. By permission of the publisher(136, 138).

Jensen, Ingeborg Dahl, *Wonderful, Wonderful Danish Cooking.* Copyright © 1966 by Ingeborg Dahl Jensen. Published by Simon & Schuster, a division of Gulf & Western Corporation. By permission of the publisher(107).

Johnson, Alice B., *The Complete Scandinavian Cookbook.* Copyright © Alice B. Johnson 1964. Published by Macmillan Publishing Co., Inc. By permission of the publisher(157).

Johnson, Ellen Foscue, *The Garden Way Bread Book.* Copyright © 1979 by Garden Way Associates, Inc. Published by Garden Way Publishing Co. By permission of the publisher(145, 152, 156).

The Junior League of Fayetteville, Inc., *The Carolina Collection.* Copyright © 1978 by The Junior League, Fayetteville, North Carolina. Published by the Junior League of Fayetteville, Inc. By permission of the publisher(163).

The Junior League of Greenville, Inc., *300 Years of Carolina Cooking.* Copyright © 1970 by the Junior League of Greenville, Inc. Published by The Junior League of Greenville, Inc. By permission of the publisher(145 — Mrs. J. Cranston Gray).

The Junior League of Jackson, Mississippi, *Southern Sideboards.* Copyright © 1978 by Junior League of Jackson, Mississippi. Published by Junior League of Jackson. By permission of the publisher(144 — Mrs. Ward T. McCraney Jr.).

The Junior League of Little Rock, *Little Rock Cooks.* Copyright © 1972 The Junior League of Little Rock, Inc. Published by The Junior League of Little Rock, Inc., Little Rock, Arkansas. By permission of the publisher (108).

The Junior League of Tampa, *The Gasparilla Cookbook.* Copyright The Junior League of Tampa, Inc. 1961. Published by The Junior League of Tampa, Inc. By permission of the publisher(127 — Mrs. James H. Kennedy).

Käkönen, Ulla, *Natural Cooking the Finnish Way.* Copyright © 1974 by Ulla Käkönen. Published by Quadrangle/The New York Times Book Company. By permission of Times Books, a division of Quadrangle/The New York Times Book Company(91, 109, 141).

Kamman, Madeleine, *The Making of a Cook.* Copyright © 1971 by Madeleine Kamman. Published by Atheneum Publishers. By permission of the publisher(159).

Karsenty, Irène and Lucienne, *La Cuisine Pied-Noir (Cuisines du Terroir).* © 1974, by Éditions Denoël, Paris. Published by Éditions Denoël, Paris. Translated by permission of the publisher(121).

Katzen, Mollie, *The Moosewood Cookbook.* Copyright 1977, Mollie Katzen. Published by Ten Speed Press, Berkeley. By permission of the author(161).

Kaufman, Ted and Jean, *The Complete Bread Cookbook.* Copyright © 1969 by Coronet Communications, Inc. Published by arrangement with Warner Books, New York. By permission of Warner Books(142, 152).

Kiehnle, Hermine and Maria Hädecke, *Das Neue Kiehnle-Kochbuch.* © Walter Hadecke Verlag (vorm. Süddeutsches Verlagshaus), Weil der Stadt, 1960. Published by Walter Hadecke Verlag, Weil der Stadt. Translated by permission of the publisher(95, 111, 115).

Klever, Eva and Ulrich, *Selber Brot Backen.* © by Grafe und Unzer GmbH., München. Published by Grafe und Unzer GmbH., Munich. Translated by permission of the publisher(99).

Kowalska, Lili, *Cooking the Polish Way.* © Paul Hamlyn Limited 1964. Published by Paul Hamlyn Limited, London. By permission of The Hamlyn Publishing Group Limited(126, 129).

Kürtz, Jutta, *Das Brot Backbuch.* © Copyright 1975 by Verlag Wolfgang Hölker. Published by Verlag Wolfgang

Hölker, Münster. Translated by permission of the publisher(113).

Lincoln, Mrs. Mary J., *The Boston Cook Book.* Published in 1912 by Little, Brown, and Company, Boston(151).

Llanover, The Right Hon. Lady, *Good Cookery.* Published by Richard Bentley, London, 1867(95).

Macdonald, Duncan, *The New London Family Cook (or Town and Country Housekeeper's Guide).* Published by Albion Press for J. and J. Cundee, London, 1812(106).

McNeill, F. Marian, *The Scots Kitchen.* First edition 1929. Second edition 1963. Published by Blackie and Son Limited, London and Glasgow. By permission of the publisher(135, 142).

Macnicol, Fred, *Hungarian Cookery.* Copyright © 1978 by Fred Macnicol. Published by Penguin Books Ltd., London. By permission of the publisher(132).

Magyar, Elek, *Kochbuch für Feinschmecker.* © Dr. Magyar Balint. © Dr. Magyar Pal. Originally published in 1967 under the title *Az Inyesmester Szakacs Konyve* by Corvina Verlag, Budapest. Translated by permission of Artisjus, Literary Agency, Budapest(106).

Mann, Gertrude, *A Book of Cakes.* © Gertrude Mann, 1957. Published 1957 by André Deutsch, London. By permission of the publisher(102).

Manning, Elise W. (Editor), *Country Fair Cookbook.* Copyright © 1975 by Farm Journal, Inc. Published by Doubleday & Company, Inc. By permission of Farm Journal, Inc.(155, 157).

Manyan, Gladys, *The Country Seasons Cookbook.* Drawings by Doug Anderson. © 1974 by Gladys Manyan. Published by Bonanza Books, a division of Crown Publishers, Inc. By permission of Crown Publishers, Inc.(160, 162).

Menichetti, Piero Luigi and Luciana Menichetti Panfili, *Vecchia Cucina Eugubina.* Published by Tipolitografia Rubini e Petruzzi, Città di Castello, 1976. Translated by permission of Piero Luigi Menichetti, Gubbio(112).

Mérigot, Madame, *La Cuisinière Républicaine.* Published by Mérigot jeune, Libraire, Paris, in the third year of the Republic (1795)(117).

Miller, Amy Bess Williams and Persis Wellington Fuller, *The Best of Shaker Cooking.* Copyright © 1970 by Shaker Community, Inc. Published by Collier Books, a division of Macmillan Publishing Co., Inc. By permission of Macmillan Publishing Co., Inc.(137, 138, 159, 161).

Monod, Louis, *La Cuisine Florentine.* Published by Éditions Daniel Morcrette, B. P. 26, 95270 Luzarches, 1977. Translated by permission of the author (116).

Montagné, Prosper, *The New Larousse Gastronomique.* English translation © 1977 by The Hamlyn Publishing Group Limited. Published by Crown Publishers, Inc. By permission of the publisher(149).

The New London Cookery and Complete Domestic Guide, by A Lady. Published by G. Virtue, Bristol, c. 1827(130).

Nichols, Nell B. (Editor), *Homemade Bread.* Copyright © 1969 by Farm Journal, Inc. Published by Doubleday & Company, Inc. By permission of Farm Journal, Inc.(101).

Norberg, Inga, *Good Food from Sweden.* Published by Chatto and Windus, London, 1935. By permission of Curtis Brown Ltd., London, agents for the author(92).

Older, Julia and Steve Sherman, *Soup and Bread.* © 1978 by Julia Older and Steve Sherman. Published by The Stephen Greene Press, Brattleboro, Vermont 05301. By permission of the publisher(118, 137).

Olney, Judith, *Comforting Food.* Copyright © 1979 by Judith Olney. Published by Atheneum Publishers. By permission of the publisher(108). *Summer Food.* Copyright © 1978 by Judith Olney. Published by Atheneum Publishers. By permission of the publisher(113, 116).

Ortega, Simone, *Mil Ochenta Recetas de Cocina.* © Simone K. de Ortega, 1972. © Alianza Editorial, S.A., Madrid, 1972. Published by Alianza Editorial, S.A. Translated by permission of the publisher(150).

Ortiz, Elisabeth Lambert, *Caribbean Cooking.* Copyright © Elisabeth Lambert Ortiz, 1973, 1975. Published by Penguin Books Ltd., London. By permission of the publisher(146). *The Complete Book of Mexican Cooking.* Copyright © 1967 by Elisabeth Lambert Ortiz. Reprinted by permission of the publisher, M. Evans and Company, Inc., New York 10017(141).

Pascoe, Ann, *Cornish Recipes Old and New.* Published by Tor Mark Press, Truro, Cornwall. By permission of the publisher(139, 143).

Pearson, Haydn S., *Country Flavor Cookbook.* Copyright © 1962, 1956 by Haydn S. Pearson. Published by W. W. Norton & Company, Inc. By permission of the publisher(156).

Peck, Paula, *The Art of Fine Baking.* Copyright © 1961 by Paula Peck. Published by Simon & Schuster, a division of Gulf & Western Corporation. By permission of the publisher(158).

Petits Propos Culinaires I. February, 1979. Copyright © Prospect Books 1979. Published by Prospect Books, London and Washington, D.C. By permission of the publisher(139).

Petits Propos Culinaires IV. February, 1980. Copyright © Prospect Books 1980. Published by Prospect Books, London and Washington, D.C. By permission of the publisher(118).

The Picayune Creole Cook Book. First published in 1901 as *The Original Picayune Creole Cook Book.* Reprinted in 1971 by Dover Publications, Inc.(138).

Porter, Mrs. M. E., *Mrs. Porter's New Southern Cookery Book.* Introduction Copyright © 1973 by Louis Szathmary. Published by Arno Press, A New York Times Company. By permission of the publisher(138, 157, 163).

The Receipt Book of Ann Blencowe. (A.D. 1694) Published by Guy Chapman, The Adelphi, London, 1925(128).

Reich, Lilly Joss, *The Viennese Pastry Cookbook.* Copyright © 1970 by Lilly Joss Reich. Published by Collier Books, a division of Macmillan Publishing Co., Inc. By permission of Macmillan Publishing Co., Inc.(158).

Robbins, Ann Roe, *The Seven-Ingredients Cookbook.* Copyright © 1968 by Ann Roe Robbins. Published by Chilton Book Company. By permission of the publisher(111).

Robertson, Laurel, Carol Flinders and Bronwen Godfrey, *Laurel's Kitchen: A Handbook for Vegetarian Cookery and Nutrition.* Copyright 1976 by Nilgiri Press, Petaluma, California 94953. Published by Nilgiri Press. By permission of the publisher(162).

Robotti, Peter J. and Frances D., *French Cooking in the New World: Louisiana and French Canadian Cuisine.* Copyright © 1967 by Frances Diane Robotti. Published by Doubleday & Company, Inc. By permission of the authors(143, 147).

Rombauer, Irma S. and Marion Rombauer Becker, *Joy of Cooking.* Copyright © 1931, 1936, 1941, 1942, 1943, 1946, 1951, 1952, 1953, 1962, 1963, 1964, 1975 by The Bobbs-Merrill Company, Inc. Published by the Bobbs-Merrill Company, Inc., 1975. By permission of the publisher(142, 146).

Rosser, Linda Kennedy (Editor), *Pioneer Cookery around Oklahoma.* Copyright 1978 Linda Kennedy Rosser. Published by Omniplex (Oklahoma Science and Arts Foundation, Inc.), Oklahoma City, 1978. By permission of the author(150).

Rundell, Mrs. Maria Eliza, *A New System of Domestic Cookery.* First published 1806. 65th edition remodelled

and improved, by the addition of nearly one thousand entirely new receipts (contributed by Mrs. Emma Roberts), 1841(128).

Schapira, Christiane, *La Cuisine Corse.* © Solar, 1979. Published by Solar, Paris. Translated by permission of the publisher(127).

Scheibler, Sophie Wilhelmine, *Allgemeines Deutsches Kochbuch für alle Stände.* Published in Leipzig, 1896(123).

The Settlement Cook Book. Copyright © 1965, 1976 by The Settlement Cookbook Co. Published by Simon & Schuster, a division of Gulf & Western Corporation. By permission of the publisher(163).

Shulman, Martha Rose, *The Vegetarian Feast.* Copyright © 1979 by Martha Rose Shulman. Published by Harper & Row, Publishers, Inc. By permission of the publisher(122).

Singh, Dharamjit, *Indian Cookery.* Copyright © Dharamjit Singh, 1970. Published by Penguin Books Ltd., London, 1970. By permission of the publisher(139, 140).

Snow, Jane Moss, *A Family Harvest.* Copyright © 1976 by Jane Moss Snow. Published by The Bobbs-Merrill Company, Inc. By permission of Collier Associates, New York, for the author(148).

Stamm, Sara B. B., and the Lady Editors of Yankee Magazine, *Favorite New England Recipes.* Copyright © 1972 by Sara B. B. Stamm and Yankee, Inc. Published by Yankee, Inc., Dublin, New Hampshire. By permission of the publisher(122, 152).

Straub, Maria Elisabeth, *Grönen Aal und Rode Grütt.* © LN-Verlag Lübecker Nachrichten GmbH., Lübeck 1971. Sixth edition 1977. Published by LN-Verlag Lübecker Nachrichten GmbH. Translated by permission of the publisher(125).

Sverdrup, Elise, *Norway's Delight: Dishes and Specialities.* © Elise Sverdrup 1957. Published by Johan Grundt Tanum Forlag, Oslo, 1968. By permission of Forlaget Tanum/Norli A/S., Oslo(141).

Tarr, Yvonne Young, *The New York Times Bread and Soup Cookbook.* Copyright © 1972 by Quadrangle Books, Inc. Published by Quadrangle/The New York Times Book Co., Inc. By permission of the publisher(93, 97, 153, 161).

Tendret, Lucien, *La Table au Pays de Brillat-Savarin.* Published by Librairie Dardel, Chambéry, 1934. Translated by permission of Jacques Grancher, Éditeur, Paris(119).

Thorne-Thomsen, Kathleen and Linda Brownridge, *Why the Cake Won't Rise and the Jelly Won't Set.* Copyright © 1979 by Kathleen Thorne-Thomsen and Linda Brownridge. Published by A & W Publishers, Inc. By permission of the publisher(149).

Tibbott, S. Minwel, *Welsh Fare.* © National Museum of Wales (Welsh Folk Museum). Published by National Museum of Wales (Welsh Folk Museum), 1976. By permission of the publisher(121, 148).

Tschirky, Oscar, *The Cook Book by 'Oscar' of the Waldorf.* Copyright 1896 by Oscar Tschirky. Published by The Werner Company, Chicago and New York(105).

Uhle, Margret and Anne Brakemeier, *Eigenbrötlers Brotbackbuch.* © 1975 Mosaik Verlag GmbH., München. Published by Verlagsgruppe Bertalsmann GMBH., Vienna. Translated by permission of Mosaik Verlag GmbH.(103, 109, 110).

Valente, Maria Odette Cortes, *Cozinha Regional Portuguesa.* Published by Livraria Almedina, Coimbra, 1973. Translated by permission of the publisher(120).

Vence, Céline and Robert Courtine, *The Grand Masters of French Cuisine.* Copyright © 1978 by G. P. Putnam's Sons. Originally published in France as *Les Grands Maîtres de la Cuisine Française,* copyright © 1972 by Bordas. Published by G. P. Putnam's Sons. By permission of the publisher(100, 102).

Vielfaure, Nicole and A. Christine Beauviala, *Fêtes, Coutumes et Gâteaux.* © Christine Bonneton, Éditeur. Published by Christine Bonneton, Éditeur, Le Puy-en-Velay. Translated by permission of the publisher(101, 123).

Viola, Pauline and Knud Ravnkilde, *Cooking with a Danish Flavour.* Copyright © 1978 by Pauline Viola and Knud Ravnkilde. Published by Elm Tree Books for Danish Agricultural Producers, London. By permission of Hamish Hamilton Ltd., London(133).

Volpicelli, Luigi and Secondino Freda (Editors), *L'Antiartusi: 1000 Ricette.* © 1978 Pan Editrice, Milano. Published by Pan Editrice, Milan. Translated by permission of the publisher(153).

Walker, Lorna and Joyce Hughes, *The Complete Bread Book.* © Copyright The Hamlyn Publishing Group Limited 1977. Published by The Hamlyn Publishing Group Limited, London, 1977. By permission of the publisher(103, 143).

White, Florence, *Good English Food.* Published by Jonathan Cape Ltd., London, 1952. By permission of the publisher(98).

Widenfelt, Sam (Editor), *Favorite Swedish Recipes.* Published by Dover Publications, Inc., New York, 1975. By permission of the publisher(124).

Witty, Helen and Elizabeth Schneider Colchie, *Better than Store-Bought.* Copyright © 1979 by Helen Witty and Elizabeth Schneider Colchie. Published by Harper & Row, Publishers, Inc. By permission of the publisher(94, 96, 98).

The Woman's Auxiliary of Olivet Episcopal Church, Franconia, Virginia, *Virginia Cookery — Past and Present.* Copyright, 1957, by the Woman's Auxiliary of Olivet Episcopal Church, Franconia, Virginia. Published by the Woman's Auxiliary of Olivet Episcopal Church. By permission of the publisher(163).

Wurtzburger, Janet E. C. (Editor), *Private Collections: A Culinary Treasure.* Copyright © 1973 by The Walters Art Gallery, Baltimore, Maryland. Published by The Women's Committee of the Walters Art Gallery. By permission of the publisher(104, 162).

Yianilos, Theresa Karas, *The Complete Greek Cookbook.* Copyright © 1971 by Theresa Karas Yianilos. Published by Avenel Books by arrangement with Funk & Wagnalls. By permission of Harper & Row, Publishers, Inc.(147).

York, George K., *Division of Agricultural Services, University of California Leaflet 2420.* Published by the University of California Cooperative Extension, Davis(110).

Zaniboni, Maria Rivieccio, *Cucina e Vini di Napoli e della Campania.* © Copyright 1975 Ugo Mursia Editore, Milano. Published by Ugo Mursia Editore, Milan. Translated by permission of the publisher(116, 120).

Acknowledgments

The indexes for this book were prepared by Louise W. Hedberg. The editors are particularly indebted to Gail Duff, Kent, England; Dr. R. Carl Hoseney, Department of Grain Sciences and Industry, Kansas State University, Manhattan; Elisabeth Lamers, Accokeek, Maryland; Peter Ort, Master Baker, Bedfordshire, England; Ann O'Sullivan, Majorca, Spain; Dr. R. H. Smith, Aberdeen, Scotland; Dr. James L. Vetter, Donald K. Dubois, American Institute of Baking, Manhattan, Kansas; Stacy Zacharias, Alexandria, Virginia.

The editors also wish to thank: Christine Adams, London; Dr. Earl G. Alexander, Arrowhead Mills, Hereford, Texas; Mary Attenborough, Essex, England; Maura M. Bean, U.S. Department of Agriculture, Berkeley, California; Guy K. Benson, National Pretzel Bakers Institute, New York, New York; Sara Bodi, *Americana,* New York, New York; Liz Clasen, London; Bernard Clayton Jr., Bloomington, Indiana; Emma Codrington, Surrey, England; Dr. Bert D'Appolonia, Department of Cereal Chemists and Technology, North Dakota State University, Fargo; Department of Home Economics and Nutrition Education, The Flour Advisory Bureau Ltd., London; Faye Egan, Standard Brands Incorporated, Wilton, Connecticut; Mimi Errington, London; Robert D. Fondahn, American Corn Millers Federation, Washington, D.C.; Dr. William D. Garvey, Johns Hopkins University, Baltimore, Maryland; Frank E. Goeckel, Standard Brands Incorporated, New York, New York; Fayal Greene, London; Rae Hartfield, The Rice Council, Houston, Texas; Maggie Heinz, London; Stella Henvey, London; Brenda Jayes, London; Maria Johnson, Hertfordshire, England; Rosemary Klein, London; Lyle E. Lahman, Mennel Milling Company, Fostoria, Ohio; Jean Wickstrom Liles, *Southern Living,* Birmingham, Alabama; Sue McFarland, Milton Keynes, England; Pippa Millard, London; Sonya Mills, Kent, England; Dilys Naylor, London; Henry Ng, Western Regional Research Center, Albany, California; Dr. Yeshajahu Pomeranz, Dr. Carl Finney, Dr. Byron S. Miller, Donald Bechtel, U.S. Grain Marketing Research Laboratory, Manhattan, Kansas; Joan Reynolds, Wheat Flour Institute, Washington, D.C.; Dr. G. Terry Shaarer, National Museum of American History, Washington, D.C.; Cathy Sharpe, Annandale, Virginia; Margaret Spader, J. Walter Thompson Company, New York, New York; Fiona Tillet, London; Tina Walker, London; Nigel Warrington, London; Helen A. Wilber, *The Providence Journal* and *Evening Bulletin,* Rhode Island; Tiggi Wood, Sussex, England; Dr. George K. York, Cooperative Extension, University of California, Davis.

Picture Credits

The sources for the pictures in this book are listed below. Credits for each of the photographers and illustrators are listed by page number in sequence with successive pages indicated by hyphens; where necessary, the locations of pictures within pages are also indicated —separated from page numbers by dashes.

Photographs by Tom Belshaw: 10, 11 —top and bottom center, 32, 34-35 —top, 40-52, 56-57 —top, 58-59, 62-63, 64 —top and bottom left, 65 —top and bottom right, 68-69, 78-79 —bottom, 80-81 —bottom.
Photographs by Aldo Tutino: 16-17, 29, 36-39, 54-55, 61, 66-67, 70-71, 76-77, 78-79 —top, 80-81 —top, 84-88.
Other photographs (alphabetically): David Davies, 74-75. Alan Duns, cover, 4, 11 —bottom left, 12, 14-15, 18-22, 23 —bottom, 24, 25 —top and bottom left, 26-28, 30-31, 34-35 —bottom, 56-57 —bottom, 60, 64 —bottom right, 65 —bottom left. John Elliott, 23 —top, 25 —bottom right. Louis Klein, 2. Bob Komar, 11 —bottom right, 72, 82-83.
Illustrations: From The Mary Evans Picture Library and private sources and *Food & Drink: A Pictorial Archive from Nineteenth Century Sources* by Jim Harter, published by Dover Publications, Inc., 1979, 90-167. Mary Staples, 7.

Library of Congress Cataloguing in Publication Data
Time-Life Books.
    Breads.
    (The Good cook, techniques & recipes)
    Includes index.
    1. Bread. I. Title. II. Series: (Good cook, techniques & recipes)
TX769.T57   1981   641.8'15   80-22396
ISBN 0-8094-2902-0
ISBN 0-8094-2901-2 (lib. bdg.)
ISBN 0-8094-2900-4 (retail)